CW01497003

Adventures of a
Light Dragoon
in the Napoleonic Wars

Adventures of a
Light Dragoon
in the Napoleonic Wars

A Cavalryman During the Peninsular &
Waterloo Campaigns, in Captivity and at
the Siege of Bhurtpore, India

George Farmer
as narrated to
George Robert Gleig

LEONAUR

Adventures of a Light Dragoon in the Napoleonic Wars
A Cavalryman During the Peninsular & Waterloo Campaigns,
in Captivity and at the Siege of Bhurtpore, India
by George Farmer as narrated to George Robert Gleig

Originally published in 1844

Published by Leonaur Ltd

ISBN (10 digit): 1-84677-056-4 (hardcover)
ISBN (13 digit): 978-1-84677-056-2 (hardcover)

ISBN (10 digit): 1-84677-040-8 (softcover)
ISBN (13 digit): 978-1-84677-040-1 (softcover)

http://www.leonaur.com

Publisher's Notes

In the interests of authenticity, the spellings, grammar and place names
used have been retained from the original editions.

The opinions of the authors represent a view of events in which he
was a participant related from his own perspective,
as such the text is relevant as an historical document.

The views expressed in this book are not necessarily
those of the publisher.

Chapter 1

As I cannot imagine that among such as may honour these pages by a perusal, there are any who would take much interest in the personal history of one so humble as myself, I think it best to pass over all the incidents of my early life, and to come at once to the period of my enlistment. Who I am, where I was born, to what class of society my father and mother belonged, are points with which I alone am concerned. And for the rest, it is fair to avow, that if the incidents of my boyhood were all strung together, they would not make up a tale worth telling, far less a narrative which would for a single hour be remembered.

I entered the service in the summer of 1808, by enlisting as a private in the 11th regiment of Light Dragoons. The corps being at that time stationed in Ireland, I was sent with several recruits besides, to the depot at Maidstone; where for some time I ran the career which is appointed for recruits in general, and acquired some knowledge of the darker shades in human nature, if I learned nothing better. It unfortunately happens, however, that our first experience of this great book is not often favourable to our morals; and I confess that I am not an exception to the general rule. My extreme youth -- for I was not more than seventeen years of age -- exposed me to many and great temptations. The same circumstance laid me open to chicanery and deceit on the part of those around me; and I lament to say, that I became the victim as well of my own folly as of the knavery of others. How I suffered from the former of these evils, it is not worth while to tell. Young men would scarce take the trouble to follow my details, were I to give them; and if they did, I am quite sure they would never condescend to be warned by them. But it is not impossible that they may think it worth while to attend to such of my admonitions as seem to bear upon the behaviour of others; and I accordingly request that they will take good heed of the following aphorisms:

1. When you join your depot, you usually arrive with a good deal of money in your pocket; that is to say, you get your bounty as soon as you have passed, and appear in your own eyes to be enormously rich. Be assured that it is quite possible to run through as much as ten or twelve guineas: and don't take

the trouble to throw your shillings and halfcrowns at people's heads, as if they were of no value.

2. You find a comrade particularly civil: begin to suspect he has fallen in love -- not with you, but your money; and button up your pockets in exact proportion to the zeal which he manifests for trying their depth.

3. Non-commissioned officers are in an especial manner to be shunned, whenever they profess to hold you in favour, or seem to relax the bonds of discipline, in order that you may not be distressed by them. These harpies desire only to make a prey of you. They will first suck you dry, and then grind you to powder.

4. Endeavour to begin your career as it is your wisdom not less than your duty to go forward with it. Aim at the character of a sober and steady man, and you will, without doubt, succeed in deserving it.

5. Keep your temper, even if you be wronged, especially when the wrong is put upon you by a superior. Truth and justice are sure to prevail in the end; whereas, it often happens that he who is eager to anticipate that end is crushed in the struggle.

6. Finally, be alert in striving to acquire all necessary drills, and an acquaintance with your duty in general. It will be of far more benefit to you to be well thought of by a few good men, and by your officers, than to to be called "a capital fellow" by scores of scamps, who will only laugh at your remorse so soon as they have succeeded in bringing you into trouble.

But I am fast getting into a prose, so let me pull up; otherwise I may fail to carry, as I intend to do, public interest along with me.

Well, then, I enlisted in London; and, marching to Maidstone, underwent the customary examinations; after which I was attested before a magistrate, and had my bounty paid with strict exactitude. Unfortunately for me, however, the society into which I was thrown bore no resemblance at all to a well-regulated regiment. The barracks were filled with small detachments from a countless variety of corps, and the serjeants and corporals, on whom the internal discipline both of regiments and depots mainly depends, seem to me, at this distance of time, to have been selected from the very scum of the earth. Like a band of harpies, they pounced upon us recruits, and never let us loose from their talons till they had thoroughly pigeoned us. We were invited to their rooms of an evening, -- introduced to their wives, who made much of us, -- praised, favoured, screened, and cajoled, till our funds began to run low, and then they would have nothing more to say to us. Under these circumstances, we were sufficiently well pleased when the order came to join the regiment at Clonmel: and, being put in charge of one Corporal Gorman, we began our journey, profoundly ignorant both of the route we were to follow, and the extent of funds which would be allowed us during the continuance of the march.

An admirable specimen was Corporal Gorman of the sort of land-sharks out of which the staff of the recruiting department used long ago to be formed. His first step was to extract from each of us, in the shape of a loan, whatever happened to remain of our bounty. His next, to defraud us of the better half of our marching-money, by paying over to us, respectively, day by day, one shilling, and applying one shilling and a penny to his own use. Like bad men in general, however, whom long impunity has hardened, he committed the mistake, in the end, of overshooting his mark, and we having been much irritated by his tyrannical behaviour, reported him, when at Lichfield, to a magistrate. It appeared that he was not now about to form his first acquaintance with that functionary. His worship knew him well; and, by a threat of bringing the case before the general commanding the district, soon forced the knave to pay back the money which we, in our simplicity, had lent him. The arrears of our marching-money on the other hand, we never succeeded in recovering. He promised, indeed, from stage to stage, that all should be cleared off; and prevailed upon us, on our arrival in Dublin, to sign our accounts, which he himself had made up, and by which we acknowledged that we had been fully settled with. But he entirely forgot to return, as he had pledged himself to do, the sum that was needed to render the acknowledgment accurate; and, quietly handing us over to a worthy not unlike himself, took his passage in the packet for Holyhead, and left us.

I joined the head-quarters of my regiment at Clonmel at a mo-ment when both town and country rang with the exploits of two celebrated robbers, called, respectively, Brennan and Hogan. Brennan, as all the world knows, was originally a soldier -- unless my memory be at fault -- in the 12th Light Dragoons; from which regiment he deserted in consequence of some quarrel with one of the officers, that he might take, after the fashion of Dick Turpin of old, to the road. His courage was as reckless as his presence of mind was astonishing;

neither of which, however, would have much availed, had he not, at the same time, been thoroughly acquainted with the locale of the scene of his operations; but in this respect his advantages were fully as remarkable as in others, for there was not a hole or crevice in the counties of Cork, Tipperary, and Wexford, with which he seems not to have been familiar. Moreover, Brennan displayed, in the management of his reckless business, quite as much of sound policy as of hardihood. He was never known to rob, or in any way to molest, a peasant, an artisan, or a small farmer. He made war, and professed to make war only upon the rich, out of the plunder taken from whom he would often assist the poor; and the poor in return not only refused to betray him, but took care that he should be warned in time, whenever any imminent danger seemed to threaten.

The consequence was, that for full five years -- a long space of time for a highwayman to be at large, even in Ireland -- he continued to levy contributions upon all who came in his way, and had always about him the means of satisfying his own wishes. As might be expected, a great clamour was raised. Government was petitioned for troops wherewith to hunt him down. Large rewards were offered to any persons who should betray him: and day and night the magistracy of the counties were abroad, with dragoons at their heels, striving to intercept him. I heard that on one occasion, when Lord Caher, the most indefatigable of his pursuers, ran him hard, his horse became spent ere it could carry him to the Kilworth hill; and that it was only by quitting the saddle, and diving into the recesses of a wood, close by, that he managed to make good his escape. His favourite roadster fell, on that occasion, into the hands of his enemies; and he never ceased to lament the circumstance as a very grievous calamity.

Of Hogan I am unable to say more than that common.report spoke of him as a pedler, whose brave resistance to Brennan's attack originally won for him the friendship of the outlaw. It is said that the bandit fell in with his future associate one day when the pressure of want was peculiarly severe upon him. He had alighted, for some purpose or another, when the pedler came up; and, not anticipating any resistance, he carelessly desired the latter to render up his pack. But the pedler, instead of obeying the command, closed instantly with his assailant. A fierce struggle took place between them, neither having time to appeal to the deadly weapons with which both, it appeared, were armed.

"Who the devil are you?" said Brennan at last, after he had rolled with his antagonist in the dust till both were weary. "Sure, then, I didn't think there was a man in all Tipperary as could have fought so long with Bill Brennan."

"Och, then, blood and ouns!" exclaimed the other, "if you be Brennan, arrah! then, arn't I Paddy Hogan? and if you cry stand to all the world in Tipperary, sure don't I do that same to the folks in Cork?"

This was quite enough for Brennan. He entertained too high a respect for his own profession to exercise it in hostility towards a brother of the order; so he struck up, on the instant, an alliance with the pedler, and the two thenceforth played one into the hands of the other.

Of the manner in which Brennan was accustomed to do his work, the following anecdote will give a just idea:

Once upon a time, when the regiment of Militia lay in quarters at Clonmel, two of the officers drove, in a one-horse chaise, to Fethard, where they bad engaged to be present at a public dinner that was to be eaten at the principal inn in the place. They joined the company as they had proposed to do, and sat till a late hour at night, when, their companions departing, they likewise ordered their gig, and walked into what was called the travellers'-room till it should be brought round to the door. There were several strangers in the room; one of whom, a well-dressed man, stood by the fire. But of these the militia officers took no notice, their heads, as it appeared, being filled with anticipations of what might befal on their way back to Clonmel. One, indeed, did not hesitate to express regret that they had sat so late.

"These are troublesome times," observed he; "and who knows but we may encounter Brennan himself?"

"What of that?" was the answer. "You and I are surely not afraid to encounter one man. We have a brace of pistols: only let the scoundrel show himself, and see how I'll handle him!'

The stranger who lounged over the fire looked up as these words were uttered, but took no notice of them. Only, when they quitted the apartment he withdrew also, -- no salutation or mark of courtesy having passed between them.

The gig being by this time brought round, the two militia officers took their seats, and in high goodhumour and excellent spirits drove off. They continued their journey for a while without meeting with any adventure; till all at once, just as they had reached a peculiarly

11

dismal part of the road, a man sprang from one of the ditches, and seized the horse's head.

"I'll trouble you, gentlemen," said he, presenting a pistol towards them at the same time, "to alight. I should be very sorry to hurt either of you; but by my soul! if you don't do as I bid you, or try to open the locker, I'll blow your brains out in a jiffy. It shall be no joke to you, anyhow."

The officers sat stockstill, staring at each other, and not knowing what to make of it; but at last one, less flabbergasted than the other, exclaimed --

"And who the devil are you, that we should accommodate you in that manner?"

"Gentlemen," was the reply, "my name is Brennan."

There was magic in the sound of the word. Not another question was put, not another remonstrance offered, but, making all possible haste, both of them sprang to the ground, and stood as if waiting the bandit's further orders. Brennan, however, was by no means a sanguinary person; and in the present instance he had a whim to indulge as well as a booty to collect. He instantly assumed the vacated seat, and gathering up the reins, looked down upon his discomfited foes, and cried, "The next time you happen to make mention of my name, you'll probably treat it with more respect." So saying, he wheeled round, and wishing the militia-men good night, drove off.

A comfortless tramp these heroes had of it, over a dozen miles of muddy road, ere they reached Clonmel. They slunk quietly to their barrack-rooms, however, being extremely desirous of concealing their own shame, and Brennan's triumph from the knowledge of their brother-officers; and for a space of not less than six months they succeeded. But at the termination of that period, when the regiment stood under arms at evening parade, a boy entered the barrack-yard, leading in his hand a horse and gig, both of which were familiar to every one present. The boy walked up to the commanding officer and handed him a note, which he read with evident astonishment. This, of course, increased the curiosity of the rest, who gathered round their colonel, while our two chap-fallen heroes slank away, and took refuge in their own quarters. The colonel was desired to read aloud. He did so; and then the boy being questioned, the whole secret came out. Amid shouts of laughter from the audience to which he addressed himself, the urchin imitated Brennan's style of telling the story, and then, not without some substantial marks of the officers favour, he was permitted to withdraw. It is scarcely necessary to add, that the two worthies who, carrying arms, forgot at the moment of trial, to make use of them, never showed themselves again in the ranks of the militia.

Brennan's career, though a very remarkable one, could scarce, in the nature of things, terminate otherwise than in his own destruction. Many a narrow escape he made, many a feat of daring and activity he performed; but in the end, accident proved more fatal to him than all the designs and projects of his pursuers. It happened, one day, that a gentleman riding along the high-road, observed two men creep through a gap in one of the hedges, and disappear on the other side. He instantly conceived the notion that they might be Brennan and his ally, the pedler; so he hurried off to Lord Caher, and told both what he knew and what he conjectured. His lordship's eagerness to effect the capture of the bandit had not abated a jot, and, thinking it highly probable that his informant's suspicion might be well founded, he gave orders for a detachment of the 11th to mount their horses, and directed, at the same time, the Sligo militia to march with all haste, and extending their files to surround the spot. For within this hedge, through which the mysterious strangers had been seen to pass, was a new house, as yet incomplete, with a stack or two of furze cut down and piled up for fuel; and his lordship justly concluded, that if he could make of these the centre of a circle, of which the radii should be respectively half a mile in length, he might pretty surely count on picking up every living thing that might have established itself, either by accident or design, within the circumference of that circle.

I well remember that I formed one of the mounted detachment, which performed the service of which I am now speaking, and the strange excitement of the chase, I shall never, till my dying day, forget. The militia marched as they were directed, and, extending their files, soon placed the unfinished domicile, with its appurtenances, within a cordon. This was gradually narrowed, while our mounted men kept a lookout in the rear, and made ready to start off in desperate pursuit, should the game be sprung, and trust to speed of foot for escape. By-and-by the infantry closed upon the house, searched it through, and found it empty; it may be imagined there was an expression of blank astonishment in every face, till one of our men suddenly exclaimed, "You haven't examined the chimney; you way depend upon it you'll find him there." It was no sooner said than done; for the speaker sprang from his horse, ran inside, poked his head up the kitchen chimney, and in an instant withdrew it again. It was well for him that he did so, for almost simultaneously with his backward leap, came the report of a pistol, the ball from which struck the hearth without wounding any body. It is impossible for me to describe the scene that followed. Nobody cared to get below the robber; nobody fancied that it would be possible to get above him; and threats and smooth speeches were soon shown to be alike unavailing to draw him from his hiding-place. But the marvel of the adventure did not stop there. While a crowd of us were gathered about the house, some shouting on Brennan to surrender, others firing at the top of the chimney, a sort of salute which the robber did not hesitate to answer, -- one of the Sligo men suddenly called out from the rear, that he had pricked a man with his bayonet among the gorse. In an instant search was made, and sure enough there lay Brennan himself, on his back in a narrow ditch, with a brace of pistols close beside his feet, of which, however, he did not judge it expedient to make use. He was instantly seized, disarmed, and put in charge of a sufficient guard; while the remainder of addressed ourselves to the capture of his companion, concerning whom we could not for an instant doubt that he was Hogan.

When Brennan gave himself up, he did so with a singularly mild and serene aspect. There was no expression of ferocity in big countenance; no look which could be understood to imply either bitter agony because of the fate which had overtaken him, or a desperate resolution to sell his life at the highest. His whole bearing, on the contrary, was that of a man perfectly reconciled to his fate; not, indeed, very hopeful, yet far from desperate; and, therefore, little disposed to shed either his own or any other person's blood unnecessarily. Hogan, on the contrary, resembled one of the wild beasts, which in Norway, or some of the other countries where battues are carried on upon a scale more magnificent than in England, the hunters contrive to hem within their toils, seeking to capture him alive rather than kill him; for Hogan would not listen to any proposal of surrender. He mounted, on the contrary, to the very edge of the chimney, making of its brick-work a sort of parapet to protect him from our bullets, and fired pistol after pistol, till his ammunition became exhausted, and he was forced, with extreme reluctance, to descend. "In the name of common sense," said Lord Caher, "why did you offer such a useless resistance? you knew all the while that you must be taken at last -- why then wantonly put your own and other men's lives in jeopardy?" But Hogan would not condescend to reply. He drew up his tall muscular figure to the utmost, and looking disdainfully upon the throng that surrounded him, he continued silent.

Brennan and Hogan were placed each on the croup of a horseman's saddle, and in this manner, under a sufficient escort, were conveyed to the watch-house in Caher. It seemed to me that Hogan evinced manifest tokens of satisfaction, as soon as he ascertained that he stood not alone in misfortune; a strange disposition, yet the reverse of uncommon, and indicative of no extraordinary ferocity on the part of him who is swayed by it. But however this may be, the prisoners rode on contentedly enough, and were in due time safely lodged in their narrow quarters.

It seemed, however, that neither the inconveniences attached to the cell, nor their anticipation of the fate that was before them, had any power to work mischievously upon their humour. How Hogan conducted himself I cannot so decidedly describe; but of Brennan, it is fresh in my recollection, that he was throughout singularly cheerful and confiding. He told us many stories of his own narrow escapes. He pointed out several of our men who had more than once been in pursuit of him, and whose lives, he declared, had over and over again been in his hands, though a sense of what was right would not permit him to take them. "Why should I shoot you?" was the tenour of his appeal. "I have been a soldier in my day, and know that a soldier must obey whatever orders he may receive. No, no -- I should have the guilt of Cain on my soul, had any one of your regiment died by my hands; and yet more than once you had wellnigh forced me to the extremity." Then he would launch out in praise of his favourite mare, whose death he deplored as the severest calamity that ever befel him, and invariably wound up by expressing his conviction, that after all he would never be hanged. "There is no proof against me," was his argument. "There's nobody to swear that by me he was ever wronged; and were the fact different, I am sure that the people will not permit me to be put to death." In this respect, however, Brennan had deceived himself; for the law, when it puts forth its might is, even in Ireland, stronger than the mere will or caprice of a mob.

Having been detained in the guard-room of Caher all night, the prisoners were removed next day to Clonmel, where, in due time, the assizes came on, and they were put upon their trial. Many charges were brought against both, and especially against Brennan; yet the robber was so far in the right, that nobody could be persuaded to swear to his identity. At length a quaker, whose carriage had been

15

robbed near Fermoy, mounted the witness-box, and went so far as to declare a belief, that he saw in Brennan the individual who had stopped it. He would not, indeed, assert positively that the case was so, -- he only believed that Brennan was the man. On this evidence, not very explicit we must allow, yet, without doubt the best which could, under the circumstances, be procured, Brennan was found guilty; and both he and Hogan, who, on some such evidence, was in like manner convicted, received sentence of death. How shall I describe the scene that followed? Multitudes from all parts of the surrounding country, and from the distance, in some instances, of fifty-miles from the town, had flocked in to witness the trial; and now that their idol was doomed to die, their grief and consternation exceeded all conceivable bounds. Bearded men wept in the court-house like children. There were groans, deep and bitter, rising from every quarter; and more than one, especially among the women, fainted away, and was carried out. Meanwhile the troops, anticipating an attempt at rescue, stood to their arms, and the whole night long the streets were patroled; but no disturbance took place. After indulging for an hour or two in useless howling, the crowd melted away, and long before midnight a profound calm pervaded every corner of the town.

At last the terrible day of execution arrived, and Brennan, with his associate, being placed in an open cart, passed about half-past nine in the morning, under a strong military escort, beneath the arched gateway of the gaol. Again had formidable preparations been made to meet and repel violence, should any be offered: but again the thunder-cloud dispersed, without any outburst of its fury. The crowd, to be sure, was prodigious; but what can a mere crowd attempt or hope to accomplish against even a handful of disciplined and well-armed soldiers? and where, as happened to be the case that day, the soldiers are numerous, then must even the thought of resistance be scouted. Not a hand was raised in defence of the prisoners during all the progress from the prison to the gallows, and round the gallows the multitudes that assembled stood, if not mute, at all events motionless. It was curious at the time to mark the difference of character that showed itself in the bearings of the two men: Brennan gazed cheerfully round him all the while he was in the cart, and recognising in the crowd several of his friends, perhaps followers, he nodded and smiled to them gaily. Hogan, on the contrary, though equally self-collected, was far more reserved, for he never bestowed upon any of the throng one mark of recognition, nor once addressed a word to his fellow-sufferer. Yea, and

after the cords had been adjusted, and the unhappy men stood, waiting for the signal which should carry the vehicle from beneath, and
leave them to die between earth and heaven, -- even then Hogan
turned aside with undisguised contempt and loathing, from the hand
which his associate offered to his pressure; and wrapping himself up in
his own thoughts, sternly and resolutely prepared for the issue. It was
not long of coming. At a given signal the cart drove away, and amid
yells, more loud and terrible than men ever utter, except in the Emer-
ald Isle, the souls of these two noted malefactors were wrenched from
their bodies. I must not, however, forget to mention, that the two renowned highwaymen suffered not alone. A young man, found guilty
of forcibly carrying away a girl from her home and the protection of
her parents, was the same day executed in pursuance of his sentence;
and he chose to die in a garb which excited not only our surprise,
but our ridicule. He came to be hanged in a garment of white flannel,
made tight to the shape, and ornamented in all directions with knots
of blue ribbon, rather more befitting a harlequin on the stage, than a
wretched culprit whose life had become forfeit to the offended laws.

Chapter 2

Throughout the whole period of my sojourn in Tipperary, amounting to not less than seven months, the peace of the county was disturbed, and men's lives put in continual jeopardy, by the prevalence of party feuds, far more desperate in their nature than any with which the present generation seems to be familiar. There were two factions in particular, the Shanavests and Caravats, who waged one upon the other an unceasing wax of extermination. Every day brought to our quarters the report of some murder or horrid personal outrage – – every night made known to us that some act of incendiarism had been perpetrated. Highway robbery, too, was very frequent, insomuch that the mail never passed from point to point, except under an escort of dragoons; while smuggling was carried on to such a degree, that the trade of the licensed distiller brought him no returns. A melancholy time of it had we under such circumstances. What with constant demands to protect a gentleman's house, or calls upon us to assist in extinguishing the flames that had been applied to it; what with escorts to protect the mail, parties to put down a still, patrols to keep the roads safe, and guards to preserve the peace at different fairs, neither we nor our horses knew what it was to have four-and-twenty hours on which we could count, as disposable for purposes -- I do not say of relaxation, but -- of ordinary regimental or common duty. Our entire life was one of alarms, excursions, and disappointments; for I cannot deny, that we became in the end extremely irritated towards the people whose misconduct thus harassed us; and, as a necessary consequence, were deeply mortified as often as we failed in making prisoners of the wretches whose violations of the law broke in so often upon our repose.

Among the various painful duties, which then engaged me, there is not one on which I now look back with more unmixed abhorrence that the operation of still-hunting. There was no hour of the night or day at which we could consider ourselves free from the chance of being roused and sent forth, we knew not whither, under the guidance of an excise officer. Unless my memory mislead me, too, these demands upon our activity came with much greater frequency during the night than when the sun was shining; while winter seemed to be the season when the smuggler chiefly plied his trade, doubtless with the laudable desire of rendering our researches among the mountains as little agreeable to us as possible. How often have I been roused from my warm bed, required to saddle and mount my horse amid pitchy darkness, and sent forth, I could not tell in what direction, to achieve a conquest over an iron pot and tin worm! Ay, and what is more, the conquest, contemptible as in the ear of the civilian it may sound, was not always achieved. It is marvellous with what accuracy the distillers received information of our movements -- often when we flattered ourselves that we were least open to the eye of scrutiny. Over and. over again, I have ridden long miles through the mountain passes, my horse floundering in the snow, or tripping over pits and holes, to the imminent risk both of my neck and his own; and after all, when we reached the spot where the seizure was to have been effected, we found nothing save the traces of an extinguished fire, and two or three peasants, who never omitted to laugh at us. In like manner, the duties of escorting the mail were by no means agreeable. Amid thickets, or in the ditches, parties of armed men would lie, who would sometimes kill both men and horses with their fire, while for us to search for them, except through the medium of our carbines, was impossible.

It is not, however, because of these annoyances alone that my rec-ollection of service in Ireland is any thing but agreeable to myself, or creditable to the temper of the people. I admit that provisions were cheap, that whiskey was abundant, and that I never saw an individual Irishman of a temper, which may not deserve to be described as gen-erous, and hospitable, and open. But as a people they were perfect savages, not merely in their mode of dealing with those against whom they entertained a feud, but against persons in whose society they set out with professing to take delight, and with whom they got drunk in all the glee imaginable. The case, for example, was not unfrequent of a party coming in to a public-house to drink, carousing together in perfect goodhumour till their senses became confused, and then quar-relling vehemently, they could not tell why. Forthwith came into play, poker, shovel, tongs, benches, and knives, till many a time the floor of the tap-room swam with blood, and of the persons frequenting it not a few were borne off grievously, sometimes mortally, wounded. Then their fairs and wakes were invariably of such a nature, that troops were sent to observe them, and to hinder the commission of all manner of violence. Yet even this precaution was not invariably found to avail. I remember, for example, that not far from the town in which we were quartered, an event befell, of which even now it is not easy to write without a shudder. There had been a funeral, which, coming from some remote corner in the country, was attended by a score or two of ragged peasants, all of whom followed the corpse, howling as is their wont, and nowise insensible to the stimulating influence of strong drink. The mourners having deposited their deceased friend in his grave, adjourned, as a matter of course, to the whiskey-shop, where they pledged his memory in as many draughts as the state of their finances would allow. Having exhausted these, and thoroughly inflamed themselves, they set out to return home; and well would it have been had they followed up this resolution, without looking either to the right hand or to the left.

The persons who carried the corpse to its grave, belonged to one or other of the rival factions, I cannot tell which. That, however, is a matter of no moment, for both were alike ferocious, and either would have been guilty in this particular instance of the horrible crimes of which I am about to make mention. Having drunk freely, as has been stated, the mourners set out to return home, and came, as they proceeded, upon the house of a respectable farmer, who owed allegiance to a party hostile to their own. Like madmen, they sprang within the inclosure, burst open his door, and meeting the servant girl in the passage, instantly put her to death. They then rushed into the kitchen, where the farmer and his wife were seated, an aged couple, from whom no molestation could be apprehended: them they pierced with many wounds; after which, they slew the cows in the stall, the horses in the stable, and the very dog and cat that wandered about the premises. In a word, a more atrocious massacre never was perpetrated, even in the county of Tipperary, though Tipperary has in all ages been renowned for the little value which its inhabitants put either upon their own lives, or on the lives of other people.

After this account of the duties which were imposed upon us, and the sort of life which we led while quartered at Clonmel, it will scarcely be wondered at when I say that the order which one day reached us, to march forthwith upon Dublin, was by me greeted with unqualified satisfaction. The 23rd light dragoons having been directed to proceed on foreign service, it became our business to supply their place; and this we did early in the spring of 1809, our respective squadrons meeting, on more than one occasion, as they moved, -- we to the capital, they towards Cork harbour. We occupied Dublin for something more than a year; and had the satisfaction, such as it was, of witnessing there the celebration of the great Jubilee. I need scarcely add, that the Jubilee of which I speak commemorated the fiftieth year of the reign of George III, and was kept up with extraordinary spirit in all parts of his majesty's dominions. I greatly question, however, whether in any town throughout the empire, more of the external show of loyalty was exhibited than in Dublin. For three whole days men exhibited their gladness, first by a grand review of the troops in St. Stephen's Green; next by a general illumination; and last of all in a sort of carnival, where all manner of irregularities were freely perpetrated, no human being caring to find fault with them. For example, the streets were thronged both night and day with minstrels, maskers, and mummers; for whom every door was thrown freely open, and who were regaled wherever they came with vivres and a hearty welcome. Neither, as far as I know, was any advantage taken of such frankness to work evil to the persons or the property of the individuals who displayed it. Yet we had slender reason to congratulate ourselves that we happened to be present on so animating an occasion: from four o'clock in the afternoon of one day, till seven in the following morning, both we and the Scots Greys were employed to patrol the streets; one half of the town being intrusted to the care of the Greys, and the other committed to our especial keeping. We all did our duty, without doubt; yet we heartily rejoiced when the gaieties came to an end, and we were permitted to return to the ordinary occupation of our lives.

So passed the year 1809, of which my general recollections amount to this, and no more -- that if not positively an era in my existence, it has left no stamp of extreme misery on my soul. Still there was very little mourning in the corps when the arrival of the 7th Hussars set us free, and we embarked, in the same transports which brought them into the Liffey, for Holyhead. There we landed in safety: a pleasant march of twenty-two days carried us to Weymouth, where the headquarters of the regiment being established, detachments went abroad to various out-stations, of which Farnham and Porchester were two. At the latter of these posts I found myself, with twenty of my comrades, the charge being committed to us of keeping guard over French prisoners, who, to the number of 7000 at the least, were cooped up within the walls of the castle.

Whatever grounds of boasting may belong to us as a nation -- and I am the last man in the world to think of diminishing their number, I am afraid that our mode of dealing with the prisoners taken from the

French during the war scarcely deserves to be classed among them. Absolute cruelties were never, I believe, perpetrated on those unfortunate beings; neither, as far as I know, were they, on any pretence whatever, stinted, in the allowance of food awarded to them. But, in other respects they fared hardly enough. Their sleeping apartments, for instance, were very much crowded. Few paroles were extended to them, (it is past dispute, that when the parole was obtained, they were, without distinction of rank, apt to make a bad use of it,) while their pay was calculated on a scale as near to the line of starvation, as could in any measure correspond with our national renown for humanity. On the other hand, every possible encouragement was given to the exercise of ingenuity among the prisoners themselves, by the throwing open of the castle yard once or twice a week, when their wares were exhibited for sale, amid numerous groups of jugglers, tumblers, and musicians, all of whom followed their respective callings, if not invariably with skill, always with most praiseworthy perseverance. Moreover, the ingenuity of the captives taught them how, on these occasions, to set up stalls, on which all manner of trinkets were set forth, as well as puppet-shows, and Punch's opera, -- in witnessing which, John Bull's good humour was sure to be called into play. Then followed numerous purchases, particularly on the part of the country people, of bone and ivory nicknacks, fabricated invariably with a common penknife, yet always neat and not unfrequently elegant. Nor must I forget to mention the daily market, which the peasantry, particularly the women, were in the habit of attending, and which usually gave scope for the exchange of Jean Crapaud's manufactures for Nancy's eggs, or Joan's milk, or home-baked loaf. This, though it took place at an early hour in the morning, was day after day an interesting spectacle to us, who, not seeking to pry beyond the mere surface of things, were apt to quit the castle-yard with a notion, that, after all, the prisoners had no great cause to be dissatisfied with their lot.

A prisoner, however, is always dissatisfied with his lot -- how indeed can he be otherwise? and we at Porchester, like others employed on a similar duty elsewhere, were in due time taught the truth of this axiom. It happened one night, that a sentry, whose post lay outside the walls of the old castle, was startled by a sound as of a hammer driven against the earth beneath his feet. The man stopped, listened, and was more and more convinced, that neither his fears nor his imagination had misled him; so he reported the circumstance to the serjeant, who next visited his post, and left him to take in the matter such steps as might be expedient. The serjeant, as in duty bound, having first ascertained that the man spoke truly, made his report to the captain on duty, who immediately doubled the sentry at the indicated spot, and gave strict orders, that should so much as one French prisoner be seen making his way beyond the castle walls, he should be shot without mercy. Then was the whole of the guard got under arms; then were beacons fired in various quarters, while far and near, from Portsmouth not less than from the cantonments, more close at hand, bodies of troops marched upon Porchester. Among others came the general of the district, bringing with him a detachment of sappers and miners; by whom all the floors of the several bed-rooms were tried, and who soon brought the matter home to those engaged in it. Indeed, one man at last was taken in the gallery which he was seeking to enlarge; his only instrument being a spike nail wherewith to labour.

The plot thus detected was a very extensive, and must, if carried through, have proved a desperate one to both parties. For weeks previous to the discovery the prisoners, it appeared, had been at work, and from not fewer than seven rooms, all of them on the ground-floor, they had sunk shafts twelve feet in depth, and caused them all to meet at one common centre, whence as many chambers went off. These were driven beyond the extremity of the outer wall; and one -- that of which the sentry was thus unexpectedly made aware -- the ingenious miners had carried forward with such skill, that in two days more it would have been in a condition to be opened. The rubbish, it appeared, which from these several covered ways they scooped out, was carried about by the prisoners in their pockets, till they found an opportunity of scattering it over the surface of the great square. Yet the desperate men had a great deal more to encounter than the mere obstacles which the excavation of the castle of Porchester presented. Their first proceeding, after emerging into upper air, must needs have been to surprise and overpower the troops that occupied the barracks immediately contiguous; an operation of doubtful issue at the best, and not to be accomplished without a terrible loss of life, certainly on one side -- probably on both. Moreover, when this was done -- and that it might, and probably would have been done, no thinking man will doubt -- there remained for the fugitives the still more arduous task of making their way through the heart of the garrison town of Portsmouth, and seizing a flotilla of boats, should such be high and dry upon the beach. Yet worse even than this remained, for both the harbour and the roads were crowded with ships of war, the gauntlet of whose batteries the deserters must of necessity have run; and out of which no reasonable man among them could hope to escape with life, supposing him to hazard life, rather than give up all hope or chance of liberty. In all sincerity, then, I am inclined to believe that the detection of this plot was to both parties a merciful arrangement of Divine Providence, inasmuch as the struggle would have been desperate, the mortality very great, and in all probability the whole would have resulted in the recommittal of the survivors of those who began the fray, to a more rigid confinement than that from which they sought to escape.

About a month after the occurrence of this adventure I got a furlough to visit my friends, with whom I spent several weeks very agreeably. I then rejoined the regiment, which had received orders only the day before to prepare for foreign service, and no great while afterwards it began its march towards the point of embarkation. There occurred, during the progress of that journey, a circumstance which not only distressed me a good deal at the moment, but in some sort affected the whole of my subsequent career of life. In my troop there were two non-commissioned officers -- a Serjeant Waldron and a Corporal Rents, as different in their tempers and habits one from another as if they did not belong to the same species. Corporal Rents was a very noble fellow -- sober, steady, kind, generous, and open-hearted. Serjeant Waldron was a cross-grained, ill-conditioned creature, who delighted in nothing so much as to annoy the "Johnny Raws;" the elegant name which it was his pleasure to bestow upon all who might have recently joined the regiment. With Corporal Rents I had early formed an intimate friendship, and it was the great object of both that we should be placed on parade as comrades; but the matter, somehow or another, was not arranged when the order to proceed upon foreign service was promulgated. On the march, however, we made a point of being as much as possible together. There was, indeed; but one man between Rents and myself in the order of files, and him I easily persuaded to change places with me; so that all the while we were upon the road I enjoyed the advantage of my friend's conversation, as he enjoyed the advantage of mine. Nevertheless, we were not long permitted to proceed thus unmolested; Serjeant Waldron took little pleasure in our discussions, inasmuch as they partook in no respect of the ribald and loose converse which in those days, at least, was too much in fashion among soldiers; and he marked his disapprobation of our tone, by ordering me back to my proper place in the line of march. Like a young soldier as I was, I ventured to remonstrate, saying that I merely wanted to chat a little with the corporal, and would get into my place whenever a halt should be ordered. At this he became very savage, and repeating his order, desired that I would not presume to call the wisdom of it in question. "Now, Serjeant," said I, very foolishly, "what difference can it make to you whether I or your own proper covering file ride next you?" "What!" said he in a rage, "do you still refuse to obey?" And so saying he clapped spurs to his horse, and rode off in search of the officer. In a moment a lieutenant of our troop -- a very austere man, whose name it is not worth while to mention, -- returned with the serjeant, and not waiting to hear a word that I might say, desired me to take my proper station in the column, and to be put down for the baggage-guard when the march should end. I was excessively indignant at this; but what could I do? At first I determined not to take this extra guard, to merit which I had done nothing; but a little calm reflection convinced me of the folly of such a resolution, and I made up my mind that it would be best for me to submit with patience to whatever load my superiors might impose.

I took my proper place in the line of march, and at the close of the movement received notice that at ten o'clock it would be my turn to mount sentry under the market-place. Meanwhile I adjourned with my comrades to the quarters which had been assigned us, and drinking freely with them, never thought of stirring till the clock had struck ten. Then, however, I jumped up, paid my reckoning, and ran off to the market-place, which, being close at hand, I must have reached within a minute or two of the time appointed for my appearance there. A corporal was in command, greatly resembling in his habits and temper my friend Serjeant Waldron. "Are you aware," said he, "how late it is? You are a full half hour behind your time, and I have put another man in your place as sentry. I shall confine you, and make a report of the circumstance to the captain in the morning. You are drunk, sir, as well as late."

It was to no purpose that I assured the corporal of my absolute innocence of the offence with which he last charged me; and protested that the clock had just struck ten in the quarter whither I had been sent. He would not listen to me for a moment, but, putting me under arrest, stated the case, doubtless in terms as strong as he could find, to the captain. I was at this time a very young soldier -- neither, from the hour of my enlistment, had I ever been confined before; so the

25

disgrace sat heavily upon me, and I fretted over it. But no important evil arose, at least directly, out of it. The following morning I took my place in the ranks, which I was permitted to retain all the way to Honiton, and from which, it is right to add, I was never, after all, removed. While we lay in this place, however, waiting for the transports to be fitted up, which were destined to carry us to the seat of war, the captain sent for me, and severely reprimanded me for the crimes of which I was charged with being guilty. He said that he was not only vexed but surprised to hear such things of me, whom he had taught himself to consider as one of the most sober men in the troop; and he charged me, as I hoped for encouragement, and desired not to incur its opposite, never to be found in so disgraceful a situation again. Hard, hard was the task of gulping all this down, while my own conscience told me that the charges were quite groundless; yet I felt at the moment that to deny them would be profitless -- so I put the padlock on my soul, and remained silent. I earnestly advise all young soldiers first of all to win the good opinion of their captain, and then, at every sacrifice of immediate gratification, to preserve it. The captain has every thing in his power, both to promote and to retard the soldier's advancement; and if you once get into his black books, it will cost you many a day of anxiety, and a considerable display of luck in your favour, to get out of them again.

I remember that about this time I received a very acceptable present from home, in the shape of various articles that would be useful during the voyage, as well as some money and tobacco, which I freely divided with my comrades, and for which they were very grateful. This was hardly done, when we proceeded to Plymouth, where the ships were fitted up and lying to receive us; but of their state of preparation we could very little avail ourselves, inasmuch as the wind was, and long continued to be, adverse. Under these circumstances, it was a sort of privilege to me, that, having for my comrade a young man intimately acquainted with the mysteries of boatmanship, I was joined to him, and had it in charge to execute the officers' commissions, as well as to purchase vegetables daily for the men in the same transport. I recollect, too, that the doctor having taken his passage on board of our ship, was, by my comrade and myself, pulled, day after day, round the different vessels among which our people were distributed; and that our excursions were not always unfruitful, at least in the accession of creature comforts. But this order of things was happily not destined to last for ever. The wind shifted in due time, and an enormous fleet, amounting, on a moderate computation, to not less than one hundred sail of all sizes and descriptions, hauled in their anchors at a given signal, and, under a very slender convoy, put to sea.

Generally speaking, there is not much in the voyage from England to the seat of war, which, in the life of a soldier, deserves to be recorded. In my own particular case, however, the rule can scarce be said to have held good; for, first, having on a certain occasion towed a dead horse ashore, I was one of a boat's crew that with difficulty regained the ship again; and next, my old enemy, Serjeant Waldron, put me to a very great strait. It happened one day that he saw me playing with my comrades on the forecastle, and that, being in a singularly bad humour, he ordered me below to look after the horses. I told him that I had done that duty the day previously; yet he would take no refusal, and affecting once more to regard me as a mutineer, he desired that I would remain below till he should give me leave to show myself upon deck. As a matter of course I obeyed, though the old hands pitied me much, and protested that had the dispute occurred with one of them, they would have carried it through very differently. Still I went to the stables, and abode there three whole days, and emerged again into upper air only when it became manifest, both to myself and others, that my health would suffer from longer confinement. A very angry man was Serjeant Waldron, when his eye encountered mine near the mainmast. He swore vehemently against my outrageous behaviour, would have forced me below again, had not the rest of the men openly withstood him, and ended by hurrying off to the officer in command, and making a highly-coloured report of the whole proceeding. It is not to be wondered at if the officer should have adopted the serjeant's view of the case, he being an old man and I a young one; or that, being assured of my turbulent and mutinous disposition, be should have consented to punish me next day by the infliction of a picketing. But, though Serjeant Waldron got all things ready, my comrades sustained me with the assurance that they would not permit the slightest wrong to be put upon me; and their good will, fortunately attained its object, without bringing any individual of the number into jeopardy. It chanced that a smart gale came on that night, so that in the morning, when the parade was formed, the ship rolled heavily, and the serjeant going to call the officer, found him deadly sick. With the utmost difficulty he was persuaded to rise, but he never got to the place where the instruments of punishment were arranged. A heavy sea struck the vessel -- the officer reeled and fell, and both he and Serjeant Waldron were in an instant covered with an ointment less odoriferous by far than that of which Arabia is the source. Poor fellow! our commandant was very much ashamed of himself, as well as extremely wroth with the person who had drawn him into the scrape. He accused Serjeant Waldron of having occasioned his disgrace, desired in a pet that the prisoner should be set at liberty, and diving once more into his own cabin, permitted both the crime with which I stood charged, and the punishment that had been threatened, to be forgotten.

Chapter 3

There occurred very little during our passage to Lisbon of which it is worth while to take notice, or concerning which it may with truth be said that it differed in any respect from the ordinary adventures that attend men during the progress of sea voyages in general. We had the customary alternations of fair weather and foul, bringing with them their usual accompaniments of comfort and its opposite, the whole being summed up by a seven days' calm, off the coast of Vigo; and, as that was not the age of steam navigation, the seven days in question rolled but heavily away. Neither can it be said that a cruise in the jolly-boat, after an enormous log of mahogany, which with some labour we overtook, but were unable to turn to an account, gave much agreeable variety to the scene. Let me then carry my reader forward to the Tagus; our entrance into which struck me as it does every stranger, with astonishment. I say nothing of the prodigious width of the river at its mouth; nor of the myrtle-clothed hills that greet your eye as you ascend: for it is on Lisbon itself so soon as it rises, like a queen, out of the water, that your gaze is with irresistible interest turned. And never, surely, has the young man's hopes more cruelly differed from the realities of life, than this fair city differs, as soon as you plant your foot upon its quays, from what it appeared to be while yet looked at from a distance.

As seen in the far-off horizon, Lisbon looks like a city of palaces. The dazzling whiteness of the houses, which catch and reflect the sun's rays, -- the series of terraces along which they are built, rising, in the fashion of an amphitheatre, from the river's brink, -- the many spires and towers which adorn its churches, -- all these give an air of magnificence to the place which prepares you to encounter, at every turn, marks, not of squalor, but of wealth. How cruelly the result disappoints you! Walls stuccoed over, with the stucco crumbling to pieces, -- narrow streets, choked up with filth of the most horrid kind, -- miserable wretches crowding about, as if they lacked not only the inclination but the physical power to exert themselves, -- all these, with a thousand symptoms besides of indolence and squalor, and a national character utterly degraded, left us, on landing, no room to inquire how far our expectations in reference to the Portuguese capital had outrun the reality. And yet Lisbon was in perpetual bustle during that season. Day after day ships arrived, bringing men, or stores, or munitions of war from England. The quays were continually crowded with soldiers, sailors, and camp-followers, while the river itself seemed to support a very forest of masts. Indeed, I never shall forget the splendour of the panorama on that day when our little squadron stemmed its strong current; for we met full in the teeth an enormous fleet, under convoy of the Caledonia, 110, and did not make our way through the throng without both giving and receiving some serious damage.

Black Horse Square will doubtless be familiar to many who honour these reminiscences with a perusal. It was there that, according to custom, we brought up; and there, after time had been given to arrange our accoutrements and get our harness in order, the regiment was formed. I was not so fortunate, however, as to march with my corps; for a serjeant's party having been directed to proceed on foot with the officers' baggage, it became necessary to intrust their horses to the care of some of their comrades, and my old friend, Serjeant Waldron, doubtless to show that I was not forgotten, committed to me the care of his charger. Now Serjeant Waldron was an extremely careless man. He had tossed his saddle, bridle, &c., he did not know where, on first embarking; and it took so much time to find them that long before I was in a condition to move, the last of the horse-party had departed. Moreover, when I did find them, they, or rather the saddle, was in a deplorable condition; for it had got into the horse's crib, and he, of course, had not spared it in any way. With some difficulty, however, I fastened it upon his back; and mounting my own, began, with the serjeant's charger in my hand, to thread my way in the best manner I could towards Belem. But such a journey! The horses being young and skittish from long confinement, pranced and kicked so that I could scarcely command them; and more than once the saddle on which I sat turned, through my inability to sit straight. I question, indeed, whether I should have reached my destination at all, but for the kindness of an English soldier who happened to come up just as, for the sixth time, my saddle had gone round and compelled me to dismount; and he volunteering to hold the serjeant's, I was enabled so to adjust my own beast that all his pranks proved insufficient, from that time, to incommode me in my seat. Then, following the guidance of my friendly comrade, I pushed on; and, finally, to my extreme delight, found myself delivered from a hateful office, and once more in comparative comfort, because restored to my regimental duty.

I am not going to swell these pages by describing matters of which a thousand accounts, more or less accurate, have appeared already. Lisbon was to me what it seems to have been to my countrymen in general, -- a scene of very little enjoyment; for though the climate is delicious, and fruit and wine are abundant, the manners of the inhabitants were, and I doubt not still are, preeminently disgusting. Of the lower classes I am bound to state, that they are at once the most indolent and filthy portion of the human race with which I have ever formed an acquaintance. With the exception of a peculiar tribe, called Galegos, who are not, by-the-by, Portuguese, but Spaniards, there does not seem to be anywhere the smallest disposition to industry among them. The consequence is that these Galegos, though despised and shunned by their townsmen in general, are by far the best-dressed and healthiest-looking people in the city; and, as always occurs in such cases, they are likewise the most civil and the best informed. In like manner, the women appear to entertain very indefinite notions as to the duties which devolve upon mothers and sisters in families. They have no idea of keeping their habitations tidy, but move about among the filth, which both within doors and without surrounds them, as if the atmosphere produced by it were not only familiar but agreeable. But woe to the individual, whether male or female, who ventures to walk the streets by night. Unless he be sheltered by an umbrella, not even a progress along the crown of the causeway will save him; for the good folks of Edinburgh are lame in the art, compared with the Lisboners -- who discharge their vessels without even a "gardeloo," and seldom miss their mark, provided there be a living thing beneath to aim at.

Nobody can have visited Lisbon without being struck with the frequency and magnitude of the religious processions which are there conducted. Of these, therefore, I need not take notice. But there was another ceremony -- in its purpose, without doubt, humane and excellent, though in its results of doubtful utility -- of which I am bound to make mention. I was struck one day with the sight of a string of eight or ten cars, each drawn by four fat oxen, before and after which went a crowd of persons, some well-dressed, others very much the reverse, among whom went sundry monks, bearing baskets in their hands, which they held up to the doors and windows of the better sort of houses as they passed. Into these the charitable threw loaves of bread, and other victuals, the whole of which being laid

31

up in the cars, are transported, by-and-by, to one of the churches. There the monks mix the whole into caldrons, and convert them, with other ingredients, into soup; for which dense crowds of ragged and miserable looking wretches wait eagerly at the doors. I found, upon inquiry, that the process went on -- I do not exactly remember how often -- but at stated intervals; and that the multitudes who looked to this precarious source for a large share of their subsistence were very great.

Of the dresses of the women, both high and low, why should I make mention? Wrapped up in their loose cloaks or mantillos, the former walk only to church, with faces so covered that a pair of bright black eyes are alone to be seen, and feet and ankles of excellent symmetry. Each of these is followed at a respectful distance by an aged attendant, or duenna. Whereas the poorer sort walk alone, in a mantle, formed frequently of scarlet cloth, with black velvet trimmings, long sleeves, and white handkerchiefs about their heads. Long black veils are likewise much worn, chiefly by respectable tradesmen's wives and daughters -- who, not unattended by their duennas, pass to and fro without scruple in the dirty streets -- and from the merry becks and nods which these girls cast upon you as you pass, you are apt, if a stranger, to form but an indifferent opinion of their virtue. But in this you are quite mistaken. The Portuguese women are naturally frank and good-natured; so that a bearing which among us would tell against a young woman on the score of immodesty, is among them the common method of marking their good will towards the party saluted.

I have spoken of Lisbon as being, at that time, a scene of perpetual bustle and great confusion. The arrival of fresh troops, and the departure of men unfit for service, were matters of hourly occurrence; while a sadder spectacle by far met us day by day, when on the beach we beheld multitudes of unhappy women, who, not having been permitted to follow their husbands to the front, were waiting till their respective turns came, that they might return home. Of these all interrogated eagerly each new-comer from the seat of war, as he arrived; though their inquiries seldom referred to others than the individuals on whom they respectively depended. Poor creatures, it made my heart bleed to listen to the shrieks of some, when told that their husbands were killed; and to the sad low moaning of others, to whom the vague reply was given, that the party appealed to was incapable of satisfying their wishes. And then to hear them deplore their wretched fate -- that they had not been able to follow the one human being to whom they were attached -- that they must go back to a country where nobody cared for or knew them. I declare that, though little given to the melting mood, I have often been obliged to hurry away, lest my feelings should quite overpower me in the very middle of the throng.

One anecdote more I crave permission to transcribe, ere I pass on to other and more stirring matters. It will not, I dare say, be forgotten by any who visited Lisbon in 1810, that the river was night and day crowded with country boats, the owners of which made a harvest by landing passengers from the ships as they came in, and would not make way for the ships' boats; which, on the contrary, they obstructed. It chanced, on a certain occasion, that an officer, charged with important despatches, endeavoured in a man-of-war's boat, to make good his landing at Belem Slips. The Portuguese watermen, as usual, blocked up the passage, and neither his threats nor his entreaties, nor the assurance that he was proceeding on urgent duty, could prevail upon them to give way. At last he stood up, and called upon one of these people, who had placed himself directly between the boat and the shore, to move aside. The man insolently refused, and, grasping a boat-hook, made signs that he would resist the farther advance of the Englishman by force. The officer lost all patience at this, and, drawing a pistol, shot the man dead on the instant. There was no delay after this in opening for him a passage. To the right and left the panic-struck boatmen drew aside, and he, landing, proceeded, on foot, unmolested to the place of his destination. But though the watermen were too cowardly to resent the death of their companion when it occurred, they made a prodigious fuss about it immediately afterwards. The corpse was carried in procession, unwashed, and in the dress in which it fell, through all the streets of the city; and money was collected from every passer by, in order to defray the expenses of the funeral. I never heard that any consequences more serious than this arose out of an affair which, in almost any other town in Europe, must have produced a bitter feud between the strangers and the natives. At the same time it is but fair to add, that there is no reliance to be placed either on the forbearance or the generosity of a Portuguese. If you happen to offend him, and a convenient opportunity offer, he will thrust his knife into your body without scruple; and where the odds in number are much against you, the sooner you take to your heels the better.

After a sojourn of ten days in the capital of Portugal, we received orders to march to the front; and went forward on our way in the highest possible spirits, and full of anticipations of glory and enjoyment. We crossed the Tagus in open boats, to a place called Aldea Golegas, and proceeded thence to Estremadura. There a furious thunderstorm overtook us, with rain so incessant and heavy, that in an incredibly short space of time the whole town became inundated; the water running in the streets a depth of a foot at the least, and sweeping into the cellars, where most of the poorer people dwelt, with the fury of a river. Our condition was of course cheerless enough, yet we bore it without murmuring, and would have been truly thankful, so early as the following day, to take it back in exchange for that which then befel us; for at the village where we halted there arrived on cars, about 700 wounded men from Albuera, whose plight was as pitiable -- I might have used a stronger expression, and said horrible -- as it is easy for the human imagination to conceive. No doubt they had received, when first taken in hand by the surgeons, all the care which the nature of their condition would allow. But they had performed since that period a long journey, through a barren country, and under a broiling sun -- and their wounds remaining undressed all this while, were now in such a state as to defy description.

There was no lack of willingness on our parts to assist them. We soon cleared out the best houses in the place; spread straw, and, where we could find it, linen, for them on the floors, and gave ourselves up to the business of cleansing their hurts, the smell proceeding from which was fearful. Over and over again we were forced to quit the miserable patients in a hurry, and run out into the open air, in order to save ourselves from fainting; while they, poor fellows, reproached us, with a degree of bitterness which none of us cared, even in thought, to resent for a moment. I need scarcely add that among that mutilated crowd there were here and there strange specimens of frail humanity. One pair of wretches I particularly remember, an Irishman and a Frenchman, who travelled in the same car, both of whom had lost their legs -- not partially, but entirely -- and who yet ceased not to abuse and revile one another from morning till night. It was melancholy to hear them railing, in their respective tongues, and threatening one another in a manner strikingly characteristic of the two nations. Paddy doubled his fist from time to time, and shook it at Jean Crapot, while Jean would put his hand towards his left side, as much as to say, "Would that there were a sword in mine hand, for then would I slay thee."

We did our duty faithfully by our mutilated countrymen; so faithfully, indeed, that weeks passed away ere I was able entirely to overcome the effect which the distressing occupation had produced upon me. I could neither eat nor sleep, for every thing seemed to be tainted with effluvia from those cankered wounds, and my dreams were all such as to make sleep a burden. Fortunately for us, however, we were not long condemned to the torture; for war must be fed for ever with new victims, and we turned our backs upon those already smitten, on the morning after we had met them. Our next stage was Elvas, where, in a beautiful olive-plantation, we formed our camp; and beyond which we were not destined, at least for a time, to proceed. Moreover, as if fate had determined to console us in some sort for the distressing rencounter of the preceding day, we met this morning, while on the march, about 500 French prisoners; who, under an escort of Portuguese, were proceeding to the depot at Lisbon, and ultimately to the hulks. Poor fellows, we pitied them too; for the Portuguese ceased not to insult and abuse them -- flourishing their swords over the captives heads, and heaping all manner of offensive epithets upon them. Beyond this, however, they did not venture to go, because by this time English discipline was in some measure established in the Portuguese army; and English discipline, as well as English feeling, sanctions no act of cruelty towards a discomfited foeman.

Chapter 4

Of Elvas and its beauties, including the fertile plain out of which it rises, the noble aqueduct which brings its supplies of water from the neighbouring mountains, and the forts by which it is commanded, I have nothing to tell which has not been told at least a hundred times already. Moreover, mere description is, in my opinion, of very little use in such cases; for things which appeal to the outward senses, must by the senses alone be examined -- that is, if the party curious concerning them be indeed desirous of having his curiosity gratified. Besides, were it otherwise, I am no master of the art of description. Mine was a humble, albeit a somewhat varied career, to detail which alone I have been induced to take up the pen; and so leaving the description of Elvas to those more competent, in their own estimation, to deal with it, I pass at once to the details of a private dragoon's life, as that is spent in the immediate presence of an enemy.

I am induced to think that the change from home service to real campaigning is much more striking, as well as far more difficult to realize, in the case of the light horseman, than in that of the infantry soldier. The infantry soldier finds himself, it is true, deprived, when he takes the field, of his comfortable barrack-room; while his provisions, instead of being served out daily, and by measure, may fall short from time to time, or utterly disappear. Then, again, he mounts guard -- not over a stout brick building, which nobody dreams of assailing -- but in the open fields, where all his wits must be about him, in order to prevent an active enemy from passing his line, cutting him and his picket off, and bringing ruin on the army. In every other respect, however, his life is pretty much what it ever was. He must keep his arms and accoutrements clean, himself tidy, attend parades, perform marches, and fight battles as often as to his own leader, or to the leader of the adverse host, a battle may be desirable. But, except in the matter of fighting, he must do all this at home likewise; and if his bed be often the wet ground, and his canopy the lowering sky, why there is no help for it; he must make the most of them. The light horseman on the contrary, has not only his own wants, but those of his charger, to attend to; and the difference to the horse in the sort of life, which on service he is required to lead, is infinitely greater than the difference to his rider -- supposing both to have been reared in England. In Portugal, for example, we had Indian corn served out as forage, which our horses would not taste, and which we could not get them to taste till we tried the experiment of soaking: moreover, we had to seek their litter where we could find it, to cut for them green meat, and train them to sleep picketed and in the open air, under which not a few broke down; and to bestow upon them in general a much larger portion of our care, than we had ever been taught, in the process of home duty, to consider requisite. In like manner, it was new to us to go on picket, and to sit on horses as videttes, for two hours on a stretch. It was equally new to our horses to have their saddles and housings fastened on for twenty-four hours together, and to receive their food with the bits hanging at their chests, and every thing prepared for action at a moments notice. I do not mean to say, that where men's feelings or imaginations are interested, all this is not very delightful; on the contrary, there springs up between the rider and his horse, a companionship, to which there is no parallel in any one of the many varied connexions which human life in its progress enables us to form; and such companionship is always pleasant, whether the cord binds us to a brute, or to our fellow-man. But some imagination is requisite in order to carry us into this train of feeling; and hence you invariably find, that in the light cavalry at least, your imaginative people make the best soldiers. Moreover, as the light cavalry are always employed, wherever the nature of the country will allow, at outposts, both men and horses are forced to acquire habits of vigilance, such as to be rightly understood, must have been both witnessed and experienced. The cavalry soldier sleeps, like his charger, with one eye and one ear always open. Both must be quick to perceive the first flash of a carbine, or the first blast of the trumpet; and both must be in a condition to take their places in the ranks, within a minute or two after the alarm is given.

Then again, patrolling, which is an especial duty, puts the metal both of men and horses to the test. You must move forward as if you had a hundred eyes: you must be cool and collected, and prepared for every conceivable adventure. Neither hedges nor ditches must offer insuperable obstacles to your progress, whether you be required to take ground to the front or rear; and you must be quite as ready and as willing to gallop off when to convey intelligence is your business, as to fight with carbine or sword, where you are desired to delay an enemy's progress. In a word, both the light dragoon and his horse are called upon, as soon as they take their station in the front of an army, to acquire, as if by intuition, new ideas on every subject; for, except in the formation of column or line, and the art of breaking up into order of march, and closing into squadrons again, the home drill -- at least in 1809 and 1810 -- had not taught us much of our real duty.

The light horseman who lays himself out to become a useful member of his profession, is sure to succeed. He will first of all devote himself to his horse; and then his horse as if grateful for the kindness shown, will do for him in return innumerable services. Thus, during a night march, when the dragoon, overcome by fatigue, drops asleep, the faithful animal will slacken his pace, or sway from side to side, in order to prevent his master from falling. In like manner, if they be passing in the dark through broken and dangerous ground, the horse will often refuse to obey either spur or rein: his superior instinct directing him to avoid the perils, into which the ignorance or over-anxiety of his master was about to hurry them. Moreover, the horse knows his master's voice: it eats out of his palm, lowers its head for the well-known caress, and licks his hand like a dog in acknowledgment. And when it comes to this, let not the light dragoon be afraid to trust his charger in every thing. If they be the attacking party, his horse will carry him bravely on: if it be necessary to fly, there is no fence which he will refuse, or which, unless it actually exceed his physical powers to surmount, he will not by some means either overleap or scramble through.

I was always fond of a good horse; and no sooner became aware of the necessity for exertion that was imposed upon me, than I gave up my undivided care and attention to the noble animal which I rode. He was young, but full of spirit; and though like the rest he soon fell away in flesh, I had the happiness to see, from the condition of his coat, and the spirit and alacrity which on all occasions characterized him, that his health was excellent: there was plenty of muscle and bone in him, with a fair portion of blood; so that set us to what work they would, I always got well through it. It was not so with many of my comrades; not a few of whom seemed to regard their horses as incumbrances, always except at the moment when the value of the horse was most felt, and when, of course, theirs, in nine cases out of ten, failed them. Let me not, however, be understood as applying this reproof to a ma-jority, nor indeed to any large number of the men of the 11th; on the contrary, it was only among the drunkards and other bad characters that this indifference to the animal, on whose efficiency their own depended, displayed itself; and such men, place them in what situation you might, would have been sure to disgrace themselves. Still, I think that there were few who took so much pains with their horses as I did; and that I lost nothing by the superior knowledge in grooming, which this fondness for my own beast gave me, will be abundantly shown, as the reader goes on with my narrative.

We had occupied our encampment some time, taking our turns in outpost duty, and occasionally skirmishing with the enemy, when there arrived at our lines one day a body of persons, whose uncouth appearance and strangely anomalous equipment excited in us to the full as much of wonder as admiration. They were guerillas, or armed peasants, whom the French not unaptly describe as brigands; of whom some had once been regular soldiers belonging to the broken armies of Spain, while others were petty farmers, or the sons of farmers, chiefly from the mountains of Estremadura. Of the composition of these corps, enough has been said in other quarters to convey to the minds of my countrymen in general a tolerably accurate acquaintance with the subject. Created partly by the war, partly by the smuggling habits of the people, the guerillas did here and there excellent service; by attacking convoys, harassing columns in their march, and cutting off detachments which were either numerically weak, or separated themselves too much from the corps on which they depended. As was to be expected, I found, on becoming more familiar with the Spaniards, that there was no end to the tales of daring and of cruelty, of which one or two of the guerilla chiefs had been the hero. Moreover, it must not be supposed, that when I speak of the guerilla chiefs, I allude only to such men as Mina, Don Julian de Sanchez, or such like. Every town and village in Spain had its regular chieftain, whose exploits the youths and maidens loved to recount; and who, in the eyes of his admiring neighbours, was of infinitely more use in clearing the Peninsula of its invaders, than Lord Wellington and all his generals put together. Neither was it an unusual thing to find a priest at the head of his own band, of whom, by-the-by, it is asserted, that if they were the most courageous -- of which there seems to be little doubt -- they were likewise the most merciless of all who waged war, not, as soldiers but as robbers. I heard it said, that about Irun and other frontier towns, the inhabitants used to keep a regular account of the strength of the different French corps as they entered Spain, as well as of the convoys of sick and wounded, which were told off to quit it; and that on the information derived from this source, the guerillas were accustomed to act in almost all the most successful of the enter-prizes, which gave a character of its own to the late Spanish war.

Our friends the guerillas did not long abide among us, whose method of waging war accorded very little either with their habits or their wishes. They sought for plunder, and liked it the better when they won it at the cost of a great many lives to the enemy. We faced the French squadrons fairly in the field, and never dreamed of molesting them, unless some important operation should be in progress. It came out, however, in due course of time, that the French were not yet disposed to act on so lofty a principle; and indeed, though we were the sufferers, I cannot find in my heart seriously to blame them. The circumstances of the case were these: --

While we lay in the vicinity of Elvas, the enemy began to show in and around Badajos a large force, of which a considerable portion were horsemen. It was our business to watch them; and as the 11th, with a detachment from the 3rd German Hussars, constituted the entire amount of cavalry then on the spot, our vigilance as well as hardihood was more than once put sharply to the trial. For the most part we came pretty well out of these affairs; but in the end, the troop of which I was a member suffered all but annihilation. It happened that when we were on picket, a trooper belonging to the Germans deserted to the enemy; and carrying with him accurate information relative both to our position and our strength, enabled them, without hazard, to arrange a plan for cutting us off. They marched, after night-fall, with the greater part of their cavalry, -- threw a strong body into a wood on our extreme right, -- and, keeping it there concealed, made their appearance at dawn in our front, with a force greatly superior indeed to ours in point of numbers, yet nowise so formidable as to justify us in our own eyes were we to flee before them. Accordingly a smart skirmish began; which lasted without intermission three hours, and the excitement of which hindered us from paying any particular attention to what was going on all the while in our rear. At last, however, some of us chancing to look back, beheld a formidable line drawn out, in such order as to bar our way completely, were we to think of retreating upon the regiment; for the left of the line rested upon a river, and the right leaned upon the wood from which the whole had, during the progress of our affair, emerged. It is marvellous how slow men generally are to perceive that they have got into a scrape. We never for a moment supposed that these were Frenchmen; we took it for granted that they were Portuguese brought up, we did not care to inquire from what quarter, but placed where they were, manifestly for our support. On, therefore, we went with our amusement, till the enemy in our front suddenly called in their skirmishers, and with four squadrons advanced to charge. We were quite incapable of making head against such disparity of numbers; so we gave ground section after section, turning to check the advance, and still keeping up a warm skirmishing fire as opportunity offered. "Retire upon the Portuguese, men," exclaimed the captain; "when they perceive that we are overpowered they will advance; and then, hold for another push at these rascals."

We did retire upon what we believed to be Portuguese; neither did we discover our mistake till something less than a hundred yards of ground divided us; and then what was to be done. The odds were out of all calculation; yet we were nowise disposed to be taken; so at the captain's orders we closed our files, and rode right at them. Never were men so entirely confounded. It was clear that they expected nothing of the sort; for they sat still, looking us in the face, and never made a movement to meet us. The consequence was, that coming upon them at speed, with all the weight and activity of our more powerful horses, we literally knocked them down like nine pins. Over they went, the horse and rider rolling on the ground; while we, cutting and slashing as we rode, broke through. But, alas! for us, there was a second line behind the first, which behaved differently. We in our turn were charged, and the battle became in a few seconds a mere affair of swords, where there was no room to move either to the front or the rear. The result could not be doubtful for five minutes. Outnumbered and hemmed in, we were almost to a man cut off. Eight were killed on the spot, twenty were wounded, and sixty-three good soldiers on the whole, lost to the service. The only man, indeed, who escaped to tell the tale, was one of our officers, who, being particularly well mounted, made a dash at the enemy's line; and laying about him, opened a way for himself, though not till he had received a severe wound in the shoulder.

In the course of that mélée, many feats of gallantry were performed; indeed, the enemy's loss in killed and wounded was far greater than ours, inasmuch as not fewer than fifty, belonging to the latter class, were brought to the hospital of which we became inmates. But there was one man in particular, who died so nobly, that I feel myself bound, as an act of justice to his memory, to speak of him. His name was Wilson. In temper and disposition, he was the quietest and most inoffensive creature in the troop; who never had a cross word with any one, nor ever, as far as I could perceive, was put even slightly out of his way. Nothing could induce Wilson to lose his temper -- nothing put him into a hurry; whatever he did was done as if the doer were a piece of clock-work, and the matter to be arranged something which could not possibly miscarry. Wilson was, besides, remarkably sober: he never drank even his allowance to an end. But if he did not drink he ate with a voracity which I have seldom seen equalled. Bread was his favourite food; and before his single pair of jaws whole loaves would disappear, as often as he succeeded in laying hand upon them. But Wilson's career, both of fighting and eating, was destined this day to end; and he fell thus:

I saw him engaged hand to hand with a French dragoon: I saw him -- for I was by this time disabled by a severe wound, and stretched at length beside others of my suffering comrades -- give and receive more than one pass, with equal skill and courage. Just then, a French officer stooping over the body of one of his wounded countrymen, who dropped at the instant on his horse's neck, delivered a thrust at poor Harry Wilson's body, and delivered it effectually. I firmly believe that Wilson died on the instant: yet, though he felt the sword in its progress, he, with characteristic self-command, kept his eye still on the enemy in his front; and, raising himself in his stirrups, let fall upon the Frenchman's helmet such a blow, that brass and skull parted before it, and the man's head was cloven asunder to the chin. It was the most tremendous blow I ever saw struck, and both he who gave, and his opponent who received it, dropped dead together. The brass helmet was afterwards examined by order of the French officer, who, as well as myself, was astonished at the exploit; and the cut was found to be as clean as if the sword had gone through a turnip, not so much as a dent being left on either side of it.

The fighting was now over, and there began a scene, of which I cannot think without blushing for the chivalry of our adversaries. Not content with taking our horses and arms, or even the purses and watches of such as possessed them, they proceeded to strip us of our jackets, boots, and even of our overalls; apparently bent, as it seemed to me, on leaving us nothing whereby we might be distinguished as British soldiers. I do not know how far the system might have been carried, had not our captain, who spoke French fluently, remonstrated with the officer in command; upon which an order was given to put a stop to the plunder; and to most of us our jackets, at least, were restored. But of watches, money, and boots, no account was taken; and we were marched off, some of us in a very sorry plight, to the rear.

The wounds inflicted in this trifling affair were all very ghastly. Being inflicted entirely with the sword, and falling, at least among the French, chiefly upon the head and face, the appearance presented by these mangled wretches was hideous; neither were we, though in almost every instance pierced through, one whit more presentable. It is worthy of remark, that the French cavalry, in nine cases out of ten, make use of the point, whereas we strike with the edge, which is, in my humble opinion, far more effective. But, however this may be, of one fact I am quite sure, that as far as appearances can be said to operate in rendering men timid, or the reverse, the wounded among the French were much more revolting than the wounded among ourselves. It is but candid to add, that the proportion of severely wounded was pretty equal on both sides; indeed, I suspect that there was a greater number of our people than of the enemy, whom it was found necessary to transport to the hospital, by slinging them over the backs of horses.

I was somewhat surprised at the moment, and I confess that the feeling has scarce left me yet, that the French should have been permitted to carry off a whole troop of dragoons, in the face of a corps, with infantry and cavalry at least strong enough to interrupt them in the operation. I dare say, however, that the reasons which dictated so much supineness to the lookers-on were adequate, -- at least, I am bound to suppose so; but, be this as it may, we were, after the fashion which I have just described, carried of under the noses of our reserves; the whole of which had turned out, and now stood quietly to observe the issue. We did not go, however, without misfortune having wrought its accustomed changes in the moral positions of those who partook in it. When I was lying wounded, for example, near the spot where the captain stood, (a lucky accident for me, by the way, inasmuch as it saved me from undergoing the same process of plunder with the rest,) I saw not far from me, my old enemy, Serjeant Waldron, covered with his own blood, and so disfigured that, till he spoke, I could not recognise him. He knew me, however, and calling me by name, besought me to lift him up. I plead guilty to the crime of having allowed the remembrance of ancient wrongs to come across me even then; and, in the height of my indignation, I answered him with an oath, and told him that I would have nothing to say to him. But my better feeling gained the mastery immediately afterwards; and I was in the act of moving towards him, when a number of the enemy pushed in between us, and I was hindered from fulfilling my intention. He recovered from his wounds, and died the following year at Briançon in France. My friend the corporal, too, who reported me on the march, fell in this skirmish. He was endeavouring to force his way through the interval between two French squadrons, when one of the enemy's officers, perceiving his intention, thrust at him with his sword, which entering under one ear, and coming out at the other, killed him on the spot.

Finally, it may not be out of place to record, that the lieutenant, who, to say the least of it, showed me no great kindness, lost his arm. Thus, the only three men in the corps whom I found austere, suffered in this affair, from which, with the exception of a severe wound in my sword-arm, I escaped unhurt.

Chapter 5

Our destination was Badajos, into which we had so sooner entered than we were all interrogated respecting our names, ages, and length of service; and the answers which we gave being entered in a sort of register-book, we were forthwith dismissed to our respective destinations. The wounded had an option between the hospital and the prison; and, strange to say, many preferred the latter, partly, I suspect, because they had no great faith in either the skill or the tenderness of French attendants, partly because they preferred the society and companionship of their countrymen to that of foreigners. I was among the number of those who foolishly preferred the prison; -- and great and lasting reasons I had to repent of it; for in the hospital we should have had at least regular dressing for our hurts; whereas in prison we could only apply to each other's wounds portions of chewed tobacco. To me the consequence was, that the wound healed too fast upon the surface, and skinning over ere a cure had been effected at the bottom, it soon suppurated, and broke out again. I need not assure those to whom such subjects are familiar, that a wound which breaks out after having been once ostensibly cured, is always a thousand times more troublesome than at the beginning. For a full month after mine took this turn, I despaired of saving the arm; and I am indebted for it at this moment chiefly, I believe to a good constitution, into the vigour of which no excesses of any kind had made an inroad.

During our stay at Badajos, we suffered a good deal by reason, not only of the indifferent nature, but of the scanty allowance, of the provisions issued out to us. Each man received, per diem, four ounces of bad goat's flesh, with six ounces of black bread; but neither wine nor vegetables were served out; and as to salt, we never knew that such an article had existence. I believe, however, that in point of feeding we were not by many degrees worse treated than the French themselves, who could derive no supplies at all from the surrounding country, and into whose magazines time had already made grievous inroads. Indeed, it was melancholy to see the whole face of the surrounding country in flames; for the Spaniards, aware that they would not be able to reap the corn for themselves, set it on fire as soon as it approached to ripeness, in order that the enemy might not be benefited by it.

Our sojourn in Badajos was brief -- only four days; at the termination of which we set out, on foot, for Merida. We suffered as may be imagined, terribly during that march; for, besides that several of us were wounded, cavalry soldiers are but little accustomed to pedestrian excursions, and the heat was quite overwhelming. Our lieutenant, indeed (for there was no distinction made in the treatment of officers, from that awarded to privates), became at last so weak that he fainted. Still, there was neither time given to rest, nor horse, nor mule, nor vehicle of any kind furnished for his conveyance. The French guard brought him to by shaking; and he was forced at the bayonet's point to struggle on -- the captain supporting him as well as he could, till we reached a halting-place.

It was a miserable, ruined village, without inhabitants, or provisions, or accommodation of any kind; and into one of the dilapidated huts we were unceremoniously thrust. We were all famishing; for no food had been issued ere we quitted Badajos, and nothing of the sort was to be had here; yet we had endeavoured to provide against the extremity, too, by gathering vetches on the road-side as we passed along. Neither were the means of dressing them wanting, inasmuch as I had exchanged my boots with a French soldier for a cooking-kettle and a pair of shoes; and the vetches being duly boiled, we endeavoured to make a meal upon them, but none of us could eat them: they were so bitter, that our gorges rose, and we threw them away in despair.

The next morning by break of day, the drum called us from our lairs; and a morsel of black bread having been handed to each, we fell in, and the march began. It was neither so long nor so fatiguing as that of yesterday; and it ended at a solitary shed -- a sort of long room, in which the farmer, whose house stood a little way off, seemed to have been accustomed to store his oil, for there were a good many large jars in one corner, all of them empty. Into two of these a couple of our men crept during the night -- so cleverly, that the fact of their having done so was unknown even between themselves; and as we did not discover their absence till we had performed a good portion of a day's journey, they were fortunate enough to make good their escape.

The third day brought us to Merida, which we entered by crossing a long bridge, built, I believe, by the Romans, and still used in the common traffic of the town. We were halted in the market-place, where crowds, both of the inhabitants and of French soldiers immediately surrounded us. The former expressed great commiseration for our fate -- the latter gloried in our capture and were not backward in saluting us with such epithets as marked a feeling for us both of hatred and contempt. But they did us no serious injury: and as we were permitted to halt here a day, our jaded limbs gathered a good deal of refreshment from the indulgence. On, however, we went at last, towards Madrid, changing our escort every third or fourth day, and leaving behind us one or more of our comrades at almost every hospital which we reached. Among others, a Portuguese major had on one occasion the charge of us -- a deserter, as I need scarcely add, from the ranks of his own army; and if, in some respects, he appeared inclined to show us kindness, in others he cost us a prodigious deal of unnecessary trouble. Moreover, his was the only command which give birth to any tbing like an adventure. It was this:

We were not far from Truxillo, when groups of strange-looking men, that kept hovering about our flanks and in our front, caused an alarm. They were all mounted; but either because they considered our convoy too strong to be attacked, or that they wished to draw us deeper into a wild and uninhabited country, they held, for a time, so far aloof that none of us could quite determine what their occupation might be. We, that is, we English prisoners, believed, because we hoped that they were guerillas; whereas the major, though manifestly ill at ease, scouted the idea. But he was not destined to remain very long under a mistaken impression. The numbers of the stragglers increased: they halted on the road before us, and, spreading off to the right and left, bore down in a sort of irregular line.

The major no sooner saw this, than he detached a portion of his mounted force to oppose them. The cavaliers soon met, and forthwith a fire of carbines and pistols left us no room to doubt that a body of marauders were around us, and that our fate depended entirely on the courage with which they might push the enterprise. A council of war was promptly held among the English; and we agreed that, as soon as the affair should grow warm and close, we would rush upon the dismounted guard, which observed us, seize their arms, and give assistance to the guerillas. I do not know how far our intentions might have been divined by the major, for he appeared all this time in a state of the most pitiable alarm; yet he gave his orders with perfect propriety; and when in our rear a fire was likewise opened, he detached people in that direction also to sustain the guard. Then began a scene of awful confusion. We were a large convoy: there might be perhaps sixty laden mules, besides cars of various descriptions filled with goods; while our escort consisted of at least three hundred men, of whom upwards of one hundred were cavalry. But corps of even three hundred Frenchmen entertained the greatest dread of the guerillas, and the muleteers and attendants went very far beyond them in the exhibition of their terror. In a moment, the latter began to cut away the baggage, and to prepare for a more rapid flight on the backs of the mules. The cars, too, were in various instances emptied, and the bullocks goaded into a trot; while the parties both in front and rear gathered strength every minute, and the noise of the strife waxed vehement. It was then that the major halted; and seeing us collect into groups, advanced towards us. He used no threats; probably he guessed that we Englishmen were not likely to be swayed by them; but be implored us for our own sakes, and for his, to lie down upon the ground and keep quiet. We did as he desired, by no means relinquishing our own purpose; -- of which the execution, by the way, seemed every moment to become more easy; for the guards, like their commander, took fright, and crept in among us as it seemed for protection. But, alas! for the realization of our hopes, the guerillas, as usual, fought for booty, not for honour. They appeared, also, to be perfectly well acquainted with the nature of the convoy -- even to the particular waggons which contained the treasure; and these having been abandoned, whether purposely or not, I cannot say, they gathered round them in a crowd, and advanced no further.

I have no language in which to describe our mortification, when we saw the Spaniards turn the waggons on the road, and drive them to the rear. The French, on the contrary, seemed beside themselves with joy; while our commandant did not fail to praise us for our good behaviour, and to assure us that we should by no means be the losers by it. This was a poor compensation to us for the loss of our liberty. Yet we had not advanced half a league, ere we had reason to congratulate ourselves on our prudence, inasmuch as there met us there a battalion, which the officer commanding in the next town had sent out to meet us. Thus escorted we entered Truxillo, every window being crowded with heads as we passed beneath; and, being marched to the prison, we were there left for a brief space, to speculate on the sort of treatment that might be afforded us.

We had not indulged these anticipations many minutes, when the Portuguese major paid us a visit, to renew his expressions of satisfaction at our behaviour during the attack of the guerillas, and to promise us the indulgence of a day's rest as our reward. He assured us, likewise, that care would be taken to supply us with an abundance of provisions: and he was as good as his word; for, in as short a space of time as was necessary to bake the bread, a store of new loaves was handed in, with an allowance of fresh meat. But the Portuguese major was not the only person who seemed to feel for our wants, and to be desirous of relieving them. As evening closed, a quantity of loaves were thrown in at our window by the inhabitants, till we soon had enough to last us, not for the day alone, but for a whole week, supposing the means of transport to have been accessible. In like manner two live sheep were given to us early on the following morning, which we lost no time in slaughtering, with bread more and more abundant, all the gift of the inhabitants; and a fire being lighted, and the carcases duly cut up, we counted on a day of, to us, extreme enjoyment; but in this we were disappointed. The major, either jealous of the good will shown to us by the Spaniards; or, which is not improbable, fearing that an attempt might be made to rescue us, suddenly revoked his promise of a day's halt, and ordered the prisoners to be paraded. It was to no purpose that we protested against such a palpable breach of an engagement. The major had the power, and he chose to exercise it; so there remained for us only to pack up as much of our meat as we could carry, and to take our accustomed places in the convoy.

Seven long leagues under a burning sun we accomplished that day; of which the effects were made apparent in the utter decomposition of our meat. Not having any other means of conveying it except suspended in lumps from sticks, it soon began to spoil; and had become, when we halted, so offensive, that we were forced to cast it away. Our evening's meal was therefore made, as usual, upon bread and water. Neither was there anybody in the miserable hamlet where we slept who possessed the power, whatever his inclination might be, to render our fare more nutritious. On the morrow, however, after traversing the field on which the battle of Talavera had been fought, we entered Talavera itself; and experienced, in a degree more gratifying than ever, the liberality and kindness of the Spaniards. Far be it from me to detract from the excellency of the motives which swayed these generous creatures. I do not for a moment doubt, that we English, had we come alone, would have been dealt by exactly as befel, yet it is proper to observe that we did not come alone. From the different towns through which we passed, our commandant gathered together all the Spanish prisoners that were in confinement, of which the number, when we reached Salamanca that day, had swelled to 300 at the least.

It is quite possible, therefore, that the inhabitants, commiserating their countrymen, extended to us, in like manner, a share of the feeling, -- in which case we were much the gainers by the misfortune of our fellow-captives. But, however this may be, soup, bread, wine, and fresh hay to lie down upon, were all brought in ample quantities to the prison; and of the three former luxuries we partook abundantly, and with extreme gratefulness. The latter, however, we were not permitted to enjoy; for again the jealousy of our commandant stood in the way; and, just as we had stripped and laid ourselves out for a night of sound sleep, the horrid drum called us to the muster. It was a cruel outrage this upon our exhausted strength. We had performed a fair day's journey since morning, and were ill able to endure the fatigue of a night march; nevertheless, endure it we did, over six leagues of deep sand; and then, just as the dawn was beginning to break, we halted. Not yet, however, was any permanent rest afforded to us. The last stages between Talavera and the capital were, it appeared, peculiarly dangerous to convoys like ours; and our commandant was directed, in consequence, to steal a march upon the Spaniards, of whose intention to deliver us some rumour had got abroad. Accordingly, at the expiration of two hours we were roused from our beds on the sand, and commanded to push on; nor did we stop, even for a moment, till the suburbs of Madrid were gained.

It was the common practice of the French to show off their prisoners to the Spaniards, with the greatest possible ostentation. For this purpose they used to march us by circuitous routes, in order to carry us through the larger towns, and always took care to enter these at an hour when the mass of the inhabitants should be abroad. This good custom, it was not to be supposed that they would omit in the capital; and hence, though we arrived within half a mile of it so early as three o'clock, we were kept lying by the wayside till six, the season -- especially on a Sunday -- when high and low, rich and poor, are to be found in the public promenades, or seated at the balconies. Meanwhile, our guards set to work, furbishing up their arms, washing their faces and hands, and otherwise getting rid, as far as circumstances would allow, of the stains and soils of travel; and, finally, when the proper moment came, we were ordered to take our places.

I never shall forget, as long as I live, the circumstances which attended our entry into Madrid. We -- that is, the English -- were in a truly pitiable state. Covered with dust and sweat, ragged, unshaven, and foot-sore, we made but a sorry appearance, even beside the escort; and they, be it observed, were not over-nice in their persons. Yet we were surrounded, so soon as we passed the gate, by crowds of well-dressed people, whose very commiseration -- and I believe that most of them pitied us sincerely -- became, by reason of the earnestness with which they pressed forward to give vent to it, an intolerable burden. For myself, I was certainly not in a condition to receive gracefully the salutations of the fair. I had taken off my overalls on the march, and now stood in a pair of flannel drawers, -- very black, be it observed, and somewhat scanty, -- without shoes or stockings on my lower limbs, and having the upper part of my person covered by a helmet and a military jacket. As to my face and beard, these were what weeks of toil had rendered them. And yet I was quite unconscious of the ridiculous figure which I must have presented, till an old woman, forcing her way through the throng, suddenly caught me in her arms, and, weeping aloud, covered me, to my extreme horror, with kisses. It was in vain that I struggled to shake her off. She held me with so tight a grasp, that I began to dream of dying by suffocation: nor could all my efforts succeed in forcing the hands asunder which she had twined round my neck. Poor creature! I never could make out why these marks of affection were shown to me, -- whether I resembled her son, or was to her nothing more than a stranger in distress, -- but that she meant well, the termination of the adventure sufficiently indicated. Having indulged her feelings as long as was agreeable to herself, she suffered me to go, and, slipping a pisetta into my hand, disappeared amid the crowd.

The proceedings of this old woman caused me naturally to turn an eye upon my own person, and I confess that I never felt so ashamed in all my life; for, of the multitudes who flocked round to gaze, a large proportion were young women, before whom I had little ambition to appear in the character of Don Quixote. Well pleased, therefore, was I, when the officer, after a quarter of an hour's halt, gave the word to move on -- and more satisfied still, when the building which had been set apart as our place of confinement appeared in view. It was not very inviting, to be sure, in its exterior, yet it promised at least to hide us from an inquisitive crowd; and I therefore entered beneath its portal with a lighter step than I had as yet planted since I first turned my back on the position of the British army.

Chapter 6

Of all the places of confinement into which I ever was thrust, this at Madrid was the most horrible. It had been originally a barn or storehouse; it measured about twenty feet by ten; and there was no other opening in it except the folding-doors by which we were admitted, and which at night were secured upon us. We found in it several infantry soldiers, belonging chiefly to the 3d Buffs; and the state in which they were may be guessed at when I describe the sort of furniture with which the prison-house was garnished. Some trusses of hay there were to lie down upon, not only worn, from long usage, into powder, but literally alive with vermin. Then, again, as the upper part of the cell was used for purposes which I need not particularize, the stench was horrible, while the squalid appearance of our countrymen told a tale of very hard fare, and the general absence of soap and water. With respect, again, to our diet, it consisted of the prison allowance, namely a pound and half of bread per day, -- not made from wheat, but almost entirely from beans, and soaked, if we chose it, in cold water.

I have heard a good deal of the harsh treatment which French prisoners were accustomed to receive in the hulks at Portsmouth, and in other depots through Great Britain; but I defy any set of men to suffer greater hardships than those which were inflicted upon us during the whole period of our sojourn in this prison of the Spanish capital.

Our comrades of the Buffs seemed to have been long enough in confinement to tame down, in some degree, their spirits to their fate. They lay down, night after night, on the living straw, and showed no disposition to refuse us a share of it; but we could not bring ourselves to follow their example. On the contrary, we swept a portion of the floor, next to the entrance, as clean as we could make it; and there, on the hard stones, found such rest as they were calculated to afford. At the same time let me do justice to our captors. They did not prevent us from walking backwards and forwards, during the day, on the space in front of our prison, round which sentries were planted; and, slight as the indulgence may appear to persons more happily circumstanced, by us it was very highly esteemed. I verily believe, indeed, that but for these promenades, not one-half of us would have lived to tell how the enemy used to treat us.

We had occupied our quarters but a few days, when an officer, evidently of high rank, -- for his dress was richly embroidered, and a numerous staff attended him, -- paid us a visit. I am inclined to suspect that he was a person more elevated than he wished us to believe: indeed, I mistake the matter much if I did not see him, on a future occasion, enact the part of Majesty itself. But, however this may be, he read -- whether Joseph or not -- a sort of proclamation from a paper, with the purport of which an interpreter who accompanied him made us acquainted. It was an invitation from the intrusive king to join his service. It set forth that he was in want of volunteers, and especially of men accustomed to the duties of the cavalry; and it gave assurance of liberal treatment, and promotion, so soon as they should earn it, to such as might close with the offer. There was but one feeling excited amongst us by this precious document, and we did not scruple to make it known. The reader was greeted with murmurs and groans of disapprobation. Indeed, I went so far as to hiss, a salutation in which I was immediately joined by my comrades. One would have thought that an officer, even if be felt disappointed by the result, would at least have had respect for the sentiment of honour which dictated ever so unmannerly a refusal: but it was not so with the personage before us. He flew into a violent passion; insisted on being told by whom the hissing was begun; and threatened in case we sought to screen the culprit, that he would inflict a severe punishment upon the whole. I confess that I was not without apprehension, lest some of my fellow-prisoners would betray me; and I own that I expected such an issue from the infantry, -- but I did them injustice, -- to a man they refused to speak. Yet I am sorry to say that, in another respect, they were not all so true to their own honour. Two men -- one belonging to the buffs, the other wearing the uniform of the 49th regiment- stepped out as volunteers for King Joseph's service; and, being carried away by the still angry officer, visited us no more.

King Joseph, if indeed it were he, kept his promise to our hurt. We were shut up in the prison for three whole days -- a terrible punishment, it must be confessed, even if our offence had deserved it. But at the expiration of that period his wrath appeared to subside, and we found the barn-door thrown open, as it used to be. We did not, of course, fail to take advantage of the privilege; yet, except to myself, this little promenade was not the source of any adventure: and mine seems, at this distance of time, so ridiculous that I scarcely know in what terms to describe it. But describe it I will.

To the right of the prison-door was a street, which communicated with one of the great squares of the city, though by what name called, or by what class of persons inhabited, I never had an opportunity to ascertain. The street in question was entered through an archway, over which was a suite of apartments, and close beside it a flight of stone steps, where, during the three weeks that I remained in Madrid, I was accustomed to spend no inconsiderable portion of my time. A corporal of the 13th Light Dragoons being, like myself, a prisoner, contracted, for me a great liking, and lent me a book, which I read with avidity, believing all the while that its details were authentic. The book was neither more nor less than Gil Blas; and it took the faster hold of my imagination, because I made acquaintance with it, for the first time, on the spot where many of the hero's adventures are laid. With Gil Blas in my hand, then, I was in the daily practice of repairing to the flight of stone steps, where I used to sit down, and in following the fortunes of an imaginary person, cease for some hours to speculate on what might be my own. My perseverance in this custom at length attracted the notice of the people who dwelt in the apartments above the archway, and more than once I could distinguish the drapery of a female, who seemed to watch me from the casement above. Gentle reader, have some mercy upon a youth, whose head was so full of the stories of Spanish devotion and Spanish intrigue that he quite forgot to take into account the absolute unfitness of his own bearing to enact, at that moment, the part of a cavalier. I confess then, that rags, and filth, and squalor notwithstanding, I took it into my wise head that some fair creature, dwelling in that elevated chamber, had fallen desperately in love with me. How I hugged the blessed vision to my soul! How brilliant were the pictures which I drew of her youth, her beauty, her extreme gentleness, her lofty spirit, and, dearest and sweetest of all, her absolute devotion to me! Gil Blas! Gil Blas was a commonplace character compared with me. I was on the brink of adventures which would throw all his into the shade. Accordingly, day after day I repaired to my wonted station, with a heart so full of its own musings that if ever I was myself in love at all, which is very doubtful, I was in love then with a being which my own imagination had created.

Not a syllable did I breathe of my happy state to any of my comrades. Even the corporal of the 13th remained in ignorance of the results to which his book had largely contributed; indeed, my plan was to become master of my fair prize in the first instance, and then to establish a claim on the gratitude of my countrymen, by making them all in some sort, partakers in my good fortune. For away upon the wings of the wind my fancy carried me, till I became a Spanish grandee at the least, and the prison-house was emptied of its inhabitants. Well, then, day by day, I repaired to my station, and each time I saw, fluttering behind the opened casement, the same feminine robe which had originally set my heart in a flame.

At length a hand and arm covered by a long black glove, were thrust out. They made a sign to me -- to me! beyond all question; and when I returned it, by rising and bowing my head, the hand was instantly withdrawn. "She is coming," said I to myself; "be still, silly heart-prithee, beat not so. She is coming, and I shall require all my energies to carry me well through the interview." She was coming, sure enough; for scarcely had I resumed my seat when a door opened close behind me, and I heard a shrill cracked voice exclaim, "Signor Inglese." I turned round instantly -- but conceive my horror. There stood at the doorway a little old woman, as ugly as it is possible for woman to be, who held in her hand a bundle of cigars, and offered them, with a few copper coins, for my acceptance. Down, down, in an instant, fell the fairy fabric which for livelong days I had been building.

It was no enamoured señorita that had so often watched me. I had excited no tender passion in any bosom, young or old; but was a mere object of charity to one of the most odious-looking hags that ever wore soiled cap over unkempt locks. I declare that I was so completely taken aback by the revelation, that I could not so much as obey the old woman's signal, far less thank her. However, grandmamma was a good old lady, and would not be refused. She kept becking and becking, till at last I moved towards her, when, thrusting the cigars and coppers simultaneously into my fist, she muttered something, to which I could make no reply, and most unceremoniously shut the door in my face.

It would be idle in me to attempt a delineation of the feelings which now swayed me. First, there was a sense of keen mortification, then of the ridiculous, equally keen; and, last of all, a consciousness that I had behaved extremely ill to my aged benefactress -- who, albeit she did not bring what I expected, brought the best which she, doubtless, had to offer. I reproached myself severely because I had omitted to thank her; and passing from that to a review of my own situation, I determined not again to put myself in the way of being mistaken for one who sat to receive alms. But the most severe ordeal of all yet remained to go through. Somehow or another I could not keep my own counsel, and, telling the whole story to my troop-comrade, I got heartily laughed at for my pains. To do him justice, however, Jack was very merciful in his mirth; he contented himself with advising me to return the book, the study of which had proved too great a trial for my wits, and sharing the cigars with me, we smoked them out, often pausing to laugh again at the ludicrous issue of my most romantic day-dream.

At last the order arrived for the prisoners to be mustered, and marched with a convoy which was then about to return into France. Well pleased were we when this announcement reached us; for though the term "French prison" seemed to insure for us an indefinite period of confinement, our sufferings in Madrid had been such as to reconcile us even to that prospect, provided it brought not in its train a renewal of the hardships that were passed. Our arrangements for the journey, moreover, were very soon made. We had no baggage to pack, and, as to other matters, with these we had little concern. Unfortunately for me, however, my friend, the old woman, having, I presume, got scent of what was in progress, made me a present of a pair of rope-shoes, which I, forsooth, imagined would, when stuffed with cotton, prove peculiarly agreeable to a pair of stockingless feet. Accordingly I slung my leather affairs over my shoulder, and tying on the old dainsel's ropes, placed myself in the line of march, and went on. But I had not proceeded many miles ere I discovered that I had committed a grievous mistake. The cotton soon got into lumps -- the rope wore my skin into blisters; and I was forced, after enduring indescribable agony, to throw the old woman's gift away, and return to my leathers. I have sometimes wondered since, whether the old jade, annoyed at the cold reception which I gave her, did not fall upon this ungenerous method of avenging herself.

Our march through Madrid was a very curious one. About 700 Spanish prisoners having been added to our force, the procession covered a prodigious extent of street; for multitudes of Frenchmen took advantage of the escort which guarded us, and, with their families and effects, wended their way home. In addition to these, we had a prodigious number of waggons, all laden with the plunder of churches, convents, and even of private dwellings; while the armed force which guarded the whole could not fall short of 500 men. But these were the least remarkable features in the conduct of the little drama. No attempt being made to clear the streets, enormous crowds choked them up, -- whose business, almost undisguised, it was to aid their countrymen in escaping. Thus, from time to time, a wave of human being would break in upon the escort, with the efflux of which some half-dozen Spanish prisoners were sure to be carried off; and as these were instantly denuded of whatever articles of military clothing they might happen to wear, and had ordinary peasants' dresses thrown over them, it was impossible for the guard, bluster as they might, to recognise and recapture them. Then, again, holes were here and there cut in certain brick walls, along which our route lay, and prisoner after prisoner, leaping through, disappeared, and was heard of no more. I firmly believe that ere we cleared the capital not less than a third part of the Spanish prisoners had escaped; and I have more than once been surprised at myself that I did not attempt, by a similar process, to recover my liberty.

Our progress through the town, and for some little way after we quitted it, was full of interest; for we might say with perfect truth that it brought us acquainted with the entire Spanish nation. There, in their carriages, drawn each by eight or ten mules, went the proud and indolent hidalgos, their imbecile-looking countenances exhibiting no expression at all, and themselves attracting no marks of respect from their inferiors. Here walked the Castilian gentleman, wrapped up in his ample cloak, with all the dignity of an ancient Roman. Close beside him strode the muleteer from La Mancha, carrying a goad in his hand, and wearing a sort of kilt made of hide. He was followed by a group of Andalusians, whose long brown vests, checkered with blue and red, and their hair tied up in long silken fillets, gave to them an air and manner peculiarly their own. With prodigious volubility they were conversing, while their quick black eyes moved hither and thither, as if their speech, rapid as it was, could not keep pace with the flow of their ideas. Then again we encountered women sitting in the corners of the streets, and dressing food for these strangers. Long lines of mules, bearing burdens on their backs, and bells at their manes, which tinkled as they went; with asses by the score, which one man was leading, while he talked to them incessantly, and seemed to be fully understood. And, to sum up all, the ringing of the church bells, the strange dialects in which the crowd was speaking, the swarthy visages of most, the sonorous utterance of all, gave such complete occupation to the senses, that reason and imagination both became paralyzed. We had no time at the moment to compare one idea with another; nor was it till long after that the full extent of the information they communicated became, upon reflection, known to myself.

Before I quit Madrid, and in doing so turn a leaf in my personal history, I may, perhaps, be pardoned if I place on record here a little piece of intelligence respecting King Joseph's habits and tastes, which I picked up -- I am sure I have forgotten how -- on the spot. Probably the reader is aware that the Spanish patriots, the more to enlist the prejudices of their countrymen against him, represented Joseph, both in their writings and their speeches, as personally a deformed man. He was crooked, they said, and blind of an eye. Now Joseph might not care much about a libel on his beauty, were his beauty alone affected by it; but knowing how much importance his loving subjects attached to the circumstance, he took every means in his power to disabuse them of the fallacy. With this view he used to go a great deal into public. He walked the streets attended only by the members of his family. He carried tapers in many processions; and seldom or ever saw a person, no matter how humble, looking at him, but he turned round and stared the individual full in the face. Yet all his care availed not. The Spaniards derided the notion of his carrying a taper out of reverence for a religion which they believed that he had abjured; and, as to his blindness, they persisted, in spite of all that could be urged to the contrary, in declaring that it was real. Were the Spaniards singular in this respect? I suspect not. There is no arguing against prejudice, be the subject proposed for discussion what it may; and the conviction of the people of Madrid that Joseph was a Cyclops, amounted to a prejudice. Then let not these worthy people be held at nought in a country where men's greatest boast it is to think for themselves; and where all have been taught by experience the truth of the distich:

Convince a man against his will,
You'll find him but a doubter still.

Chapter 7

The march of a body of prisoners from one place of restraint to another cannot be expected to furnish much matter for description. Our progress, indeed, was marked throughout by a succession of hardships and sufferings, even to look back upon which never fails of exciting in me sensations the reverse of comfortable; for I hold it to be one of those popular errors which men mistake for truths -- merely because they are continually repeated -- that the memory of sorrows past brings present joy. Yet I must not withhold from my reader a few slight sketches, such as may enable him to form some idea of a condition of life, into which it is my most earnest hope that he may never, from personal experience, become initiated.

I have quite forgotten the name of the place to which our first day's march out of Madrid conducted us; but I well remember that the journey, from its commencement to its termination, was to me prolific of distress. In the first place, the sun shone out with an intensity of heat, such as constitutions worn down with hard fare and long confinement could ill sustain; while the dust, rising in clouds from each footstep as it was planted, got into our throats and lungs, and well-nigh choked us. In the next place, my feet, lacerated by the rope-sandals which the old woman had given me, became one mass of blisters. It was to little purpose that I removed the immediate cause of this evil, after the evil itself had been fairly incurred; I did not enjoy one moment's respite from acute pain throughout the whole of that and the succeeding day. Nor was it from this cause alone that I suffered. Convoys, such as that of which I then found myself a member, were accustomed to halt for an hour or two at noon, in order that the escort might be refreshed and the prisoners rested; the former by eating their dinners, the latter by sleeping on the ground. Like my companions in affliction, I threw myself down so soon as the long-wished for permission was given, but I could not sleep; on the contrary, I lay writhing in agony; and when the order came to fall in again, I was quite incapable of obeying it.

It happened that just as I was making an abortive effort to stand upright, a French officer approached, who, noticing the cause of my weakness, and greatly commiserating it, desired me to get upon a waggon laden with wool which stood near. "It belongs to our convoy," said he, "and will carry you to the end of this day's journey, at all events. Get up, my poor fellow, and take your rest."

I thanked him, and with the help of my comrade, managed to scramble to the top of the bales -- but, unfortunately, I went not alone. Two or three of the rest, seeing how comfortable I had made myself, ascended the waggon in like manner, and lay down, like me, at length. But the waggoner had not been consulted as to the propriety of these arrangements; and we were soon made to feel that he regarded the matter in a different point of view from ourselves. We were scarcely settled, when he approached the vehicle, with an expression of fierce anger in his countenance, and forthwith, without having spoken a word, he began to belabour us about the heads and faces with his whip. My comrades, more active than I, soon leaped down. For me, I suffered in silence, for the height of the bales from the ground was considerable, and the bare thought of jumping upon my bruised feet was agony. I therefore took the blows, which continued to fall in showers upon me, with all the patience which I could muster, till in the end they wore me out, and I fainted. I believe that in this plight I fell from the waggon; at all events, when I recovered my senses I found myself lying upon the road, and, on lifting my head, I had the satisfaction to perceive that the convoy was advanced a long way to the front. What was to be done? I was even less capable of exertion then than I had been ere the halt took place. My very comrade, too, had abandoned me, and the rear-guard were preparing to quit their ground. Now the rear-guard had already shown, on more than one occasion, that they were determined not to favour the escape of any prisoner who should, under the pretext of inability to proceed, drop behind the column; they had shot, without mercy, every straggler whom they found it impossible to drive before them. What should I do? - struggle on, or lie still, with the certainty of death as my reward? I declare that the weight of a straw would have turned the scale to either side that day; for if ever man felt existence to be a burden, I did. Yet there is an instinct of self-preservation within, which will not permit us deliberately to resign life, so long as the chances of saving it appear to be within our reach. I made a desperate effort to rise, and succeeded; but as to moving on, that I believe would have been impossible, had not Providence sent a means of transport to my relief.

While I tottered, rather than stood, upon my blistered feet, a Spanish coach happened to pass; fastened beneath the perch of which was a spare pole, projecting a foot or two from the rear. A rope, likewise, hung from the top of the vehicle, as if it had been suspended there for my especial use; this I seized with a desperate clutch, just as the hinder wheel rolled beyond my station. I was swung to the back of the carriage instantly; and scrambling upon the pole, I made the rope fast round my middle, and felt that I was secure. Never has human breast beaten more gratefully than mine did at that instant; for the coming up of the carriage seemed to me to have been directed by Heaven for the preservation of my life. Neither was I indifferent to the fate of others; for observing, not long afterwards that another of our men had fallen, and was, like myself, entirely exhausted, I shouted out to him so soon, as the carriage approached the spot where he lay, and invited him to join me, which, with a desperate effort, he did. I made room for him on the pole. By then untying the rope, and passing it round our middles, both were made fast, and we jogged on, uneasily enough, as the judicious reader will believe, yet very thankful for the blessing, such as it was, which a kind Providence had thrown in our way.

We had journeyed thus about three English miles, when the same officer who had advised me to ascend the waggon rode up. He instantly recognised me, but not only did not require either of us to descend, but expressed himself well pleased that I had found a substitute for the resting-place from which the waggoner had driven me. Neither did his kindness end there. The carriage was his own; it contained his wife and two children, whom he was escorting back into France, and who carried with them their own provisions, which they were accustomed to cook over night, and to eat upon the march. He ordered the driver to stop, rode up to the coach-window, made his lady pour out two cups of wine, and brought them, with some slices of bread and sausages, to us. We ate and drank with grateful hearts, and received from the repast so much refreshment, that we found ourselves, when occasion required, fully capable of walking; and the occasion did present itself somewhat sooner than we could have wished, for the coachman, to make up for lost time, drove his horses into a trot, and the end of the pole - an uneasy seat at the best - was no longer endurable. We were forced to abandon our position. Nevertheless we held on by the rope, which dragged us into a run, during which blisters and bruises were alike disregarded; and we arrived in good time at the yard within which the rest of the prisoners had been thrust, not, to all appearance, greatly more distressed than the strongest of them.

I asked for no portion of my comrades' rations that night. I was too much exhausted even to eat; but throwing myself down upon the ground, with a stone for my pillow, I soon fell asleep. At daybreak next morning we were roused as usual, and the march began; the guards pushing us forward with very little regard either to our comfort or their own reputation for humanity. In my own case, however, it seemed as if the endurance of the preceding day had hardened me for all that was to follow; for I felt, to my great surprise, comparatively well, and trudged on - not indeed at ease, but suffering far less, even from blistered feet than many of those around me. Moreover, I observed that the Spaniards, however accustomed they might be to the burning suns of their own country, were far less capable of sustaining fatigue than the English. For one of our people that dropped behind, a score of these unfortunate wretches were knocked up; and he in the Spanish garb who once gave in never found an opportunity to recover. I believe that this shocking practice of shooting their exhausted prisoners was resorted to by the French in reprisal of similar atrocities perpetrated upon their countrymen by the Spaniards. The French themselves, at least, so accounted for the barbarism; but, however this may be, I am sure that no good results arose out of it inasmuch as the mutual antipathies of the two people became only, from day to day, more confirmed. I regret to be obliged to add, that this day an English prisoner suffered the same fate - and yet I had the best reason for believing that his executioner slew him in ignorance. The facts were these:

A soldier of my own regiment, whose clothes had melted from his back, contrived, somehow or another, to get possession of a Spanish dress, which he wore upon the march; and on account of which, as it happened to be in excellent repair, he became an object of something like envy to his more destitute companions. Poor fellow! his constitution was not by nature so robust as mine; and he repeatedly declared that, let come what might, it was impossible for him to proceed further. We encouraged him as well as we could; we took it by turns to lend him our arms: but all would not do. At the foot of an enormous mountain, which it was necessary to cross, in order to reach the place of our destination for the night, the pleasant town of Segovia, he sat down by the way-side, and resigned himself to his fate. There was not strength enough in us to carry him. There were neither horses, nor mules, nor cars for the conveyance of the feeble; we had, therefore, nothing for it but to commit him to God's keeping, and to march on.

But God saw that this day he had run out the measure of time that was allotted to him; and his labours, and his anxieties, and his hopes, and his fears, were all brought to an end.

It happened that my comrade and I, feeling unusually fresh, took it into our heads to diverge from the proper line of march; and making for an elbow of the mountain, began to climb, under the expectation that we should thus head the column, and find time to rest at the summit. We were not deceived in this expectation; and yet we were both tempted, by-and-by, to regret that we yielded to the impulse: for, though we reached the mountain's brow, and found a luxurious bank of soft herbage to recline upon, the spectacle which met our gaze, as we looked down upon the plain beneath, was harrowing in the extreme. The rear-guard of a convoy, of which prisoners of war form a part, marches, be it observed, a long way behind the closing files of the column. I believe that this wide interval is interposed between them and the captives for the humane purpose of giving to the feeble among the latter as good a chance for recovery as may be; but it does not always succeed. To-day, for example, we were horrified by observing -- far, far away, in the distance -- one little column of smoke rise after another, even when by us no report of musketry could be heard. But our feelings were not yet entirely harrowed up, for we had fixed our eyes in a great measure upon the spot where our poor comrade was sitting, and we were resolved to judge, from the fate which should attend him, of that which we apprehended might have been awarded to others.

I have no power of language in which to describe the breathless anxiety with which we watched the gradual approach of the armed party towards the base of the mountain. On and on it came, -- another and another little blue column ascending -- and, by-and-by, faint and feeble, the sharp ringing in the ear which told of a musket or a carbine discharged. Still we doubted the reality; for, as chance would have it, none of these things took place anywhere within half-a-mile of the spot where our comrade was sitting. But our doubts were not destined to operate for ever.

"See, Tom! they are approaching," exclaimed I, grasping my comrade's arm with a convulsive motion. "Look, look! there is one of them stepping out from the column; and now he approaches him. See, see! he stoops over him -- he is going to assist him. Oh! yes -- they will rise him up. But why does he step back?"

Let me draw a veil over what followed. We saw the musket levelled-we beheld the flash, -- and, long ere the report reached us, our poor countryman rolled backwards to the earth.

The convoy reached Segovia, in a chapel at the outskirts of which we were halted; and right glad were we to find, when thrust into the interior, that the floor was covered with nice clean straw. We lay down, thanking Heaven for a luxury to which we had long been strangers; but the time alotted for the enjoyment of it proved very brief. One of us going to the door, overheard the sentry talking, to his great surprise, to another French soldier in English. Our guard, it appeared, had been changed; and we were now under the charge of a detachment from the Irish brigade, of which a scoundrel named Smith was at the head. He was an officer in the service of Napoleon, -- a traitor to his country and his legitimate sovereign; and, like all such renegades, remarkable for his hatred of the people whose cause he had abandoned. From what passed between the sentry and his Irish comrade in French uniform, we learned that Captain Smith was determined to take time by the forelock, and, regardless of our sufferings, to compass not less than seven leagues more ere he permitted us to rest for the night.

Now we had already traversed six leagues, of which a considerable portion lay over mountains, and the seven with which we were threatened scarcely dipped at all into the plain: our horror may therefore be imagined. Nevertheless, no good result attended our effort at remonstrance. To the deputation which we sent to implore his clemency he replied in language which I do not care to repeat, summing up all with this announcement: "I know that there is a long journey before you; but I advise you not to think of cutting it short; for I am a man of my word. No straggling, you scoundrels! remember, I have plenty of ball-cartridges."

It was useless to remonstrate with one whose nature seemed to be cast in so savage. a mould; so we packed up our miserable wallets, took our places in the column, and at the word of command moved on. With one exception, this proved to be by far the most distressing day's march which we accomplished. The road -- a mere track, which led from one hill-top to another -- soon cut our wounded feet to pieces. The rain began to fall; and we, having but our tattered uniforms to oppose to it, were wet to the skin, in half-an-hour. Moreover, we could not venture, let our necessities be what they might, to diverge, even for an instant, from the direct line; for Mr. Smith took more than one opportunity of repeating his threats; and we learned from the unfortunate wretches whom he commanded that it would give him positive pleasure to carry them into effect.

I speak of these men as unfortunate wretches, because I found, upon inquiry, that they were not all naturalized Frenchmen, the remains of Emmetts and O'Connor's bands, -- out of which, as is well known, the Irish Brigade had been formed. One, on the contrary, I recognised as an old acquaintance, who, after having lived as hostler at the Greyhound in Blandford, had enlisted in an English regiment, been taken prisoner, and prevailed upon to take service with the enemy. This man assured me that there were several in the corps similarly circumstanced with himself, not one of whom had put on the French uniform except with a view to escape so soon as a convenient opportunity might occur. But such opportunities the French took care not to afford. "We dare not go beyond our cantonments," he added, "without running the risk of death upon the spot. For the gendarmes have orders to shoot us without trial; and we know, from experience, that they are ready to obey them. If there be any in your batch that are tempted to adopt this method of delivering themselves from immediate suffering, warn them from me that no good will come of it. I cannot now return to the condition of a prisoner; but, if I could, it would not be blistered feet, nor yet hardships tenfold more severe than those which you suffer, that would tempt me again to profess myself a traitor. Escape if you can, and die in prison if you cannot; but never take service in the French army."

I trudged on, pondering with painful interest the words which my old acquaintance had spoken; till, just as twilight began to deepen into night, I found, to my inexpressible relief, that the journey of seven leagues had been accomplished. Not even then, however, did the ferocity of Mr. Smith cease to display itself. Instead of affording us the shelter of some public building, (for we halted in a town of which I have forgotten the name,) he thrust us into a stable-yard, the soil of which was become, in consequence of the rain, a heap of mud; and, without straw or litter of any kind to lie down upon, without so much as serving out a morsel of bread or a draught of water, he told us to make the best of a lodging which was a great deal too good for such as we.

Upon the sufferings of that night I shall never cease to look back except with unmitigated horror. My bed was the soft earth, -- my canopy the stormy sky; yet I slept, -- though, when I woke, it was in a state so benumbed and cold, that all power to move hand or foot was for a while denied me.

I do not know how I should have recovered strength enough to stir from my lair, had not a comrade, whose constitution seemed more hardy than my own, befriended me. This man, perceiving that I was quite chilled, ran to a sort of sutlery, which was not far distant, and purchasing a glass of brandy, returned with it to me. I drank it as a man may be supposed to drink water, who comes suddenly, in the middle of an Arabian desert, upon a secret spring. I blessed the hand likewise, that supplied the medicine, and rose in five minutes greatly invigorated by it. Yet I made but a bad march that day. My feet gave way again: I was entirely spent: and the first halt which we made, on a wild and desolate moor, I threw myself down upon the ground, and wellnigh prayed that death would come to my release.

I was in this mood, suffering extreme agony from my feet, when, on lifting up my head, I beheld, not far from me, a spectacle which -- be it spoken in all remorse and compunction of heart -- served but to aggravate my distresses fourfold. Somehow or another I had detached myself a good way from my comrades, and, lying near a waggon, I saw a man descend from it, spread a tablecloth upon the grass, and convey to it a most inviting assortment both of eatables and drinkables. To these he forthwith addressed himself: and, oh! gentle reader, if ever you have known what it was to gaze, yourself fasting, upon a feast that had been spread for others, then you will have some fellow-feeling for the agonies which, throughout the interminable space of perhaps two or three minutes, I endured. Both my appetite and my suffering were, moreover, enhanced by the sort of half conviction which took possession of me, that the happy man on whom mine eyes rested was not French, but English; for all his proceedings were redolent of the practices of that favoured land where the commonest peasant eats wheaten bread to his bacon, and never thinks of resting his jaws till his crop be thoroughly filled.

Heaven forgive me! but, over and over again, I invited myself to breakfast with the fortunate individual -- not once presuming to imagine that, be his nativity what it might, he would take the whim into his head of inviting me; yet he did. I daresay my gaze was abundantly expressive; but, however this may be, my surprise and delight defy the power of language to describe them, when all at once I heard him, after stopping the movement of his jaws for an instant, exclaim, "I say, comrade, are you peckish? If so, come and mess with me; there's lots for both of us!"

I need not say that I waited for no second invitation. The influence of fatigue seemed to pass away under the excitement of the prospect thus opened out to me; and I sprang from the earth with the agility of one who had spent the night between a pair of clean Holland sheets. I don't think many such breakfasts have been eaten, either in Spain or elsewhere, from that day to this. I declare that I felt quite ashamed of myself, so tremendous was the onslaught which I made upon the meatpasty and the flask of wine wherewith I was invited to wash it down.

Having appeased the cravings of a well-tried appetite, I entered into conversation with my hospitable entertainer, who informed me that he was a soldier of the 10th Hussars; that he had been taken prisoner, and released by a French general, who offered him a situation in his family as groom. This he did not feel authorized to refuse; and he had lived for some time with his master in a state of comfort and respectability, which made him wellnigh forget that he was an exile from the land of his birth.

Having told me all this, he went on to say, that he and his master were travelling under the escort of our convoy, into France; and that, if I liked it, he would reserve a place for me on his waggon, and use his best endeavours to treat me well throughout the remainder of the journey. It is scarcely necessary to add, that I closed thankfully with his offer.

Hiding myself under the straw, I escaped the observation of the guard, and was thus pleasantly conveyed as far as Miranda, where the cavalcade halted for the night, and where I found an opportunity of being useful to my fellow-prisoners, the bare remembrance of which makes my heart swell, at this day, with triumph. The circumstances were these:

Under the protection of my friend Joseph, I not only travelled secure, but was, at the termination of the stage, treated with marked generosity by one or two French officers who seemed somehow or another to be attached to his master's family. One of them gave me a five-franc piece; another presented me with a foraging-cap; a third supplied the place of my dilapidated uniform with a good jacket and a pair of trousers; while Joseph himself, carrying me to the stables, showed me an excellent bed laid down, of which fresh straw and two or three horse-cloths constituted the materials. He then conducted me to one or two wine-houses, where we drank, in moderation, with the French soldiers, and found them not only agreeable, but exceedingly generous, companions. For example, rations were issued out to them that night -- an allowance of bread and meat to each man; which they did not seem to value in the least degree, because, as they said, the Spaniards were bound at every stage to provide them with better. I asked Joseph whether it might not be possible to hinder the waste of throwing these viands away by begging them as a gift to the starving English prisoners. Joseph instantly stated the case to the French soldiers, and, without a single exception, they acceded to his wishes. The bread and meat were given to me. I carried them away to the bottom of a garden, lighted a fire, and, with the addition of some pot herbs, made a capital mess. With this Joseph and I made our way to the prison, and the joy and gratitude of its poor inmates filled my heart with strange feelings and my eyes with tears. I could not, however, venture to linger long among them, for I knew that, if discovered, I should be at once brought back to the condition of a prisoner. I therefore left Joseph to minister to their wants more in detail; and, after cordially embracing my comrades, retreated to the stable.

Chapter 8

From that time till the convoy reached Segovia I managed to share Joseph's waggon by day, and his excellent board and snug quarters at night. By some unlucky accident, however, I was detected, just as our vehicle was entering the latter place; and the consequences were, my immediate removal from the influence of my friend's kindness, and my return to the companionship, in every sense of the expression, of my fellow-prisoners. Not that Joseph forsook me: he visited me in our place of confinement at Segovia, bringing with him a flask of wine and a large loaf of bread, and took of me an affectionate farewell -- his master's route and ours diverging at this point one from the other. We did not part, however, till after we had exchanged assurances that, if Fortune should ever bring us together again, we would without fail renew our intimacy. I am happy in being able to record that Fortune did thus favour us; and that she was doubly kind to me, by enabling me, in a distant land, to pay back, in some sort, the favours which I received from him in this my hour of humiliation and suffering.

I do not know whence it came about, but the further we removed from the Portuguese frontier the less kind the Spaniards, as a people, showed themselves towards us. At Segovia, for example, the inhabitants, though they provided their countrymen with good things of every sort, brought little or nothing to us; and we were reduced, in consequence, to subsist as well as we could upon our scanty allowance of very indifferent bread. It was but natural that the consideration of this fact should not be without its effect upon us. We began first to envy and then to dislike our companions in exile; and seeing them flush of money, while we ourselves were penniless, the idea gradually matured itself, "Why should not we, by fair means or by foul, share in their abundance?" When men are suffering real privations, and there are profusion and waste all around them, the moralist may say what he will, but they don't readily listen to the voice which would whisper of self-denial, and patience, and abstinence. We soon discovered, for instance, that the Spanish prisoners had large sums of money at their command, which they squandered continually in gambling, as if it had been applicable to no other use than that of keeping alive a violent excitement among them. I have often seen as many as forty or even sixty dollars on the ground at a time, for which different groups were tossing, and which changed hands over and over again, according as the guess of this or that speculator proved to be correct. At first we were mere spectators of the pastime; but, by-and-by, we began to argue that the money would be at least as well applied in the purchase of a few necessaries for us, as it seemed to be in the encouragement of an idle and profitless spirit of gambling among our allies. Accordingly, having watched till a tolerably rich treasure cumbered the surface of the earth, about a dozen of us suddenly broke the ring and began to help ourselves, without compunction, to the dollars and other coins that lay scattered around us. The Spaniards, of course, raised a clamour, but they attempted nothing more; while the French, instead of interfering in their behalf, only laughed at them. The result was, that, for several days, we had tobacco to our pipes, and onions to eat with our bread, while the gamblers, if not cured, were rendered a few degrees more cautious in the exhibitions which they made both of their wealth and their cupidity.

In this manner we proceeded as far as Valladolid, where, numbers falling sick, and many more becoming lame through exertion, a halt of three days was permitted. It sufficed to fill the hospitals with invalids -- few of whom, I have reason to believe, ever quitted them alive. But, however this may be, all who were in a fit state to travel marched, on the fourth day, to Burgos -- whence a moderate stage carried us to Sallada, overwhelmed by the oppressive heat of the weather and stifled with dust. Here an event befel, of which, as it gave an entirely novel colouring to the whole of my after fate, I feel myself, in some measure, required to give a somewhat detailed account.

When thrust back into the common prison-house, I had been deprived, by the escort, of the few articles of wearing apparel which Joseph had procured for me, and was now, in consequence, more squalid and torn than ever. I had no jacket at all -- only a waistcoat out at the elbows; no shirt, no stockings, no cap: indeed, I was altogether as perfect a representation of abject poverty as the fancy of the most fanciful could well describe. In this condition I entered Sallada, and went with my comrades, to the prison yard, into which, by-and-by, came several French and English officers, the latter, prisoners like ourselves, though, of course, in better plight; and as it seemed, much thought of by their captors.

Among others, there drew near a gentleman in the uniform of a regiment of Lancers -- a man evidently of rank and consequence, whom a considerable personal staff attended, and who appeared to have some object to gain by his visit. I saw him stop beside a man of the 13th; and, by means of an interpreter who bore him company, enter with that person into conversation. Not knowing why I did so, I listened to what passed between them, and found that the foreigner was desirous of engaging the Englishman to serve him as groom, and that the Englishman, though not personally averse to the arrangement, stated a fact which at once stood in the way of its completion. He told the interpreter that he was married and had a family; upon which that personage, though with great kindness, stated that, with a man so circumstanced, the count was not desirous of entering into an engagement. He had scarcely said so, when his own and his employer's eyes falling upon me, both approached, and the interpreter opened with me the same subject. I was completely taken by surprise. I assured him that I neither could nor would listen to any such proposition, but was determined to share my comrades' fate, be it what it might, till, by the course of a regular exchange, we should be enabled to return to our regiment. It is not worth while to fatigue the reader's patience by describing how both the count and the interpreter pressed the point; for the officer of rank proved to be the German Count Goltstein, who was at that time at the head of the Lanciers de Bourg, in the service of Napoleon. But the results were, in a few words, these. I believe that I should have stood out against all his proposals, though they were both numerous and liberal, had not an English officer, who overheard the dialogue, interfered to set aside my scruples. He assured me that, if I was afraid of being compelled to take up arms against my own country, I laboured under a very groundless species of alarm; that the Count Goltstein was a man of honour -- far more attached at heart to the English than to the French; and who, let happen what might, would not only not urge, but never permit, my passing into the ranks of the enemy. Finally, he and the interpreter set such tempting offers before me, that I did not know how to refuse them. I was to be at the head of the stables; to have charge especially of an English thorough-bred mare; to be well fed, well clothed, well looked after, and to receive as wages, or pocket-money, call it which you may, one guinea per month. Surely I am not to blame for having accepted this engagement, when the sole choice submitted to me was between its acceptance, and my continuance for some indefinite, yet, without doubt, protracted, space of time, a prisoner of war. But, be this as it may, I did accept it; and I am bound to add that I never found any just cause to repent of the decision.

A sorrowful scene was that which occurred between me and my fellow-captives, when I returned the same day to the place of confinement to bid them farewell. Some envied, others pitied, but all grieved to lose me; and my own heart bled as I squeezed their hands -- not knowing whether I should ever be permitted to do so again. Yet I cherished the hope that, in my new situation, opportunities of serving them might occur, from which I secretly resolved that I should never turn away; and I thank God that I kept the resolution. Meanwhile, however, the count's interpreter, who bore me company, was beginning to exhibit symptoms of impatience.

"The count's quarters," said he, "are in a village two good leagues distant, and it is absolutely necessary that we should reach them before dark."

"But how shall we do that, sir?" replied I; "have marched six. leagues to-day already, and no consideration on earth would induce me to walk half a league farther."

"I do not wish you to walk;" answered he; and then he went on to explain, that if a horse of any kind were to be had in the village, he would procure it for me, though the arrangement might not, it appeared, be without its difficulties, owing to the alarm of the Spaniards in this quarter, who invariably abandoned their houses on the approach of a French force. The result, however, was, that he did procure me an animal, -- a long-legged, sharp-boned mule, which he took away from a countryman when working it in a plough; and on the sharp back of which he mounted me. And thus, riding between him and his chief, (for the count himself, at the head of a troop of his lancers, waited for us in the outskirts of the village,) I made my way to my new quarters, not without having an endless variety of questions put to me respecting the strength and disposition of the English army; all of which I answered as vaguely and on as magnificent a scale as possible. But these are points on which it is scarcely worth while to touch. What can a private soldier know of the true condition of a force in which he is a mere unit? or if he did, how can the querist suppose that he will communicate his knowledge in its simplicity?

We reached the village where the Lanciers de Bourg were stationed, about nine o'clock in the evening; and I was immediately directed to the count's stables, where I was given to understand that I should find a person who was capable of conversing with me in my own language. I proceeded to the place pointed out, and was a good deal struck both with the size and excellence of the stud, and the richness of the furniture, which was scattered somewhat carelessly about the stables. But the object which chiefly attracted my attention was a pot-bellied, rubicund, and evidently half-sober man, who no sooner turned his fish-like eyes upon me, than he hailed me with the exclamation, "How do you do, countryman? You be welcome!" I could perceive, from the peculiarity of his accent, that my new acquaintance was not English; and I very soon heard from himself that he was German: that he had served in England as a private in Hompeshe's Dragoons, whence, on the dissolution of the corps, he had returned home, and passed into the count's service: for the count's estates lay round the village of which he was a native; and, unless my memory deceive me, he was himself the son of one of the count's baurmen. Moreover, I heard him, with infinite pleasure, launch out in praise of our master's generosity and honour; which came upon mine ear the more agreeably, that I did not listen to it fasting, -- for my worthy comorado produced his cold tongue and his flagon of wine, both of which passed away famously; till, by-and-by, a sense of drowsiness quite overpowered me, and I besought him to point out a place where I might lie down. He was not backward in doing this. He called a servant, ordered him to make a bed for me in a room adjoining his own; and conducting me thither, pointed out a comfortable palliasse, on which I lost no time in throwing myself. In less than five minutes I was fast asleep.

I do not know how long I may have lain in a state of unconsciousness, when the touch of a soft hand applied to one of my feet, which was covered with blisters, awoke me. There was a light in my room, which, on partially opening my eyes, I ascertained to proceed from a chamber-lamp, which a venerable-looking hidalgo, with hair white as snow, was holding in his hand, for the benefit of two young maidens in their labour of Christian charity. These gentle creatures were both employed in washing and dressing the feet and legs of me -- an entire stranger. One, indeed, they had already rendered comfortable, by cleansing it thoroughly, and swathing it in soft linen, while I was asleep: the other they were now in the act of mollifying; and tender as their touch was, even it broke in upon my rest, so lacerated was the member, and by long travel so impregnated with fragments of gravel and thorns. How shall I describe the delicacy and gentleness with which these high-born maidens extracted both from my flesh! And then they whispered words of commiseration and charity, which they would not utter aloud, because they feared to awaken me. I declare that I could scarcely credit my own senses, so entirely did the scene resemble the delusion of a dream. But the old gentleman, by-and-by, discovered that I was not asleep; and then the ladies, with natural modesty, stepped back, till he had reassured and urged them to their generous task again. The results were, that my bruised and torn limbs were thoroughly cleaned, and bandaged with the softest and finest linen; and that my benefactors pressed upon me a cup of chocolate, with some sweet cakes: after consuming which, I placed my head once more upon the pillow. And then -- and not till then -- the Spaniards withdrew.

I never saw these kind people again. I do not even know their names; nor can I guess at the motive which urged them thus to exercise, in my case, feelings of benevolence, which were manifestly congenial to their nature. But I suspect that they mistook me for a prisoner newly taken; and that their sympathies were the more powerfully awakened by the idea that I was suffering all the bitterness attendant on a recent blight of my prospects. Be this, however, as it may, I heartily blessed them in my prayers that night, -- and often bless them now, when the remembrance of their kindness come over me. Doubtless they have had, and will continue to have, their reward.

I felt so comfortable after the dressing of my legs, and slept so soundly, that it was broad daylight when I awoke; which indeed might not have occurred even then, had not my German friend Kruger called me. He had evidently been drinking, and seemed somewhat impatient for the lack of my society; for he desired me to get up without any further delay, unless I were willing to go without my dinner. Now, the very sound of the word had been so long strange in my ear, that I experienced no desire at all to neglect the opportunity of improving it; I therefore rose at his bidding, and putting on the fragments of apparel of which I could yet boast the possession, I accompanied him to an apartment, in which the whole of the count's servants were assembled. At the end of the table sat his valet or steward; next to him the coachman; then the cook, -- the very beau ideal of his nation, thin and spare, with sharp features, and a white linen cap upon his head; and by-and-by, as each could find a place, grooms, stable-boys, and menials of humbler degree. To me the seat of honour was assigned, on the right hand of the valet; for Kruger led me there as his friend, and no one showed the slightest inclination to resist or resent the intrusion; and the consequence was, that throughout the progress of the meal, I felt that there were few lots in life with which mine could be exchanged, except at a disadvantage. For my fellow-servants vied with one another in heaping civilities upon me, and in loading my plate with the most delicate morsels. Then, again, the wine was both good and abundant; we had our pipes and tobacco, with which to sum up all, and we sat conversing by means of signs, for not one word of each other's language could we utter, till nearly ten o'clock at night. At last, however, the party broke up; after which Kruger, so completely disguised that he could no longer articulate, yet sober enough to point out a horse which was intended for my riding during the march of the morrow, rolled himself on his straw, and left me to retire to my pleasant palliasse at my leisure.

When I awoke next morning, I found, somewhat to my chagrin, that the march was already begun. The count, and all his household, indeed, were gone; and on hurrying to the stable, I ascertained that the last of the grooms, after sending off the baggage, were about to follow. They had reserved, indeed, for me, my own horse; neither did Kruger appear to have forgotten me, inasmuch as a great coat and for-aging cap were laid, so as to attract my notice, in the hall. But Kruger, like all the rest, seemed to have given me the slip, whether because his own duties engrossed him, I cannot tell. To say the truth, however, the consideration of this point occupied very little of my attention. I harnessed my steed -- a Spanish jennet, and not a bad one; I took a long pull at the skin of wine, which, by this time more than half exhausted, stood in a corner of Kruger's dormitory; and, vaulting into the saddle, began my journey, I knew not whither, in a frame of mind by many degrees more joyous than I had experienced since the day of my capture.

It was a bright, clear, sunny day, and I enjoyed my excursion ex-tremely. Of my own corps, -- if, indeed, the expression be allowable, when speaking of the regiment of Lancers which my master com-manded, -- I saw nothing throughout the day; but I overtook, soon after clearing the village, a column of French infantry, which served me in some sort as a guide, though from time to time rather provok-ingly. The French, when marching will not allow any persons, except officers, to pass the heads of their columns; I was therefore stopped when making the attempt to get before the infantry, and had noth-ing for it, except to regulate my pace by theirs. Yet, I was very happy notwithstanding; and made an excellent meal, without dismounting, off the half of a cold fowl, which honest Kruger had stuffed into my great-coat pocket. Finally, at the end of about four or five hours, I reached the outskirts of a large town, on the bridge that led to which a serjeant of the Lancers was standing, who immediately recognising my horse, made signs to me to follow, while he should lead the way to the quarter in which the count had established himself. I need scarcely add that I obeyed the signal with good will: to what purpose, the reader, if his patience be not exhausted, will learn in the next chapter.

Chapter 9

Under the guidance of the serjeant I soon made my way to the house in which the count had established himself, and found that he and all his servants were fast asleep. Upon this my steps were turned towards the stable; and the appearance of the stud, in point both of numbers and breed, excellent, yet exhibiting in their dirty coats manifest tokens of neglect, greatly surprised me. It was quite evident that not so much as a wisp of straw had been applied to any of their backs since they came in; while their feet were clogged by mud, and their hoofs filled, in the hollows, with gravel. This was not at all according to my notions of a well-ordered stable; so, making choice of the English mare, I led her out into the yard, and stripping to the skin -- for, in truth, I was not worth a shirt -- I set about dealing with her according to the most approved principles of grooming.

I was thus employed -- having carefully washed her feet, and, by means of a brush, made her coat smooth and sleek -- when the count, attended by his intrepreter, came out into the yard. He was prodigiously struck with the change of appearance which my careful grooming had created in his favourite; but I thought that he looked anxious, too, and I was not long kept in ignorance as to the cause.

"Is it your custom in England," demanded the interpreter, "to strip to the skin when you work? Our master is fearful lest you should catch cold, and begs that you will think of yourself."

I replied to this inquiry, as the real state of the case required, by explaining that I stood in nature's garb for the most obvious of all reasons, -- namely, that I had not been master of a shirt since the day I was taken prisoner. Nothing could exceed the kindness and commiseration of the count when the statement was repeated to him. He sent the interpreter into the house for three of his own shirts, which he gave to me. He then presented me with a louis-d'or, and desired that, so soon as I should have completed my job, I would first refresh myself from the cook's larder, and then go and make such purchases as the state of my wardrobe might render necessary. It is scarcely worth while to add that orders so agreeable in themselves were to the minutest tittle attended to. I ate a hearty luncheon, refreshed myself by bathing in the Douro, put on one of my new shirts, and walked forth a prouder and a happier man than I had been for many a day. The next hour saw me in possession of a silk handkerchief for my neck, of four of a like texture for my pocket, of several pairs of stockings, and a hat; and, after all, I had silver enough left wherewith to treat Kruger to a good bottle of wine. In a word, my situation was as pleasant as it is possible for that of any man to be who feels that he is, after all, but a prisoner at large; and who receives at the hands of foreigners and strangers those marks of regard, which bring not with them their perfect value unless they come from our countrymen and our friends.

It is not worth while to describe how we continued our march, first to Valladolid, and afterwards to Salamanca. Pleasant excursions these were to me; for I rode my own horse, without having any other charge committed to me than to lead the English mare, which was my master's especial favourite; and not unfrequently my master himself rode by my side, and, through the interpreter, conversed with me. With respect to our living, that was of the best; and we invariably made choice of some beautiful glade or covert in which to eat our noonday meal. Moreover, in Salamanca I was measured for two entire suits of clothes; to convey which, as well as the rest of my wardrobe, a portmanteau was given to me. No man in my situation could, indeed, be more entirely comfortable; nor was I left without evidence that to others I was become the object of something like envy. But that is a misfortune from which I greatly fear that no successful candidate for advancement, in any situation of life, is free. Take the lead of your fellows, ever so slightly, and they may seem for a while to admire, -- go on, heading them more and more, and they soon come to hate. So much for human nature.

We remained in Salamanca a considerable space of time; of which I did not fail to take advantage, by visiting every object in that celebrated seat of learning which was described to me as worth the attention of a stranger. Of the general effect of the city, as it is first seen at a distance, with its endless spires, towers, and domes, I need not say much. The traveller, if he approach it while the rays of the setting sun light up its gilded cupolas, finds himself almost involuntarily led into the delusion that the home of some oriental prince is near at hand; and though the idea may wear out before the lower gate is passed, it is succeeded by others scarcely more familiar. For Salamanca, at least when I resided in it, resembled no other city which I have visited even in Spain. Its colleges were then in their integrity, -- its cathedral, pure and graceful in its architecture, uninjured; and even the dwelling-houses, which adjoined to the old Moorish walls, and overlooked, by their narrow casements, the battlements which surrounded them, had a character so peculiarly their own, that I find myself entirely incapable of describing it.

With respect again to the inhabitants, these struck me as having even more than the accustomed allowance of Spanish indolence about them. Salamanca cannot have been, at any period, a place of great trade. Like Oxford and Cambridge among ourselves, it is overhung by an atmosphere of academic abstraction; yet we naturally expect to find, where shops are abundant, some display of the spirit of barter, and neither in Oxford nor Cambridge are we disappointed. But in Salamanca the whole world seems asleep. You walk abroad in the middle of the day, and the streets are empty; you go forth in the cool of the evening to be met by hidalgos wrapped up in their cloaks, who, unwashed and unshaven, lounge from point to point, as if the act of moving were a labour all but insupportable. And then again for the women. They may have been better than the men; I verily believe that they were; but in the matter of dress, never have Eve's daughters so striven to disfigure themselves. Their long thin waists contrasted singularly with a degree of fulness both above and below, which quite surprised me; and their movements were, in consequence, such as might be expected, altogether ungraceful. I confess that I do not retain any pleasant remembrance of a city, which in its architectural arrangements presents a thousand beautiful features, and in which, as far as my own personal case was concerned, I had every motive for being satisfied with my residence.

In a place thus miserably circumstanced, it will not surprise the reader to be told, that I met with few adventures which made strong demands upon my interest. One, indeed, if such it deserve to be termed, I may be permitted to describe; even though the results were to allect me with no very pleasing ideas of the Spanish character, as connected with one of the most solemn acts in which rational creatures can take part.

I remember one day strolling into the cathedral, where I was greatly struck by the progress of a funeral ceremony, which had only just begun. The corpse was that of a young woman of some rank, which lay in its last robes upon a sort of platform in the middle of the chancel, -- pale, and with the long black hair gathered in braids over the forehead. She was somewhat gorgeously arrayed; had a jewelled ring upon one of her fingers -- possibly the gift of a betrothed, -- and

79

a golden crucifix suspended from her neck, while earrings, also of gold, were in her ears, and a brilliant clasped, or seemed to clasp, the band upon her brow. I did not get sufficiently near to judge of her beauty; but, as far as a cursory examination will enable me to speak, I should say that her features were regular; and that there was a soft, sweet, gentle expression in her sunken features.

The corpse, when I entered the church, seemed to have been just conveyed to its temporary resting-place -- a platform, on which the black bier was laid. It had scarce settled down, if I may so express myself, when certain vergers approached, and enveloped it, all below the waist, in a black velvet pall, while a body of priests performed mass at the high altar, and a crowd of Carthusian friars sang a requiem for the dead with great effect. Innumerable wax candles burned both at the head and at the feet of the deceased. Her maid was in attendance beside them; and the rapidity with which she crossed herself -- lighting and extinguishing from time to time her own taper -- seemed to indicate that she took a deep and solemn interest in the ceremony. Meanwhile, the grave, which had been prepared near one of the smaller altars, stood open; and by-and-by a monk, bearing a huge black crucifix in his hand, approached it. This he planted at the head of the orifice; and, as if his doing so had been the signal that all was ready, a huge, muscular, large-headed man, dressed in the ordinary attire of a workman, and probably the gravedigger, approached the bier. The music, suddenly ceased -- the masses were ended -- and that barbarian seized the corpse, which, without regard even to the semblance of decency, he threw up, as if it had been a bundle of rags, into his arms. He bore it thus across the aisle, and, descending with it into the grave, laid it in the coffin, which yawned at the bottom of the hole. But his business did not end there -- the monster suddenly thrust up his arm, and drew towards him, first, the lid of the coffin, and next the black pall, with which he entirely shrouded both himself and his future proceedings; it is therefore impossible for me to say what he might have done during the half hour that he lingered in the grave; but I own that my imagination turned towards the jewels and the golden crucifix, none of which could I conceive it probable that he would leave to be devoured by the tomb. Nor was this the only transaction that disgusted me in the winding up of what, in its commencement, was an exceedingly striking ceremony. No sooner was the dead body removed out of sight, and the candles that stood beside the bier extinguished, than a spirit of extreme levity appeared to take possession of all whom the building contained. I heard the murmur of a light, and, as it seemed, a frivolous conversation pass through the crowd, while laughter, scarcely suppressed, told where each joke had taken effect, and spoke very little in favour either of them who uttered or of those who received it. Perhaps it might be prejudice on my part, but I own that I was thoroughly disgusted. I turned away, and walked home, not without a conviction that, after all, there is more of real sublimity in the simple and affecting burial service of my own church than in all the mummery of masses and requiems with which the feelings of the heart seemed to be quite at discord.

Nothing could exceed the total disregard exhibited by the French for every thing which a Christian people are apt to consider sacred. Of the churches in Salamanca very many had been converted by them into barracks, and even into stables. In the former, you might see bands of soldiers cooking their provisions over fires, which they had lighted on the paved floors of the very altar-places, and fed with gilded wood, broken from the altars themselves. The smoke, of course, having no outlet except the doors and windows, rose and curled about the Gothic pillars, blackening the walls, and defiling the carved work with which the roofs were ornamented; while the loud laugh, the coarse wit, and coarser song, sounded peculiarly hideous in a place whence the voice of prayer and praise might alone be expected to proceed. But if the churches in which the infantry had quarters were hideous, a thousandfold more disgusting was the spectacle presented by those into which corps of cavalry had been thrust. There, not the men only, but the horses, defiled God's house, in a manner, to look back upon which makes me shudder. The floors lay a foot deep in manure and litter: the marble pavements were beaten into fragments by the hoofs of the animals. No care was taken to preserve the brass monuments, which, in one church in particular, must have been, a short while previously, both numerous and singularly beautiful; while into the very stone walls rings seemed to have been driven, to which, here and there, a brute more restive than the others was tied up.

They whose thoughts are continually turned towards the field of battle or the toilsome march, draw for themselves but an imperfect representation of the horrors that attend a state of warfare. It is when armies force their way into the haunts of civilized life, -- when soldiers and citizens become incongruously huddled together, -- when armed bands, that are accustomed to the touch of deadly weapons, stretch themselves forth to commit havoc, -- and domicile and fane, and temple and town-hall, are alike polluted by the sounds and sights that appertain only to the camp -- then it is that war offers to the gaze of the looker-on its most hideous features; and our visions of glory, and renown, and high prowess, are all obscured by the contemplation of suffering and much wrong. I freely confess, that I used to pass these desecrated churches by in a frame of mind quite unbecoming the occasion. I said to myself, over and over again, "The miscreants who thus defile the temples of the Living God do not deserve to triumph, and triumph they assuredly will not."

There was a very large French force at this time in and around Salamanca, -- according to their own account, at least seventy-five thousand men. It had been collected for some time, for the avowed purpose of driving the English into the sea; and now preparations were made for the immediate accomplishment of this much-desired object. Of these, while they were going on, I saw, of course, very little; though the extra work performed in all the bakehouses did not escape me. But by-and-by the truth came out, and the count himself disclosed it.

"We march to-morrow," said he, one morning to me, "on an expedition from which I, for one, augur no good. We are going to advance towards Lisbon; and, the better to ensure celerity for our movements, all our baggage is to be left behind. We shall carry nothing with us, either on the men's backs or by the cars except twelve days' provisions; and, before these are expended, your countrymen, it is assumed will be driven to their ships. But, as I greatly doubt the issue, I don't mean to take you along with me. Remain where you are; take good care of the horses; and, depend upon it that, ere many days pass, we shall meet again."

I thanked my master for the consideration which induced him to screen me from the disgrace of even following in the train of an armed force which was going to march against my countrymen; and determined that, as far as diligence and care on my part could avert the evil, he should find no reason to complain that his horses had been neglected.

The prediction which Count Golstein ventured to make ere the march began was verified to the letter. I saw the columns of infantry and cavalry defile from Salamanca, with all the pomp and circumstance of war.

The horses were in good condition, -- the men fresh, well-appointed, and in excellent spirits. The bands of the several regiments played favourite airs, and flags and banners floated to the breeze, -- for the movement was begun with extraordinary magnificence. How different was the order of their return! In an inconceivably short space of time they came back, crest-fallen and dejected, having suffered quite as much from the lack of provisions and forage as from the sword; for the system adopted during the first retreat to Torres Vedras was still rigidly acted up to. Every town and village was deserted on the approach of the French, -- every morsel of bread carried away, -- every animal removed, or else slaughtered; while the very corn in the fields was set on fire and consumed in order to prevent it from falling into the enemy's hands. The consequence was, that each league which they traversed in advance served but to involve them in deeper difficulties; and, long ere the twelve days were expired, on which they had counted as securing a triumph, both leaders and followers saw that the case was desperate.

The historian has recorded in what manner the retreat to Salamanca was conducted. Horses died by scores -- men foundered, and were taken or put to death by the peasantry, guns and carriages were abandoned at every pass. There was distress and anxiety everywhere. I shall never forget the soil-stained and demoralized appearance which the different regiments presented when once more they entered the town. The spirits, too, and tempers of all ranks were broken; and they seemed ripe for almost any species of outrage.

"I told you how it would be," exclaimed my master; "I was sure that evil would come of it. Your countrymen are as obstinate as the rocks on which they have planted themselves. They have handled us very roughly; neither have I, in my own proper person, come of scot-free. That scoundrel, Kruger, has deserted with one of my best horses, and a portmanteau filled with some of the most valuable portions of my wardrobe. However, here we are; and we must make the most of it. How does the mare go on?"

Chapter 10

There never lived a kinder or a more generous man than the Count Von Golstein. His own losses, his own privations, were invariably the subjects which engrossed the smallest share of his attention; and never was the disposition more completely shown, than now, on his return to Salamanca. The French had brought back with them very few prisoners; but among these there happened to be some men of my own regiment, of whose condition my master immediately informed me, desiring me at the same time to visit and relieve them as far as I was able. I went instantly to the tower in which they were shut up; and the emotions to which they all gave way, for they recognised me in an instant, I cannot undertake to describe. Poor fellows, they were footsore, and half naked; and as men's hearts are generally softened by the sort of misfortune to which they were subject, they lifted up their voices and wept, when they saw me come among them. But I did not come merely to pry. Having ascertained their number, I hurried off, and my kind master supplying the funds, I purchased a quantity of meat and bread, which the cook and I made ready between us. With this, and half-a-dozen bottles of brandy, I made my way back -- not indeed without considerable risk of annoyance from the French soldiers -- who were quite as badly off as their captives, and whom the steam of the savoury mess excited wellnigh to violence. But as I had taken the precaution to ensure the convoy of the servant of one of the officers on guard, I succeeded in conveying my treasure in safety to the prisoners' tower; and the eagerness with which the food was devoured, and the keen relish with which they drank the liquor, sufficiently testified that to luxurious living they had long been strangers. Happy men were they in a few minutes: they sang, they chatted, they capered, and danced. In a word, and with the thoughtlessness which belongs to their calling, they forgot the evils that were past, and shutting their eyes to the certainty that evil would come again, they made themselves exceedingly comfortable in what the present hour could offer. I rejoiced, as may be supposed, in the work of my own hands; neither did my power to serve them end there. My master desired me to select one out of the number, who might supply the place of Kruger, and be a companion to myself; and as my troop-messmate -- by name

Judd -- happened to be there, I could not of course hesitate as to the individual whom I should select. Judd thankfully closed with an offer, of which I made him fully aware of the value; and accompanying me home, became forthwith both an active and a willing assistant in the work of the stable. Of the remainder, I never saw more till the peace of 1814: they were marched away early in the morning succeeding the day of what they called "the feast;" and Judd and I could give them no more than all the little money we had about us, and our best wishes for their welfare.

My mind was full of the situation of my poor comrades, when one day as I was riding through the streets, I found myself accosted in good set English, by a "How do you, countryman; what make you here?" I looked about, and saw a dapper little fellow in a civilian's dress; who, following up his first salutation, approached, and made immediate acquaintance with me. He told me that his name was Smith -- that his father had married a Frenchwoman, and now followed the French army as a sort of travelling bootmaker, and that, by every body of every nation who made trial of his skill, he was admitted to be a first-rate workman. "But, come to the house where my father and mother live," continued he, "and I will introduce you to scenes that will amuse, if they do not greatly edify."

"I'm the man for your father and mother," replied I; "depend upon it I shall visit you shortly," and so we parted.

I confess that I had forgotten my new acquaintance altogether, when on the following evening he visited me at the stables; and as I had nothing better to do, I agreed to accompany him to the paternal mansion. It was a very mean apartment, in a very mean street, through the excessive gloom of which, I could with difficulty discover three human beings seated, two of them upon stools, the third in an arm chair; two were men, who appeared so entirely engrossed with cobbling, that they scarcely lifted up their eyes when we entered; while the third was a woman -- as curious a specimen of the genus, as these eyes of mine have ever beheld. I could not hope, by any description, to convey to the minds of others an idea, even partially just, of the squalor of her appearance. I say nothing of her filth, though that was extreme, nor yet of her complexion, in comparison with which, saffron deserves to be accounted pure; neither will I speak of her apparel, which no Jew from Rag Fair, whom I, at least, have ever encountered, would have admitted within the portals of his storehouse. But there was a strange intermixture of cunning and simplicity in her eye, which would have tickled me much, but for the tiger glance which from time to time superseded it.

"I've brought a countrymen to drink tea with us, mother," said Joe.

"He's welcome," was the reply; " make him sit down."

I sat down, and forthwith two broken cups were produced, by means of which, and a crazy teapot, we managed to discuss some pint or so of slops. It was not Joe's cue, however, to let the jollification end there. He gave me a hint, which I did not fail to take, by offering myself to stand treat for some brandy -- to procure which, Joe, after a few modest denials on his mother's part, was sent abroad. Doubtless the reader has anticipated much of what is to follow. The old lady drank cupfuls of raw spirit, encouraging her husband and journeyman to do the same, till the two latter fairly rolled from their stools insensible, and she gave evident tokens of a rapid approach to the same state of helplessness. I looked disgusted and somewhat alarmed, but Joe only laughed at me. "Ply her well," said he; "she is a perfect bag of sand, and a good deal is needed to bring her to the proper point; but once there, and for as long as three or four weeks on a stretch, she will continue in a state of absolute helplessness. Here, mother, take another cup; it will do you good."

The old hag muttered something, drank, and was conveyed by her hopeful child to bed. She complained of thirst: he gave her a fresh dose; and she fell asleep in a moment, muttering something about a stocking all the while.

Joe clapped his hands, and laughed aloud, while he exclaimed, "Now, my boy -- now, we have done it; and you, as well as I, shall have your reward." So saying, he drew from beneath the cushion of the arm-chair a stocking crammed with silver and copper coins, dollars, half-dollars, quarter-dollars, and I don't know all what. "This is nothing," said he, pouring some of them out; "at the bottom of all are certain doubloons and louis-d'ors, for which I think that I can find a far better use than any to which she dreamed of applying them. Come, friend, help yourself: don't be bashful; nobody ever throve in the world that could not help himself."

I positively refused to touch a stiver; at which Joe laughed heartily; and, when I proceeded to remonstrate with him, his mirth only increased. "Why, man," said he, "this sort of thing occurs regularly at stated periods. The old woman dearly loves both her money and the brandy-bottle: as long as she has resolution enough to keep the latter at a distance, the treasure accumulates, for she starves us all, and makes us work like galley-slaves; but, when the stocking becomes full, we always have a spree, which ends, as you see that this is going to do,by my making myself master of its contents. The old hag will not awake for these three weeks at least; that is to say, she will merely open her eyes and ask for drink -- which I shall faithfully give her. And when she does get up, every thing will be forgotten, except that which I choose to tell her; -- that she has spent all her savings in liquor. Why, then, should I scruple to enjoy myself, since nobody suffers?"

"But she is your mother," said I, in remonstrance; " how can you thus work upon her vices and abuse her infirmities?"

"She is as much my mother as she is yours," replied the hopeful; "and if she were, what then?"

My friend Joe's notions both of morals and manners were so very different from mine, that, with the termination of what he called "the spree," our intimacy ended. I frequently met him in my walks and rides, and learned from him that his mother kept to her time; that she slept soundly for three weeks, and rose at their termination a greater screw than ever. But neither his arguments nor his entreaties could prevail upon me to share with him in the amusements which the plunder of the stocking procured. On the contrary, I felt something like compassion for the wretched old couple; and there, again, was in due time taught that I had been exceedingly weak for my pains. When consciousness returned to that amiable family, they found themselves, as a matter of course, destitute. To work they accordingly set, and, very much to their satisfaction, the old man received an order to wait upon an officer of rank, and measure him for half-a-dozen pairs of boots. But Smith the elder was destitute even of a coat wherewith to cover his upper man; and I, in an evil hour, was persuaded by his help-mate to lend him a new cloak which I had purchased. I never saw the mantle again, except at a distance; and then it enshrouded the form of Madam Smith herself, while she sat in her little donkey-cart, and accompanied the army on its march from Salamanca to Valladolid. I would have taken it from her on the spot; but she saw me coming, and with rare skill contrived to hand it over to her husband, who, being on foot, glided round some of the baggage-cars, and was at once lost to my vision. At Valladolid I made another attempt to recover my property; but it proved equally unsuccessful; indeed, I was overwhelmed on this occasion with such a torrent of abuse, that I had not the courage to face a similar infliction, even if the recovery of the cloak had been ensured. Besides, the brutes had utterly soiled and misused it; for it was their coat by day and their bed by night. I therefore gave the beldame a hearty benediction, and went my way.

We had not long occupied our new quarters in Valladolid, when intelligence of a rising in Astorga reached us, and a considerable corps, of which my master's regiment formed a part, received orders to proceed, by forced marches, for the purpose of repressing it. If the forced marches of the French army be conducted at all times in the order which distinguished this, it must be confessed that they make but light of the sufferings both of man and beast. We were formed every morning, and actually en route by three o'clock. At eight we halted and breakfasted; at nine we again moved on, and halted again at two to dine, and a couple of hours were then afforded to refresh; but at the termination of these the column moved: and it was always eight -- often as late as nine or ten -- ere we halted for the night. The halt, however, was not, at least at all times, a season of rest. There were cattle to be procured, killed, and cooked, for the morrow. There was forage to be collected, and the horses to be fed. There was not unfrequently the process of baking to be carried through; for we depended everywhere upon the supplies which the country could afford for our maintenance. Many a time have we found ourselves so occupied, by the necessity of attending to these wants, that midnight came ere we could throw ourselves on the ground, and catch an hour's broken sleep beside our horses. Yet in some respects the march was not disagreeable; and it was replete with interest throughout. For example, we, of the cavalry, leaving the high-road to the infantry and the guns, struck into all manner of bypaths, which carried us through a succession of vineyards, of which the fruit hung in large clusters, ripe, and ready for gathering. Again, it not unfrequently happened that our rear and flank patrols had the satisfaction of maintaining a continued skirmish with bands of guerillas, who fired upon them from the broken ground, and hovered round them like vultures watching their prey.

Then, again, the towns and villages, but especially the latter, were all but deserted as we approached; and all sent forth, as soon as our backs were turned, fresh bodies of armed peasants to annoy us. At the same time we were invariably met at the entrance of the towns by the civic authorities, who professed either to adhere to King Joseph, or, at all events, to be neutrals in the contest; and who hoped, by these means, very generally in vain, to preserve their own and their townsmen's property from violation. For, in good sooth, the French were fearful plunderers. It struck me, too, that the officers never made so much as an effort to restrain them; and the results were, that places which we found comparatively prosperous on our arrival, we left with all the evidences of rapine and violence about them. And desperate was the revenge which the outraged Spaniard took, as often as an unfortunate French soldier fell into his hands. Neither wounds nor weakness roused his pity. He slew the straggler as if he had been a wild beast, and often added torture ere he ended him.

Sixteen days of constant marching brought us at length to Astorga; in and around which the corps proceeded to establish itself. The cavalry had quarters within the walls; the infantry and guns encamped outside; and strange and wild were the scenes which they alike enacted, -- from which, as may be supposed, the ill-fated Spaniards were the sufferers. I must, however, in common justice observe, that the Spanish authorities brought the evil, in some measure, on themselves. They assured our general, for instance, that the town was destitute of stores, and that, unless he had the means of victualling his own troops, they ran great risk of starving. This was but sorry news for men who had not tasted a wholesome or regular meal for a fortnight, and were all but desperate in consequence. But a little exercise of the ingenuity habitual to our troopers soon refuted the declarations of the alcalde. Two doors from a large house which was assigned to the lancers as a barrack, there was discovered, in the lumbre, or ground-floor kitchen, a trap-door, by raising which a man introduced himself into a capacious cellar, well filled with all manner of stores, sufficient for the relief of one entire battalion. Tanned hides were there for making shoes, flitches of bacon, large bags of caravanceros, and skins of wine in abundance. As might have been expected, the success of this individual prompted many more to prosecute their researches; and our general had soon the satisfaction to know that he ran very little hazard of starving. Now, if he had been content to appropriate these stores, while at the same time he maintained strict discipline among his people, nobody could have blamed him. The troops must be fed -- so must their horses; but he went much beyond this. The soldiers received a sort of unspoken licence to plunder; and terrible was the havoc which in their wantonness they occasioned. Moreover, the honour of the women, and here and there the lives of the men, fell a sacrifice not unfrequently. But let me not go on: -- in the camp of the infantry you might see all manner of rich hangings converted into tents. The soldiers lay, or danced and sung among the tents, arrayed in priests' robes and ladies' dresses; while the lancers, in spite of Count Golstein's best exertions to prevent it, were not altogether free from similar atrocities. Of course the town became rapidly thinned of its inhabitants, of whom all who were capable of bearing arms went to swell the amount of the Spanish forces. Yet were the French not yet cured of their propensity to evil. They persisted in carrying on the war more like savages than civilized men; and they suffered in consequence all the outrages of which their own historians too much complain.

Chapter 11

We remained in the neighbourhood of Astorga but a few days, at the expiration of which the order to march was issued; and, without having seen an open enemy, or had any opportunity of taking vengeance on a guerilla party, we began to retrace our steps towards Toro. There was no deviation either in the route, or in the rapidity with which we traversed it; and the consequence was, that our sufferings during the retreat were to the full as intolerable as they had been on the advance; and that, when we reached Toro, both men and horses -- but especially the latter -- were all but unfit for service. Among others, my kind, good master fell sick, and the skill of his physicians failing to set him on his legs again, he was ordered to try the baths at Valladolid. Thither I accompanied him, and on the interval which we spent there, I continue still to look back as on one of the most agreeable in my life of captivity. Valladolid is a large and stirring place: its inhabitants are much given to public amusements, in which I found frequent opportunities of joining; and lying, as it did, out of the broad channel of the war, both they and I were enabled to indulge our respective tastes freely and without apprehension.

My master, having derived considerable benefit from the waters, at length took his departure; and for a while we fixed our quarters, with the lancers, of which he was at the head, in the city of Burgos. Of the local situation of that fine old town I need not pause to speak, -- with its hills overlooking it on each side, and its citadel crowning a rocky eminence, as if in defiance of the enemy who dared attempt to reduce it. But the condition both of the garrison and the inhabitants at this moment was so curious, that I cannot think of omitting to notice it, -- more especially as the truth has never, to my knowledge at least, been told, by any writer, whether French or English, who has touched upon the subject.

It is well known that the hatred borne by the Spaniards towards the French had become, in 1812, bitter in the extreme. Taught by experience that they were no match for the invaders in the field, they waged war upon them by private assassination, -- insomuch that the French armies, victorious everywhere, except where the might of England encountered them, were nowhere, throughout the Peninsula, masters of a foot of ground beyond the limits of their different en-campments. In like manner, the garrisons which occupied the towns of Spain were always in a state of siege. There might be no organized force within many leagues of them, nor the smallest reason to appre-hend the arrival of any such. But each cottage in the suburbs, if not in the heart of the town itself, contained a little band of foemen, in their own way more to be dreaded by far than if they were openly in the field, and banded together in companies and battalions. In and around Burgos I soon discovered that this was peculiarly the case. At first, indeed, the manners of the people deceived me quite; for I fancied that they were content, because of the gentleness and deference with which they appeared to treat not me alone, but every Frenchman with whom they came openly into contact. But the experience of a few days taught me, that this air of meekness was put on, for the sole purpose of enticing victims into their power. There was scarcely a day passed without bringing in reports of assassinations attempted, if not perpetrated, upon our people. No man could walk half a mile beyond the town without being fired at; and even in the grand promenade, which extends along the bank of the river, and is shaded on either side by rows of noble trees, the same scenes were constantly enacted. I have ridden over and over with my master, to enjoy the refreshing breezes in that shady spot, and been driven out again by showers of bullets, which knocked the leaves about us, and came, we knew not from whence. In a word, the French were, both in camp and in quar-ters, prisoners at large, with the comfortable assurance continually forced upon them, that even within their own lines they could not count on escaping the knife of the assassin.

When we first reached Burgos, the garrison was labouring un-der a terrible and contagious fever. The hospitals were all crowded; and every morning at daylight a couple of carts traversed the streets, collecting the dead from the wards in which they were lying, and transporting them to the place of sepulture. It was a ditch dug some-where among the hills, into which the bodies were cast in heaps, no care being taken to treat them with respect, nor any mourning being made for their removal. Moreover, several detachments were by-and-by sent out to levy contributions on the surrounding districts, and Burgos became, in consequence, the grand depot of French plunder in this quarter of Spain. The Spaniards were neither unaware of this circumstance, nor ignorant of the process by which our treasures were gathered in; and in the beginning of 1812, they made a demonstration as if they had designed to appropriate them. The circumstances of the case were these:

One morning in the month of January -- I have forgotten the precise date -- an alarm spread that heavy columns of troops were advancing towards the town. We ran to the most elevated stations which we could find, and saw, sure enough, 6000 Spaniards at the least, marching in good order along the Madrid road, and apparently bent on carrying the town by a coup de main. Now, it so happened that the town was at this moment in a peculiarly defenceless state. The castle, indeed, stood above the reach of insult, not from this body of troops alone, but from their betters; but the town was no further fortified than by palisades, that blocked up the principal entrances, and light cannon so planted as to command the bridges. Then again, the garrison, enfeebled by sickness, was more than usually weak, in consequence of the many detachments which had gone out, consisting, as may be supposed, of our strongest and healthiest men, and commanded by our ablest battalion officers. Still, though mustering scarcely 400 combatants, the commandant put a bold face upon the matter. All the persons living on the southern side of the river were directed to cross, and to establish themselves and their baggage under the guns of the citadel. The hospitals were emptied of every man who might have strength enough to level a musket; and these being planted under cover of the palisades, were directed to maintain their post to the last extremity. At the same time the utmost care was taken to keep down a mutinous spirit, which the first rumour of an advance on the part of their countrymen had excited among the inhabitants. They were commanded by proclamation not to show themselves in the streets, and were told that wherever two should be found holding converse together they would certainly be shot. Every thing, indeed, was done, which in a very trying case courage could suggest, or prudence dictate; and the results were that courage and prudence prevailed over mere numbers, to direct which there was manifestly no head present.

Among other officers of merit my master chanced to be detached; and with me it mainly rested to save his property from the danger of confiscation. I was established in a house close to one of the barricades, where, up to this moment, the people had been particularly civil; but now, when I came to pack up and made preparations for moving, their tone entirely changed. They refused to lend a helping hand in any way; and not only rejected my application for a skin of wine, but told me with significant looks, that of wine I should not much longer stand in need. Such conduct of course served only to irritate; and I was forced to use the show of violence, by levelling a pistol at the padrone's head; but there was no occasion to go farther. I got my mules and horses laden; and securing about two gallons of wine, retired, with my fellow-servants, to the heights near the castle, whence we commanded an excellent view of the Spanish bivouac. Why did they not push on? Why did they halt, out of musket-shot of the palisades, and make there an idle display of their numbers? They ought to have known their enemies better than to suppose that they were the sort of people to be overawed by any thing of the sort. Had they made the attempt, bravely, resolutely, and without a check, it must have proved successful. How earnestly I wished that half the number of English troops had been there; for the booty would have been prodigious; all the treasures, with no inconsiderable portion of the stores of the whole French army, being, by some strange oversight, kept, not in the castle, but in the town.

The Spaniards either did not know this, or they held the garrison in too much respect; for they contented themselves with driving in, towards dusk, a solitary advanced post, and taking possession of the convent within which it had been established. We saw them then light their fires, and make preparations as if to invest the place, and try upon it the tedious process of a siege. But even to this plan, absurd enough it must be admitted, they failed to adhere. Throughout two days the blockade, such as it was continued. They were days to us of very considerable discomfort; for we knew our own weakness, and scarcely dared to hope that it was hidden from them: yet they came to an end at last, and with them all fears respecting the issue. The dawn of the third morning showed the Spanish lines abandoned. Not a man remained beside the fires, which had been recently trimmed and continued to burn, nor was so much as a dog left behind. Yet the Spaniards had not retreated in the proper sense of that term. Intelligence of the routes pursued by our various detachments having reached them, they broke up into parties, and hurried off, with the view of intercepting these on the march, and so winning both glory and riches from the spoil with which they were known to be laden. They succeeded, however, very imperfectly in both objects. Several of our detachments sustained, indeed, a heavy loss; and one, which, when it went abroad, consisted of a hundred men, returned with no more than fifty; but not in a solitary instance was the escort overpowered, or the booty taken away of which it was in charge. It is marvellous even now to think of the extreme accuracy with which the Spaniards were accustomed to inform themselves, not only of the movements of the French troops, but of the personal habits and circumstances of the individuals by whom detached bodies were commanded. On the present occasion, for example, there was a French lieutenant-colonel sent forth with a hundred infantry in a particular direction: he was a brave and a skilful officer, and though attacked by an overwhelming force of cavalry, he repulsed them twenty times at least, keeping his treasure always in the centre of his square. But he was known to the assailants as one who never stirred abroad without carrying all his private property in a sort of valise behind him, so that, while advancing to charge, the Spaniards would call out to him that they were determined to have his doubloons, and that he had better give them up quietly. The Frenchman held his course undaunted, and had wellnigh reached Burgos ere the fatal bullet struck him. But he died at last, from a pistol-shot in the head; and his valise, containing about a hundred-and-fifty gold pieces, became the property of the brave men who had, for twelve long hours, sustained his honour and their own in a very unequal contest.

For some time after the occurrence of these events, my master and I kept our station in Burgos. He, like others, had lost a good many men from his detachment, and one officer, whose poodle dog attached itself to me; but he had received no wound himself, and, though still delicate, was able, for a while at least, to go through with his duties. I am not sure, however, that my readers would be very deeply interested were I to detail to them the manner in which day after day was spent; let me be content, therefore, to repeat one or two anecdotes, as illustrating the sort of life which at that period I led, and then we will pass together into new scenes, some of which may possibly offer to them greater attractions than the mere transcript of a prisoner's diary.

I was one day crossing the bridge at Burgos, when, to my great surprise, I encountered a man dressed in the uniform of the 12th English Light Dragoons. We entered, as may be imagined, at once into conversation, and I ascertained that he had been taken at Grenalda; that he was a farrier by trade, and then in the service of the French General, Count d'Orsun. A very extraordinary fellow was my friend, Richard Kilby; his ingenuity as a working smith surpassed all that I have ever witnessed, and, as a horse doctor, he had either great skill or great good luck; but he was a determined drunkard -- a profound hater of the French nation -- and, beyond compare, the most self-willed and obstinate individual of his race. He and I became, as a matter of course, sworn allies: we were much together, for I helped him to turn his shoes; and, acting as his interpreter, I first procured for him from his master those supplies of money without which his genius never could have found a channel in which to exercise itself; yet I more than once had reason to regret that an intimacy was ever struck up between us, and am forced, though reluctantly, to acknowledge that, when our destinies carried us in different directions, I shed no tears over the prospect of being separated from him for ever.

My friend Richard hated the French, and never omitted an opportunity of telling them so: to be sure, he could not speak one word of their language, nor did they understand a syllable of his, so that the pleasant epithets of "coward," "scoundrel," "rogue," "thief," with which it was his constant practice to greet them, passed by unnoticed, because unknown. But in more ways than this he delighted to tease them, and he was quite indefatigable in indulging his humours. For example, his style of shoeing was so universally and justly admired that there was no end to the applications which were made to him by the French officers. He would never attend to them, except when the purse was at the lowest ebb, and even then he took care to insult the groom by holding the charger tight with one hand, and so keeping him, till the amount of the charge -- eight francs -- was put into the other. He was constantly involving himself in quarrels, from the ruinous consequences of which nothing short of his master's rank in the service could have saved him; and once, at least, even that might have failed, but for the peculiar prowess by which he opposed, and finally repulsed, the assailants. The story is this:

One Sunday, Richard and I strolled beyond the limits of the town, and entering a wine-house, drank our bottle of Malaga, on the conclusion of which Richard complained of being hungry. The woman of the house was cleaning, at the moment, a number of salt herrings, two of which Richard secured, and put upon the coals to broil. He had not perceived that some French grenadiers, who equally with ourselves chanced to be inmates of the apartment, had likewise made a purchase of herrings, and were dressing them; and, having occasion to go out for a moment, he was rendered quite furious by meeting one of these men with a couple of herrings in his hand. Richard swore that the fish were his -- wrested them from the grenadier, abused him like a pickpocket, and stripping off his jacket, challenged the Frenchman to fight. Now, the Frenchman must have stood at least six feet three from the ground, whereas the extreme height of Richard could not exceed five feet; yet there was the little farrier squaring at the giant, and so conducting himself that the latter, in absolute amazement, became rooted to the spot. The landlady, in great alarm, entreated me to withdraw my friend, and, with some difficulty, I succeeded in doing so; but it was only that he might thrust himself into another situation, to the full as perilous, and far more laughable, than this. We adjourned to an old haunt of Richard's -- to the house of a woman whom he had dubbed his mother; and who, being regularly put in possession of the whole amount of his earnings, could not refuse -- even though it was the hour of Divine service -- to open her door to her son. Accordingly, we entered, were shown into a parlour up stairs, and earnestly besought to keep quiet, otherwise the landlady must get into a scrape.

We sat quietly enough, till Dick observed a patrol of gendarmes ascending the street, and approaching the site of his mother's dwelling. His wrath against their nation was kindled, and he began first to swear and then to sing at the top of his lungs. They halted before the door, and ordered him to be quiet, but he only sang the louder. Then they knocked and tried to enter, but the door was bolted, and Dick hastened to reinforce the bolts by piling up furniture against it. The gendarmes threatened and blustered, while Dick, finding in one corner of the room a bag of large onions, opened upon them, with these strange missiles, a heavy fire. As might be expected, they were furious, and though he kept them somewhat at bay as long as his ammunition lasted, they would have certainly forced an entrance in the end, had he not plied them with water -- not scalding hot, certainly, yet neither very cool, nor in its nature very limpid. The guard retreated with precipitation before such a torrent, and Richard shouted and laughed, as they shook their ears -- for his supply had been both copious and very liberally dispensed.

Not having any particular desire to connect my own name with pranks of this sort, I escaped from Richard as soon as the coast was clear, and scarcely saw him again till within a day or two of our final separation; though I heard of him from time to time, and always heard with sorrow, that he continued to be the same reckless and unhappy man that he was when I first encountered him. Neither was his end unworthy of the earlier part of his career. Having accompanied his master to Pampeluna, and wellnigh exhausted his patience, Dick, in a drunken fit, deserted; and falling among the guerillas, was by them passed on from station to station, till he finally rejoined his regiment in Portugal. But he came with a constitution entirely undermined: against the excessive hardships which he encountered with the guerillas, a frame worn down by hard drinking, could not hold up; and within a few days after having reported himself to the adjutant, he expired. Richard left a son, like himself a farrier, who afterwards served with me on the cavalry staff, and many a day have we spent hours together in mutually detailing, one to another, anecdotes of his father's eccentricities.

I do not remember that there occurred any thing else of moment while I continued in Burgos, unless, indeed, the purchase of an Irish horse may be so regarded, which, when led in by a French groom, in a very miserable state, I instantly recognised as having once belonged to one of my troop-mates in the 11th. He was so savage a brute that neither his new master nor his servants could ride him; for a French officer had purchased him of an Englishman, in Portugal, for ten Napoleons, and the Count Golstein got him, in consequence, for the same sum that had been paid for him. But the horse knew me immediately: when I called him by his name, he turned his head and snuffed me all over, and became in my hands as quiet and tractable as a lamb. With none else, indeed, would he condescend to be familiar, -- for even my master never rode him but once; but he followed me like a dog, and neighed and whinnied whenever he heard my voice even at a distance. The count gave him to me, and I rode him constantly for two years; at the termination of which, his vicious humours wore out, so that the count's son, to whom I ultimately transferred him, found him invaluable as a charger, and received the most satisfactory proofs of his hardihood. Mulch, as he was called, carried the young Count Golstein through the whole of the campaign to Moscow and the retreat in which it ended; and, though much reduced in flesh, was still in excellent health when he came again under my care in his master's stables.

Chapter 12

After a residence in Burgos of something more than two months, the Count Golstein received permission to revisit his native country. He was accordingly directed to proceed to Vittoria, and join himself there to the sort of caravan which year by year passed, under a strong escort, through the dangerous defiles of the Pyrenees into France. I went with him, of course, and never enjoyed myself more, in every sense of the term, than during the week or two which, while waiting for the assembling of the party, we spent in the capital of the Basque provinces. Vittoria is a singularly pleasant place, -- for a Spanish town clean and tidy, and well regulated; and, being built along the side of a hill, is very healthy, besides being abundantly supplied with pure and excellent water. It struck me, also, that the people were more alive to the influences of climate than those of the more fertile plains of Castile and Aragon. The women, in particular, were both beautiful in point of feature, and singularly graceful, as well in their attire as in their movements; and the humbler classes came too near, in their habits, to what we read of the damsels of old Palestine and Greece, not to be in my eyes objects of peculiar interest. Like the orientals, they go to draw water at the public fountain; and the vases in which they carry home the pure element are at once strictly classical in their shape, and poised, with classical exactness, on the heads of the bearers. It used to excite both our surprise and interest to see with what unerring exactitude they bore their pitchers from the well to their own houses. There was no balancing the instrument by means of the hand. Planted upon the top of the head, it appeared to rest there by virtue of some balancing power inherent in the bearer; and over the roughest ground, as surely as over the smoothest, she passed without spilling a drop. I cannot tell how often I have been tempted to stand by and admire these beautiful "drawers of water," and if from time to time I was tempted to carry on with one or another a little innocent flirtation, I pray the more rigid of my readers not to judge me too harshly for the act of imprudence.

If any thing could have taught the French that their chances of reducing Spain to obedience were blank, the care which they were obliged to exercise for the purpose of passing the most ordinary convoy across the border ought to have done so. I believe that there was no instance on record of a moderately-sized party attempting that passage, and saving so much as an individual alive, to tell how it had fared with his companions. And even the accumulations of months, though escorted by a strong battalion, were glad by all manner of disguises to conceal the true moment of their starting. I found, for example, that, inclusive of sick, wounded, weary, and persons whom real business drew out of Spain, not fewer than 10,000 people were, when I reached Vittoria, assembled there, for the single purpose of being passed, under military guard, into France. Moreover, a corps of 600 infantry, with four fieldpieces, were appointed to guard them; and of waggons laden with baggage, and public and private plunder, there was no end. Yet, multitudinous as we were, it was not accounted safe to undertake the threading of those dangerous defiles, except under the protection of a stratagem. Thus there came out an order from the commandant, warning the travellers that, at a certain hour in the morning of the third day subsequently to the issue of his proclamation, they should be ready to begin their journey. As might be expected, intelligence of this arrangement spread far and wide through the provinces, and, without doubt, the guerilla were everywhere on the alert to intercept and profit by the movement. But we stole a march upon them. On the day immediately succeeding that on which the governor's handbill took its place at the corners of the streets, there appeared a supplementary command, by which we were directed to pack our baggage, and hold ourselves in readiness to move in one hour.

Never was the wisdom of any arrangement more distinctly proved than this. We had scarcely cleared the outskirts of the town, ere groups of brigands began to draw near us, which seemed to accumulate strength in proportion as we penetrated deeper and deeper among the mountains. But they never acquired such a power of numbers as to justify them in their own eyes in making a serious attack; and we, in consequence, suffered nothing from first to last except from an occasional and very desultory fire of musketry. At the same time there was enough, in the whole progress of the journey, to divert my attention for the moment, and to make a deep impression upon my memory. In the first place, the scenery exceeded, in point of grandeur, all through which I had previously passed. So bold, indeed, were the ascents, and so steep the paths by which we regained the depths of the valleys, that over and over again I used to wonder how cars, and waggons, and even horses, contrived to traverse them. And then the wood was gorgeous in the extreme: the magnificent cork-tree overshadowing the base of mountains, -- on the sides, and here and there the brows, of which waved far and wide whole forests of oak, and pine, and hazel. But that which gave to our journey its most engrossing interest was the constant proximity of bands of robbers, who, like the vultures that hover over a battle-field, seemed to track our course, and seize every opportunity that offered of molesting us. Repeatedly were we fired upon from the summits of inaccessible corries, and repeatedly threatened with more serious interruptions, which, however, our great numerical superiority, aided by the excellency of the device which had hindered them from assembling in force enough to meet us, effectually prevented. Yet the knowledge that danger was constantly at hand failed not to produce its effects as well upon the imaginative as upon the timid. And, finally, the bracing nature of the climate operated upon our nerves and spirits to an extent which I have no language adequate to describe. But the case may be judged of so soon as I state that when, towards sunset on the second day, we arrived in sight of Irun, there were comparatively few among us who did not experience a sensation not very far from regret that their perils were surmounted.

If I felt sorry at first on finding that I had quitted the salubrious air of the mountains, the feeling was at once dispelled when, to my great surprise, I found myself addressed, just after entering the town, by one who spoke to me in excellent English, and whom, in spite of the total change in his style and attire, I soon recognised as a former comrade in the 11th. I think that I have elsewhere spoken of one Nicholas Brown, an American by birth, who served in my own troop, and whose liberation from the prison at Salamanca I had been the means of procuring. But, however this may be, the person who now addressed me proved to be this same Brown, and the reception which he gave me was not more creditable to himself than it was, in the highest degree, acceptable to me. I confess that, when we first encountered, I was a good deal surprised by the elegance of his attire and bearing. Neither was the sentiment diminished when he conducted me to his apartments, -- three well-furnished rooms in the commandant's house, -- and, ringing the bell, ordered a servant to provide all things necessary for our recreation. So, also, the display of his wardrobe, his jewellery, and, though last not least, his ready money, impressed me with sentiments of great respect. But when the truth came out, my surprise, at least, suffered a remarkable diminution. The commandant's lady -- not his wife -- had, it appeared, taken a fancy to Brown. She was young, beautiful, and extremely fascinating; and Brown, acting as men in his circumstances are apt to do, readily gave himself up to the bright intoxication. All his wishes were in consequence prevented; and he very fairly told me, that, let him escape from the condition of a prisoner when he might, he would certainly not rejoin his regiment. I confess that, bearing the fact in my mind, that he was not an Englishman by lineage, I scarcely blamed him for this; but, even if I had, the fact of his meditating a public wrong to the state would have scarcely justified me, in my own eyes, for rejecting his private kindness. I spent a day with him very pleasantly; and, next morning, when we marched, as we did at five o'clock, he rode several miles in my company; neither did we part without feelings of sincere and mutual regret.

We halted for a couple of days in Bayonne, of the position and capabilities of which it is not necessary for me to say any thing. The intrenched camp, which at a later stage in the war covered and rested upon it, was not then begun; neither were the sluices taken up, nor the low ground flooded; but the permanent fortifications both of the town and the citadel were in excellent order; and being a sort of depot station for most of the regiments employed in the north and east of Spain, it could boast of a strong, if not a very homogeneous garrison. It is cut in halves, as the reader doubtless knows, by the river Adour; and can boast of a population greater by far, than the surface extent of the site would lead the traveller to imagine. But I cannot say that my remembrances of Bayonne are very agreeable; so I content myself with stating, that we turned our backs upon it with little regret; and plunging into that strange and wild district called the Llandes, passed on by way of Dax, towards Bordeaux.

The Llandes have been too often and too accurately described by other travellers to render so much as an allusion to the peculiarity of the scenery admissible from me. It is an enormous plain of sand, which extends along the sea from Bayonne to Bordeaux, and measures, at a moderate computation, at least two hundred miles in length, by fifty or sixty, or perhaps more, in breadth. In ancient times, the sands used to be quite bare, and to shift, like those of the desert of Alexandria, with every high wind that blew, till a pious monk -- whose name I heard, but have forgotten -- showed his countryman how to reclaim, by planting the waste with pine-trees. The roots of the pine served as braces to bind the sand together. The leaves and cones, as they fell and decayed, created a soil; and now we come, from time to time, in traversing a huge forest, upon extensive clearances, over which flocks of sheep and herds of cattle wander, and neat villages are scattered. It struck me, also, that the inhabitants of the Llandes were a very happy, as well as a primitive race. They seemed to have every thing about them in abundance which is necessary to sustain life, and many articles of simple luxury. Moreover, they were light of heart, free of speech, bold hunters of the wolf and of the bear; and, as I could gather as much from what I saw as what I heard, daring smugglers. Yet they appeared to be an innocent race, notwithstanding this latter propensity; and their deference for their priests was worthy of the patriarchal times. Many a pleasant dance I had with the young women, and many a pleasant chat with the old, after our tents were pitched, and our horses dressed, and our convoy established.

We traversed the Llandes in the space, if I recollect right, of five days, having been greatly interested throughout the journey, as well with the nature of the country, as with the happy condition of its inhabitants. Our resting-place was Bordeaux, of which, for the same reasons which held me back from describing Bayonne, I do not think that it is worth while to say any thing. It is a noble city, very clean, full of bustle, and adorned with many gorgeous edifices; and enriched as well as beautified by the proximity of the Garonne, which, in a fine volume of water, flows past it. Besides, the opportunities afforded me of minutely examining the place were not great; for my master having brought with him certain relics of a French general who had been a friend of his, and fallen in battle, set out, on the day after our arrival, for the château in which the widow dwelt, that he might tell her how her husband's last moments were spent, and hand over to her his treasures. I dare say, that to the poor bereaved lady the visit was sad enough, for she was a young and delicate creature, not more, as it seemed, than twenty-five years of age; and her countenance, when I saw her, told a tale of hopes altogether blighted. But to me the excursion was full of interest, and therefore I may as well make mention of it.

The château towards which our steps were turned, lay a good day's journey from Bordeaux; and to reach it, we passed through a succession of vineyards, interspersed with luxuriant groves of olive and myrtle. The highest order of cultivation, too, was present everywhere, and food for ourselves, as well as forage for our horses, was both cheap and abundant. But it was the abode of the widow and her domestic establishment that principally engaged my attention; for any thing more gorgeous, yet peculiar, I never witnessed. We reached a village towards dusk, at the bottom of which stood the château, -- a fine mansion, with extensive stables and outhouses attached, -- and our reception, so soon as my master's name had been announced, was of the most gratifying kind. The entire household seemed, indeed, to greet our arrival as a jubilee. My master was led at once into the presence of the lady; while I had the horses taken from me, and was conducted into a room, where a dozen maids were assembled, and seated forthwith as the honoured guest among them. Not one word of their language could I speak, nor one in a dozen could I understand; and as for my efforts, whether I addressed them in English, or Spanish or German, they were alike unprofitable to gain a hearing. Yet we continued to converse, amid a great deal of laughter, by signs; and as to drinking healths, that was managed by hob-nobbing our glasses at momentary intervals. It was, upon the whole, the most amusing meal that I ever ate; and the viands, as well as the wines, were excellent.

We spent two days with the French general's widow, throughout which we were treated with the greatest possible kindness. My master was sumptuously lodged, in an apartment the walls of which were entirely covered with mirrors, and the floor laid with oak, on which the polish was so fine that, till I pulled off my boots, I at least could not stand upon it without slipping. There was, too, a peculiarity about that chamber, which, on one occasion put me to some inconvenience. The door shut with a spring; and being, like the panels, overlaid with glass, I found it impossible to make my way out again, till my master, waking from his first sleep, put his hand upon the catch and threw it open. As to my own billet, it was extremely comfortable, though in a remote and gloomy wing of the castle. And then the grounds were perfectly beautiful, with parterres of flowers, terraces rising above one another, all in the formal order of the French school. But it is not worth while to continue these details any further. We abode in this hospitable mansion till the morning of the third day; on the arrival of which we bade our friends farewell, and returned the same evening to Bordeaux.

Chapter 13

Our march from Bordeaux carried us by easy stages through a very beautiful country, the whole surface of which was covered with vine plantations. We halted, likewise, for one night in a large town, of which I have forgotten the name, but which, from its general aspect, and the business in which the inhabitants were engaged, reminded me very much of Birmingham. By-and-by we reached Orleans, still famous for its statue of Joan of Arc in the market-place, and well filled, at the period of which I now speak, with English detenus. I cannot, however, pretend to give any description of a city in which my sojourn extended not beyond a single day; nor, which was at the moment still more mortifying to myself, did I on that occasion visit Paris at all. For, though the count had gone before us to the capital, his instructions to us were, that we should turn short by the road to the Rhenish provinces, without touching on the great city; and we, albeit sorely mortified at the circumstance, had no choice except to obey. Accordingly, we journeyed on, leisurely and very pleasantly, through a rich country, and under the influence of a genial sun; taking care to halt, whenever the opportunity offered, at some pleasant village for the night, and always meeting from the villagers a very friendly reception.

We (I mean the count's domestics and baggage) were attended throughout the march by a small escort of Polish dragoons. I mention this fact, because the wife of one of the party acted as a sort of sutler to the cavalcade, and by the oddity of her appearance, as well as the strangeness of her proceedings, was the occasion of a good deal of merriment and some wonder. She was singularly short, and happened to be in a state when women in general avoid horse exercise. Yet there she was, day after day, mounted cross-legged on a brute at least seventeen hands high, and laden with eggs, bottles, and glasses, out of which she dispensed, with a liberal hand, Cognac to such as required it. One day we missed her from her accustomed place. The cavalcade set forward, and she went not with it; ay, and more extraordinary still, when the halting hour came, the Circular Pole, as we called her, failed to make her appearance; so we were forced to get our schnaps, sorely against our will, at the auberge. In like manner the march of the following day began, without restoring us to our Hebe; and something like anxiety was rising among us, when all at once there was seen in the rear a tall horse at a swinging trot, and a human form, or else that of a baboon, perched upon its back. The question of humanity did not, however, remain unsolved long after the apparition arrived within ear-shot; for the old cry, "Boir, boir, monsieurs, ein glass brande-wine," soon told us that our old friend was still in the land of the living. Nor did she come alone: strapped upon her back, like a bundle of rags, was a thumping boy, which in the stable of the last halting-place had first seen the light; and which, as well as its mother, showed that it was sound in wind, whatever might be the case as to limbs. I confess that I was astounded; yet what will not Nature do when circumstances make extraordinary demands on her?

In this manner we passed the fortresses of Cambray, Valenciennes, and Avesnes, at the latter of which my fellow-servants and I came to an open rupture. They had never forgiven me the favour which our common master showed me, and here they made up their minds to let me feel the extent of their vengeance. It happened, either by accident or design, that the coachman, after washing the carriage, placed it exactly across my stable door, so that I could neither get access to the horses nor lead them out to water. I could not suppose that there was design in the matter, neither did I care to put his good humour to the test by begging him to remove it; so I wheeled it on one side with my own hands, and proceeded to arrange the horses. My work was yet incomplete, when forth from the house rushed my comrades: the valet took the lead, and a volley of abuse was instantly heaped upon me. At first I kept my temper wonderfully. I asked them what was wrong, and received in reply only fresh abuse; till, by-and-by, my anger was in its turn kindled, and I told the valet that, if he were not an old man, I would wring his nose from his face. "Would you?" cried he, "we'll see." So saying, he ran aside, armed himself with a sword, and advanced towards me in a menacing attitude. I was very much irritated, dashed into the stable, got a good broom-handle, and rushing out, prepared to do battle; but lo! my enemy was gone. I searched for him everywhere, but in vain; till at last a thought striking me that he might have ensconced himself in the carriage, I wrenched open one of the doors, and he leaped out through the other. Away he ran across a meadow, still carrying with him the naked sword, and away I set in pursuit; till, coming up with him, I knocked the weapon out of his hand, and laid him sprawling on the grass. He now cried for quarter, and I gave it; as, indeed, after soundly rating them all, I extended my forgiveness to the rest of the household; and it is but fair to add, that, having amply apologised, and promised better behaviour in the time to come, they conducted themselves towards me ever afterwards with the greatest good feeling and attention.

We did not enter Paris, but leaving it on one side, took the road by Liège, and through Brabant, towards Aix-la-Chapelle. It seemed to me as if a perpetual carnival were established. The villages, as we traversed them, were all alive with the gaieties and dissipations of a fair; and strange to say, the occurrence of each festival seemed to keep pace with our arrival at the scene of the merry-making. I was greatly pleased with all that I saw, and enjoyed both the bustle of Liège, where there are extensive iron-works, and the monastic gravity of Aix-la-Chapelle, where Napoleon's mother kept, in my day, a species of court, and divided with the tomb of Charlemagne the notice of strangers. The people did not speak in very favourable terms of her whom they described as the empress-mother. On the contrary, they represented her to be avaricious in the extreme; so much so, indeed, as to visit the market in person, and cheapen the articles that might be needed for her own household consumption.* But the circumstance which most of all gave to Aix-la-Chapelle its claims upon my notice was, that here the count, who had rejoined us near Paris, met, for the first time after three years' absence, his wife and family. And a very joyful greeting it was; for the countess came, with her two daughters and her sister, to welcome her lord to his home, and a happier group it has seldom been my fortune to witness in any part of the world.

We spent a couple of days at Aix-la-Chapelle, in order that the count and the countess might, according to etiquette, pay their respects to the empress-mother; after which we proceeded to Brael— for such was the name of my master's château, and of the grounds attached to it. The former was a baronial castle, moated and drawbridged as in ancient times, of prodigious extent, and confronted by stabling and coach-houses, where a hundred horses with a dozen of carriages might have been bestowed. The farm-yard was also capacious, and contained draught horses, cows, bulls, pigs, poultry, and all

---

* The Light Dragoon's observations agree in every respect with what higher and better authority has told us. Napoleon's mother was very stingy; yet there was a spirit of rationalism in it too. "You wish me to spend more money," was her answer to many who complained. "No, I will not. I shall have all these kings (meaning her sons) to support yet."

the usual appliances of a country-house, in abundance. So also the gardens, the orchards, and the woods were extensive; yet over the whole hung an air of neglect and desolation, such as bespoke a family in decay, or suffering from extreme mismanagement in its affairs. I have reason to believe that to the latter cause, rather than to the encroachments of time or public calamity, the dilapidated condition of Brael was owing; for the late count had, it appeared, nominated his widow to be the guardian of the property during his son's absence; and the widow, being a woman of very irregular habits, cruelly abused the trust. The consequence was, that, when making a tour of the castle, I found myself wandering from one unfurnished room to another; the very pictures themselves having been removed from the walls and sold, in order that means might be provided for the indulgence of her passion for gaming. I never shall forget the expression of the count's face when this scene of waste and desolation opened upon him. Not even the consciousness that he was again in the bosom of his family seemed for a while to afford him any relief: indeed, I was half tempted to wonder that he did not apply to be sent back to his regiment, that, in the excitement and hurry of active service, his private mortifications might be forgotten.

The count was too little satisfied with his dilapidated and unfurnished castle to make there any lengthened stay; yet a strong sense of duty urged him to visit his mother, who dwelt in another château, likewise his property, at the distance of five leagues from Brael. It was called Bolingdorf; and thither, at the expiration of a few days, we proceeded. The old lady, eccentric in the extreme, gave us but a cool reception. We abode with her, nevertheless, upwards of a week, and greatly delighted the peasants and retainers by our display both of pomp and liberality: for the count, arraying his domestics in new liveries, rode to church in state, and gave a grand supper, to which a ball succeeded, in the largest of the barns that adjoined the mansion. Going to church in state, however, much more feasting the lowly on costly viands were not at all in the countess's way; so she and her son were not slow in discovering that one house would be too small to contain them both. Wherefore our family removed to my master's town-house in Dusseldorf; and there, not unpleasantly, about a year of my existence was spent.

Having now exchanged the condition of a soldier for that of a domestic in a private family, my readers will probably agree with me in opinion, that our wisest course will be, not to adhere any longer to the form of a connected narrative, but simply to describe such occurrences as from time to time befel -- to which at the moment some measure of interest was attached, and of which the remembrance is still cherished. Let me, then, begin by stating that the year which I spent in the neighbourhood of the Rhine was that which witnessed the infliction of the first great blow upon the colossal empire of Napoleon. The Russian campaign was begun, and the drain of men and horses, not upon France alone, but upon all the States subject to French influence, was terrible. Among other districts, the duchy of Berg, of which Dusseldorf is the capital, received orders, early in 1813, to supply the grand army with a reinforcement of five thousand infantry and five hundred cavalry. Instantly the conscription was called into play. Berg had already been pretty well denuded of the stoutest and most active of its youth; but the present demand was peremptory, and was carried out in total disregard of mercy. Accordingly, the names of all the male inhabitants between the ages of fifteen and fifty being already in the keeping of the proper authorities, a sort of lottery-drawing took place, and forth from the city went the gendarmes in every direction to secure their prizes. It was shocking to see the poor wretches brought in, twenty or thirty in a string, tied round the neck with one cord, the end of which was fastened to a mounted policeman's saddle. And then for their lodging they had a particular barrack, being well and rigidly guarded there by a body of old French soldiers, every effort to corrupt whose fidelity proved as fruitless as were the endeavours to elude or deceive their vigilance. Once, and once only, a band of conscripts contrived, by rising suddenly upon the guard, to break through the barrier; of whom about two hundred effected their escape; but even they, after wandering some days in the woods, were glad to give themselves up again; for the authorities having taken care to register each conscript as he came in, noting down the exact name and residence of his father and mother, the conscript himself became from that instant a mere instrument in their hands. Had he deserted, they did not care so much as to look for him; but they sent a patrol to his father's house, seized the old man, threw him into prison, and kept him there till his son came back to his standard. There was not one of all the two hundred fugitives who was not by these means recovered: for filial piety was in those days an active principle in Germany, nor was its power to influence the behaviour of individuals ever more clearly shown than in the case of which I am now speaking.

Such was the process by which five thousand men were, in the space of a few days, brought together. To collect the horses a device not less summary was adopted. Wherever the police agents saw within the duchy an animal which seemed to be fit for military service, they, without inquiring into its age or capabilities, seized it. The proprietor might complain, but who regarded him? He received, in compensation for the loss of his beast, an order upon the treasury for seven pounds sterling, which, in ninety-nine instances out of a hundred, proved to be worth its value in paper, and no more.

The men and horses being gathered together, the next thing was to officer and drill them; the former of which measures was carried out, at least in the cavalry, by breaking up the skeleton of a lancer regiment which had served in Spain, and distributing the troopers, as captains, lieutenants, and sub-lieutenants, throughout the newly-raised levy. With respect again to the infantry, I believe that an attempt was made to place them under the command of those of their own countrymen to whom in civil life they had been accustomed to look up; but it very imperfectly succeeded. Be this, however, as it may, three short weeks were all that could be granted for organizing and training the recruits; at the termination of which the whole were pronounced fit for service, and received the rout to march into Russia. Surely there never took the field such a body of cavalry; for the men were incapable of sitting their horses, and the horses unbroken to obey the bridle, far less the sound of the trumpet; and as to the infantry, they could prime and load, certainly, and fire, and load again; but of the evolutions of a common company's parade they knew nothing. Still the cry for men was great at headquarters, and the order was issued for the Bergers to march, after their officers should have presented themselves at a grand entertainment which General Travier, the individual appointed by the authorities at Paris to superintend the equipment of the levies in this quarter, had determined to give.

I was present at the dinner, my master, Count Golstein, having purposely desired me to wait upon himself; and a scene more perfectly ludicrous, more unlike to every thing of the sort which I had ever witnessed before, never, I must admit, passed under my observation. At the upper table, where sat General Travier, my master, the civil and military authorities of the place, and several men of rank from the neighbouring districts, matters went forward pretty much as at public dinners they are wont to do; but among the gentry who crowded the long tables that stretched from one end of the hall to the other, a widely different state of things prevailed. There was scrambling and pushing while the viands were before them, -- one was heaping an entire dish of vegetables on his plate, another seizing and keeping possession of a joint or a stew. This gallant captain upset a butter-boat in his neighbour's lap, -- that newly-fledged lieutenant poured a jug of gravy over the shoulder of his friend beside him. It was everywhere "make sure of what you can reach, and never think of asking whether any body would like to share it with you." And then, when the process of giving toasts began, surely no caricaturist, in the most extravagant flight of his fancy, ever imagined aught so grotesque. General Travier, to be sure, pledged the emperor with great spirit; and, though not one in twenty understood a word of what he said, was greeted, till he sat down, with cheers. Then followed "Success to the grand army," which was prefaced by an assurance that "the gentlemen whom he had the honour to address were fortunate men, inasmuch as they were about to march to certain glory, of which the fruits would be a speedy advancement to rank, distinctions, and wealth." That, too, was cheered, not least vociferously by those who could not comprehend a syllable of the argument which the eloquent speaker laboured to establish. But by-and-by wilder and louder words were heard. The gentlemen at the lower tables, conceiving that time was precious, helped themselves in bumpers, and soon got drunk; whereupon the occupants of the high table withdrew; and even my disposition to laugh gradually exchanged itself for a sense of deep disgust, and I, though nowise required to do so, followed my master.

Next morning, at seven o'clock, five thousand Berger infantry, and five hundred cavalry, began their march towards Russia. It was a piteous spectacle that, -- for wives, and mothers, and sisters threw themselves wildly into the ranks, and the sound of lamentation rose high above the notes of martial music. But what availed it? The decree had gone forth, -- the ill-fated conscripts held their way, -- and few, if any, ever returned to tell how it fared with them amid the snows and frosts of Muscovy.

As the act of organizing this corps kept Dusseldorf in a state of extreme bustle, so the stillness that prevailed after the troops had marched struck me as something awful. You saw no human beings in the streets except women and children. Even the old men were few in number; for the conscription, like the standard of height, was often stretched; and they, like the women, seemed to be fairly bowed down with sorrow for the loss of their offspring. Every occurrence, therefore, which promised in any way to break in upon the gloom of total inaction was hailed, at least by me, as a relief; and two there did occur, very different in themselves to be sure, yet both so striking that I cannot think of passing them by unnoticed.

The first was the execution of a woman and her paramour for the murder of the husband of the former. The deceased had, it appeared, by frugality and ceaseless labour, contrived to amass some money as a maker of brooms, which brooms he was in the habit of cutting in a wood not far from the city. He, therefore, finding years increase upon him, hired a man to assist him, and his wife proceeded to form with that person an illicit connexion. They say that Love is blind, and, without all doubt, he showed himself, in this instance, to be at least fearfully shortsighted; for while the frail fair one was really a handsome woman, the gallant, if not absolutely deformed, was but by a hairbreadth removed from deformity. Nevertheless he had charms in the eyes of the broom-maker's wife, so irresistible, that at last it was agreed between them that the husband should be put out of the way.

The poor man was missed; but as his wife represented him to have gone on a visit to some relatives at a distance nobody inquired further, and for several weeks all went on smoothly. At the termination of this interval, however, a body was found, very much decomposed, yet distinguishable as that of the broom-maker, floating on the surface of a pond or small lake, which lay deep in the forest whence his bosoms used to be drawn. It was immediately conveyed into the city, and the woman and her lover being arrested, arrangements were made for putting them on their trial. How closely does the eye of Providence watch over the life of man; and how rarely are they who shed man's blood permitted to escape. Two children, the eldest only eleven years old, had, as it now came out, been spectators of the butchery. They saw the old man -- for he was full sixty years of age -- come, with his journeyman and his wife, to his accustomed spot, and stoop down, as he was wont to do, for the purpose of cutting the heather where it was longest. He was thus employed when his servant stole behind and felled him to the ground with a blow from a bludgeon. The blows were repeated till his victim ceased to struggle; and then he, with his paramour, dragged the body to the edge of the pond and threw it in. But life, as it appeared, had not been extinguished; for the guilty pair turning round, after they had proceeded some way from the spot, beheld their victim dragging himself towards the shore, by means of the bulrushes which grew in large quantities round the edges of the pond. Instantly the woman turned back, and, seizing a broom-handle, she pushed her husband back into the water, and held him under till he expired.

These facts having been proved at the trial, there could, of course, be no doubt as to the nature of the sentence. Both criminals were condemned to be guillotined; but as it was necessary in those days to get the sentence of death confirmed at Paris, several weeks elapsed ere the wretched pair were taught that with them the business of the world was ended. The woman, I was assured, made very strenuous efforts to obtain, if not a pardon, at least a commutation of her sentence. She offered to pay as much as ten thousand dollars into the imperial treasury. Yet the emperor, or his representatives, though sorely pressed for the sinews of war, refused, point blank, to have any dealings with her. Accordingly the day was fixed, and at the time appointed she and her partner in crime were brought from the prison to the scaffold, each in an open cart, and each attended by a priest, who seemed, to do him justice, most assiduous in the discharge of his duty. The wretched woman looked to her spiritual comforter with attention. Her whole demeanour, likewise, was that of one who knows that it is the reverse of a light matter to die; whereas the man, either from ignorance, or because he was more master of himself, exhibited no symptoms at all of concern. Both were, however, firm; nor did she, even when the executioner stripped her to the waist, shrink from her doom. But I must not go on. It is a horrible species of punishment. Easy it may be to the delinquent, when compared with strangulation; but on the spectator the effect is far more disgusting: for there is something frightful in the literal shedding of blood, especially as by the guillotine it is shed -- in torrents. Let me, then, be content to state, that in three seconds after they had been fastened to the machine they lay before us, successively, headless trunks; while we, or at least I, turned away, utterly sickened by the spectacle of which I had been the witness.

The second anecdote which I undertook to repeat has reference to a phenomenon on which, for aught I know to the contrary, may be founded the well-known legend which records the destruction of a tyrannical chief in his own castle, on the Rhine, by an inroad of rats. The country about Dusseldorf is subject to periodical visitations from myriads of field-mice. These tiny marauders advance in such numbers, that every effort to destroy them fails; and wherever they go they mow down the standing wheat before them, as surely and wellnigh as quickly, as a band of reapers. They feed entirely on the roots of the stalk; and, grubbing for their food, while the stalk is yet green, they utterly destroy as they go forward. Moreover, they can neither be arrested nor turned out of their direct route; but forward they go, like the hurricane, in a straight line, and their operations are scarcely than the hurricane less destructive. I tried to persuade the people that, if they would only dig a deep and wide trench across the field, the small marauders would be stopped; but they paid no attention to me. And the consequence was, that, throughout a space of several miles, -- on a plateau not very wide, to be sure, but exceedingly fertile, -- all the labours of the seed-time were rendered profitless, and the husbandmen entirely cheated of their harvest. At last the army of foragers reached a running stream, which they could not pass; and I believe that, in their efforts to do so, they all perished.

The people of Berg are very superstitious, and, in one sense of the phrase, extremely philosophical. No sooner were the mice gone, than they set about collecting the damaged grain, laying it up as forage for the cattle during the winter. And, while they shrugged their shoulders, and declared that the visitation came from God, and could not, therefore, be avoided, they comforted themselves by the anticipation of a crop, tenfold more abundant than that which had been lost, on the following autumn. I have reason to believe that the calculation in question never fails them. Whether it is that the mice manure the land as they go on, or that the removal of the grain by the process of mining spares the soil more than if it were reaped, I cannot pretend to say; but experience has shown, that the season immediately succeeding that of a visitation of the sort is invariably more prolific, by many degrees, than the seasons usually are. So bountiful is nature in all her arrangements, even when she seems at times to have declared war against us.

Time passed; and each new week -- I might have said each new day -- beheld detachment after detachment arrive from the interior of France, halt to organize itself, and provide horses for the conveyance of its baggage, and then push on, as the event proved, to certain destruction. Every animal that could move or carry a load, be it ever so trifling, was, of course, taken up, and my kind master, among others, parted with all his stud, leaving me, for the first time, since I joined him, entirely destitute of employment. It was under these circumstances, and with his entire approbation, that I consented to transfer my services to an English family, called Grainger, then resident in the place, and with them for a while I lived in great comfort, albeit certainly not in idleness. But the crisis had come, on which, at a period not remote, he would have been accounted insane who should have reckoned; and bands of stragglers, making their way back to their homes, told us of the entire overthrow of the grand army. The battle of Leipsic was fought; and the wreck of the combatants might, it appeared, be expected in full retreat for the Rhine, which they desired to interpose between themselves and their pursuers. Moreover, the vigilance of the French in guarding their prisoners, as well on the German as on the opposite side of the river, seemed to relax; and, one after another, the captives regained their freedom, though not without the endurance of much suffering. I remember one bitter cold day, in the depth of the winter of 1813-14, going out early in the morning for the purpose of washing the carriage, and encountering at the yard-gate a spectacle which greatly interested me. It was a young man, dripping with wet, from whose person the icicles were hanging, and who earnestly besought me to tell whether there was not an Englishman in the place. After a little discussion, I made myself known, and learned that he, a countryman of my own, with three others, had escaped from a depot of prisoners on the other side, and, swimming the Rhine, were now all but dead from cold, having crouched together throughout the night in a gravel-pit. I took them in, as may be supposed, carried them to the servants' hall, lighted a good fire in the stove, and from my own wardrobe supplied them with a change of dress. My master likewise behaved to them with great kindness; and, concealing them for a while, we eventually contrived to pass them on, by a route which secured to them a good chance of reaching England in safety. They had, it appeared, been mates of merchant-vessels, in which capacity they were taken; and the name of one was Robinson, from Tooley-street, in the Borough. I cannot recall to my remembrance the precise channel through which intelligence of their safe return to London reached me; yet I know that they did escape in a smuggler from Holland. I hope that they have since prospered.

The Englishmen were scarcely gone, when evidences, more and more conclusive, of the turn which affairs had taken at Napoleon's head-quarters, began everywhere to exhibit themselves. Rumour after rumour came in of fresh disasters sustained, and of a universal disposition exhibiting itself throughout the whole of the Rhenish provinces, to rise against the iron yoke under which they had so long lain. The people, indeed, were everywhere eager to be led against their oppressors; but chiefs to direct the insurrection were wanting, and the consequence was, that an outbreak which occurred at Elberfeldt was put down, with great loss to the insurgents. It was determined, also, by the victors to make an example of four of the ringleaders, by putting them publicly to death in the four most populous towns in the district; and one, an unfortunate weaver, was brought to Dusseldorf, that he might there undergo the sentence which a court-martial had awarded. I went to the great square, for the purpose of witnessing his execution; and a very shocking sight it was. The poor man, who had been wounded in the battle, was carried upon a sort of litter, by four French grenadiers, and laid down in the market-place, scarcely if at all conscious of what was going on. A coffin had already been prepared for him, and he was thrown on the ground beside it; in which attitude he was shot, I verily believe, after the breath had gone forth from the body. Neither this barbarous act, however, nor many more of a like nature, sufficed to stem the tide of events, which swept irresistibly onwards. The period of French domination was come, and the lapse of a few days made all parties, whether friends or foes, aware of the fact.

While I was looking, like all around me, for what each new day might bring forth, I chanced, once upon a time, to pass through the market-place, where I encountered a man leading a mule by the halter, whom I felt myself irresistibly compelled to examine closely. My surprise may be imagined, when I recognised, in the squalid object before me, the same Joseph, who, on my first capture in Spain, had behaved to me with so much kindness. He had, it appeared, followed his master all the way to Moscow, and shared in the hardships of the subsequent retreat, at some stage in which the General was wounded, and sent on, with others in a similar plight, to France. Joseph, however, did not accompany him, but marched with his mule, throughout that inclement season, which cost the invaders of Russia so many lives, and utterly destroyed the French army. I took him to my home, of course, and strongly urged his making his way to England through Holland; but he refused to act on my advice. "The mule is loaded with my master's property," said he, "and I cannot bear the thought of wronging him of one fragment of it. I will take my chance, penetrate into France, and, having delivered it up, return home as I best can." There was no blaming him for acting on a principle of such perfect honesty, so I contented myself with giving him a share of my worldly goods, and recommending him to keep well ahead of the retreating army, I saw him to the edge of the Rhine, and there took leave of him.

I had just parted from Joseph, when I learned from some market-people that a corps of French troops was in full march towards the town. About noon they arrived, some six or seven hundred in number, bringing with them two eight-pounders and a howitzer. They encamped outside the barrier, whither, with many more, I went to see them. Never have I beheld troops in such a pitiable plight. Their arms, I believe, were serviceable enough, but their clothes were all in tatters; and their frames, emaciated from constant fatigue, and the absence of regularity in their diet, seemed altogether unequal to any further exertion. Their morale, likewise, appeared to be affected almost in an equal degree with their physical powers, for the very name of a Cossack made them shudder, and they were evidently incapable of showing any steady front, if attacked. Nor, indeed, was it intended that they should attempt a stand on this side of the Rhine, the object of their movement on Dusseldorf being to get possession of the flying bridge, and to carry that, with every boat and barge that lay near, out of the reach of their pursuers. Accordingly, after a halt of a few days, during which period Buonaparte with his staff and body-guard arrived, and a regiment of cavalry with some more infantry joined them, the whole moved off without having offered to the town the slightest molestation, and established themselves in a camp which had already been formed along the farther bank, and from which both they and their leaders hoped to guard effectually against the passage of the Rhine by the Allies.

Chapter 14

There is something very sad in the contemplation of such a total wreck as had by this time overtaken the French armies, however
merited the downfall of the discomfited may be; and there occurred
a little incident which sufficiently proved that the inhabitants of Dusseldorf at least were not insensible to the feeling. After the last of the
boats had been carried across the river, about five-and-twenty invalid
French soldiers, whom their comrades had overlooked, and who remained in one of the hospitals, discovered that they had been abandoned, and, rushing out into the streets, exhibited amid their weakness, the most distressing symptoms of despair. They ran to the water's
edge, adjured their countrymen to save them, and, in several instances,
made an effort to throw themselves into the river. The citizens looked
on with great compassion for a while, after which they took the poor
follows to their homes, and, hiding them in places where they had
at least a chance of escaping observation, they fed and nursed them
there with great tenderness. I am glad that it is in my power to add,
that the humanity of the Dusseldorfers was not wasted. The invalids
contrived to elude the notice both of Russians and Prussians; and, being supplied with money and other necessaries for the journey, were,
on the recovery of their strength, sent home to their own country.

It was on the 13th of November, 1813, that the last of the French
army passed the Rhine; and the same day, about noon, I learned from
some countrymen whom I met in a wine-house, that bands of Cossacks were hovering about in the fields, at no great distance. Now, we
had not been taught to think too highly either of the self-denial or the
honesty of the Cossacks; and I confess that the intelligence rendered
me very uneasy, on account of my mistress and the female domestics
of the family. I therefore hurried home, warned my poor mistress --
whose husband had gone from home -- of the danger that menaced,
and gave her all the aid which I could furnish, in guarding against
it. The first thing done, was to direct the cook to have an abundant
supply of provisions ready: the next, to get up from the cellars wine
and spirits, enough to cheer the hearts of half a regiment. After this,
I persuaded the baroness to retreat with her children and nurses up
stairs into one of the bedrooms, and to barricade the door on the

inside, so as to hinder it from being easily opened. Then, having seen matters arranged, as far as circumstances would allow, I strolled out, partly to ascertain how far danger really threatened, partly to gratify the sort of nervous curiosity by which all men, so situated, are apt to be affected.

It was night when I entered the streets, throughout the whole compass of which not a living thing showed itself. The shops were all closed, every window was dark, and not so much as the stroke of a hammer broke in upon the deathlike silence. I wandered on and on, seeing nothing, and hearing nothing, except the clank of my own footsteps on the pavement. At last I turned towards a public-house, which I had been in the habit of frequenting; and finding the door shut, I knocked. For a considerable space no notice was taken of the signal; but I knocked again and again; and in the end, the sound of the bolt withdrawn from its socket reached me. By-and-by the door creaked on its hinges, and mine host stood in the very narrow aperture, holding a candle in his hand, by the flame of which I could perceive that he was pale as ashes. "What's the matter, Boniface?" cried I; "has any thing happened?" "Oh, nothing at all," replied he, drawing a deep breath;" I only thought it might be the Cossacks." From this I learned, that the arrival of these people was momentarily expected; so, having drunk a glass of wine, and conversed for a few moments with mine host, I hurried home.

It might be about nine o'clock when the first straggling party of Cossacks entered Dusseldorf. Their advance was conducted with extreme caution; for they no sooner passed one gate, than they put their horses to the speed, and galloped helter-skelter through, emerging by the gate opposite. Having thus satisfied themselves that there was no garrison in the place, they returned to the gate through which they had first shown themselves, and there formed. They marched next to the market-place where they halted. But though the inhabitants, perceiving but a handful of men, ventured to come forth and invite them into their houses, not one of these wild and wary warriors would quit his station. They sat down, to be sure, to the tables which were soon spread for them in the open air, and ate and drank as savages are accustomed to do, who have long fasted. But though they vociferated their delight as often as a cry arose, "Long live the Emperor Alexander," they steadily refused to enter beneath a roof.

Throughout the whole of that night the Cossacks continued to receive, by twos and threes, a fresh accession of numbers. At first not more than twenty or thirty had entered the town; when day broke, about 200 occupied the square; and they were soon afterwards reinforced by about 500 Prussian lancers. These proceeded, without delay, to obtain billets upon the inhabitants; and taking quiet possession of the apartments that were allotted to them, they exhibited no disposition to molest or offer injury to their entertainers. The case was very different, when a few hours later a battalion of Russian infantry, with a regiment of horse, entered the town. They did not so much as go through the form of applying for billets; but spreading themselves through the town, they took possession by parties of whatever domiciles seemed to attract their notice, or hold out the prospect of agreeable quarters. Neither did they stop there. Whole families were turned into the street: the grossest outrages perpetrated on the women: horses were put up in the very drawing-rooms, and the costliest articles of furniture broken up for firewood. As to the work of plunder, that went on without the smallest interruption, and no human being appeared to blush for it. Among others, our house was visited by two officers of cavalry and a troop of their men. They knocked furiously at the gate; and though I lost no time in opening it, they overwhelmed me with abuse because I had kept them waiting. They demanded quarters for themselves and a superior officer. I showed them into a couple of rooms in the lower story, where beds had been purposely prepared; and replied to their orders concerning dinner, that it should be forthcoming immediately. And thanks to the bravery of my countrywoman, the cook, who refused to retreat with the rest of the female servants, and stood to her utensils all day, I was enabled, within ten minutes, to set before them a sumptuous meal.

The Russians expressed themselves both surprised and pleased at the rapidity with which their wants were supplied. They drank copiously, too, from a magnum of white Burgundy, which, having no good Rhenish in the house, I set before them as choice Markobruner, and desiring that tea might be ready in a couple of hours, they walked abroad. And now began my troubles with the men. So long as the officers continued on the spot, the privates bore themselves with some show of moderation; but moderation was now at an end. They clamoured for food, drink, every thing of which they fancied themselves in need, and made a rush to storm the kitchen, which the cook defended with great resolution. At last, however, by dint of expostulation and entreaty, I prevailed upon them to desist; and a bountiful supply of black puddings and gin soon restored them to good humour.

Meanwhile, flying portions of these savages had wandered all over the house, trying every door, and entering every apartment to which they found access. Among others, they had twice or thrice lifted the latch of that behind which my mistress and her family lay; but finding it fastened, they did not burst through, very much to the relief of the parties within, who were wellnigh killed with terror. They were not, however, so delicate in their dealings with our horses: these they turned out of the stalls into the streets, putting their own under cover, and feeding them with our forage. In short, it was a day and a night of extreme anxiety even to me; of agony and terror to the rest. Nevertheless, it passed by with perhaps less of suffering than might fairly have been expected. And on the morrow, my mistress, perceiving that no personal violence was likely to be offered to her, ventured to quit her place of refuge.

Her first step was to wait upon the officers, who chanced to be at breakfast, and to remonstrate with them against the treatment which her horses had received. They did not so much as rise when she entered the apartment; but asking with a sneer, whether she thought her horses, or those belonging to the Emperor, of greater worth, they told her, point blank, that things should remain as they were. She instantly withdrew, and burst into tears. But tears were of small avail in such a situation as that into which the fortune of war had brought her, and she was condemned in consequence, throughout a space of four whole days, to sustain as she best might, the wrongs and insults to which foreign soldiers subjected her.

During four whole days this state of things continued, and Dusseldorf was the scene of indescribable misery. Each new hour brought an accession to the numbers of the troops that filled it, till by-and-by not fewer than 10,000 to 12,000 must have taken up their quarters there. As a matter of course, the inhabitants were expelled from one apartment after another, to make way for men and horses. The streets, also, were strewed with fragments of broken furniture, beds, chairs, curtains, cooking utensils; and the noise of revelry rose above sounds which told of outrage suffered and feelings lacerated. But the most curious figures in that strange scene were the Cossacks: for a Cossack accoutred for war, bears as little resemblance to a human being as it is possible to conceive. His attire consists of an accumulation of rags of all sorts fastened about his trunk and limbs, with ropes or bands of straw: his cloak is not unfrequently a bear-skin, with a hole cut in order to let his head pass through; over which again is drawn a

red woollen night-cap, so closely, as to leave no part of his countenance visible except the small piercing red eyes, or the sharp cheek-
bones. Moreover, the Cossack is so enveloped in swaddling-clothes,
that each limb appears as thick as an ordinary man's waist, and each
waist like a goodly pollarded oak. As to his arms and appointments,
these consist always of a lance, long and stout, and headed with steel;
often of a bow and a quiver full of arrows, as well as of pistols stuck in
profusion round his body. His horse again is as rough as a polar bear,
small of stature, yet exceedingly hardy; and as to the saddle, according
to the height of that, you may judge of each man's personal wealth.
For a Cossack never stuffs his plunder any where but in the croup of
his saddle, which, as he is a capital forager, grows higher and higher,
till, towards the end of the campaign, its shape is portentous. Finally,
a Cossack never undresses till the campaign has ended, nor thinks of
sleeping in a bed. He is accordingly a moving mass of filth and vermin: yet, withal, hardy, active, acute, and brave -- a very locust to the
land over which he sweeps as a conqueror, a very hornet to the flying
enemy, whom it is his business to harass.

Up to the present moment, the French had been in possession of
one bank of the Rhine, the Allies of the other; yet, by neither party
was an attempt made to break in upon the repose of its adversaries.
On the side of the French this forbearance was purely voluntary, for
they had in battery opposite to Dusseldorf, two 8-pounders, and a
howitzer. The Allies, I am afraid, could lay claim to no merit on that
score, seeing that they were destitute of cannon, and possessed not a
single boat wherewith to try the effect of a passage. But the cannon
for which they had repeatedly sent, came up at last; and one night,
orders were given to plant eight 12-pounders above and below the
town, so as to throw upon the French camp a cross-fire. Having been
made aware of the issuing of these orders, and being desirous of witnessing the effect of the first discharge, I made interest with the governor of the jail to whom I was personally known, and was by him
admitted into a cell in one of the upper stories, whence an extensive
view of the surrounding country could be obtained. I took my place
beside the barred window, just as the first gray streaks of dawn appeared in the sky, and the intensity of interest with which I watched
them gradually extend, I have no power of language to describe. At
last the morning came there was nothing remarkable in it for a brief
space; and in the French camp all seemed security and peace. The huts
had been built with great regularity: they were filled with slumber-

ing soldiers; not a man indeed appeared to be awake throughout the whole encampment, except the sentries, and horses and mules stood picketed in numbers near. In a moment afterwards what a change was there! The allied guns opened. Crash went the huts, down fell horses and mules; forth from their sleeping-places rushed crowds of men, only that they might the more expose themselves to the showers of round and grape that fell among them; while here and there a human form stretched upon the earth, or dragging itself along, gave evidence that not in vain had round and grape sped upon their course. It was a horrid spectacle, for the wretches thus cut down neither had offered, nor could offer the smallest resistance; and their retreat itself, though begun without the loss of a moment, did not carry them for some time out of the reach of their destiny.

The French appeared to have been taken so much by surprise that they made, for a while, no reply to this rude salutation. By degrees, however, their artillerists recovered their self-possession, and sharply and well their guns spoke back, sending round shot into many a house, and setting fire to more than one store of combustibles. On our side, however, as every possible preparation had been made to meet this exigency, buckets and engines were all ready, and the flames were soon extinguished. But besides that some lives were lost, more than one domicile received a mark of what war will do, in the shape of a round-shot lodged even in its inner chambers, which not to this day, I have reason to believe, have the Dusseldorfers thought it necessary to efface.

The firing continued on both sides till dusk, when the allies, having levelled the enemy's camp with the ground, ceased, and the enemy withdrew their guns from a position which was no longer tenable. But our people were not willing to let the matter end there. Having ascertained that two horse-boats had been scuttled just before the French evacuated the place, the officer commanding caused them to be raised, and in the course of half an hour they were repaired and made sea-worthy. Immediately one hundred Prussian grenadiers, headed by a brave and enterprising young officer, volunteered to make a dash upon the town of Eberfeldt, where it was well known that most of the boats removed from the Dusseldorf side had been laid up. The offer was accepted, of course; and about midnight this handful of gallant fellows shoved off, carrying with them the best wishes of their countrymen. It appeared that they managed all things with equal prudence and bravery. They landed without observation, the French suspecting nothing on that side, and therefore having no sentries planted. They crept up towards the gate of the town, and lay down, waiting till the hour of relief should come round. It struck at last: they heard the relief muster inside; they saw the drawbridge fall and the gate roll back, and then, without so much as a cry, they sprang forward. The guard were bayoneted to a man, and into the town they rushed. What can soldiers do when thus surprised? That night a battalion of five hundred men, a general, and twenty officers of inferior rank, became prisoners to this handful of grenadiers, who seized them in their beds; and, when daylight came, the inhabitants of Eberfeldt were at once astonished and delighted to see that their town was in possession of the allies.

The glad tidings soon spread to Dusseldorf, and boats coming over, crowds of curious persons hastened to ascertain how matters had gone with the party. Among others, I must needs visit Eberfeldt, and a curious scene of revelry and triumph it presented. The Prussians occupied the great square, the French having been unceremoniously thrust into the common jail, and there, with the inhabitants of all ranks and both sexes, they were carousing. But not to Dusseldorf alone had tidings of the night's work made their way. At Juliers, a place scarcely nine English miles distant, a division of six thousand French troops lay; and these, made aware of the disaster that had overtaken their comrades, hastened to avenge it. It was curious to watch the progress of things. Guns, tumbrils, ammunition-waggons, military stores of every description, quantities of bullion, of smallarms, and great-coats, were run down to the water's edge, and embarked; while, by-and-by, the idlers, whom curiosity had brought into danger, began to hurry as fast as possible beyond the reach of it. For, strange to say, though a lodgement was thus made, there existed no intention on the part of the allies to hold the ground on the enemy's bank of the river, and the hundred grenadiers received, in consequence, no reinforcement. Accordingly, the news no sooner spread that an enemy's column was advancing, than helter-skelter all ran for the beach; and, in a few minutes, it seemed doubtful whether boats enough would remain to carry back again the handful of heroes who had so well accomplished the task committed to them.

The Prussian officer, however, was a good soldier in every sense of the word. He did not neglect his line of retreat: he marched a party down to the river, which at once took and kept possession of as many boats as were judged necessary. He then coolly planted his men under cover of certain houses which commanded the road by which the French must advance, and saluted the head of the column, as soon as it arrived within range, with a volley. A smart skirmish followed, in which the Prussians lost, I think, three men; but it was not of long continuance. The officer had done his duty; he therefore retreated in excellent order, and, carrying with him his wounded, arrived on the opposite shore, amid the enthusiastic shouts of his comrades.

All this while the force of the allies continued to increase in and around Dusseldorf. Every farm-house and hovel in the neighbour-hood was filled with troops, who, with their horses, literally licked up every thing that was fit for food -- till, by-and-by, about twenty thousand men were ready to debouch by the opening which our Prussians had made. Among other arrivals, I must not omit to mention that of the Black Hussars -- a corps originally raised by a Prussian noble, whom his master, for reasons of state, had sent into banishment. These men, with their leader, had long existed by plunder, which they carried off from far and near, and stored up in their haunts among the Hartz mountains. But when the crisis came, the chief of the band made a tender of his services to the allied sovereigns: he was pardoned and accepted; and the battles of Leipsic and Hennau bear testimony to the reckless bravery which marked his own proceedings and those of his followers. His men were well mounted: he had equipped them in black, and they bore upon the fronts of their chakos the same emblems which our own Black Brunswickers used to bear -- namely, the skull and cross-bones. But though the rumour of their approach excited unspeakable alarm in Dusseldorf, I am bound to state that, when they did come, they conducted themselves with at least as much of regularity as any other body of armed men in the town. Two of their officers were quartered upon us, and we found them in all respects civil and even modest.

The Black Hussars, with the rest of the forces assembled in Dusseldorf, broke up in due time, and took the road to Paris. Other heavy columns moved simultaneously with them from Cologne and Coblentz; and the newspapers, which circulated freely, told us day by day of some fresh triumph obtained and some province liberated. Such a state of things naturally excited in my mind a strong desire to revisit the land of my birth; and as spring came on, I only waited the return of my master in order to carry this natural and cherished scheme into execution. He came at last, bringing with him a letter from my mother, whom he had seen and informed of my wellbeing; and who, erroneously conceiving that I intended to live and die abroad, proposed to sell off her little property and join me at Dusseldorf. But this kind proposal only sharpened my zeal to breathe once more the atmosphere which I had breathed in my childhood; and suspecting that my master would throw impediments in the way, I set about making my preparations very quietly. At last I told him. He was surprised, vexed, and perhaps somewhat unjust: he refused at first to let me go without three months' notice, and when I resisted this, he sent me away with less of kindness than I conceived that I had merited. I did not, however, resent the injury; but, retiring to a public-house, packed my little all into as narrow a compass as possible, and made ready to begin my homeward journey on the morrow.

Though Dusseldorf had been to me the land of strangers, there were some kind hearts there which I was loth to leave behind. This was particularly the case in reference to my first master and friend, Baron Golstein. Yet it would have been strange, had the consciousness of liberty recovered not very much outweighed these natural regrets; and I am not ashamed to acknowledge that my step was light and buoyant, as, for the last time, I traversed the streets of that ancient town: besides, I was not an object of any one's compassion. Two good suits of clothes I could call my own, besides a watch and thirty odd Prussian dollars in money; while my travelling companion was a poodle dog, whose gambols served to while away many a vacant hour, and whose sagacity was not inferior to that of his kind in general. My first day's march, which carried me to Gueldres, was performed in the highest spirits; and my reception there having been all that the heart of man could wish, my second began under circumstances nowise less propitious.

It was a fine fresh morning, the 3rd of April, 1814, when this second march began. Having a considerable distance to accomplish, I started betimes, and was passing over an extensive heath -- my pipe in my mouth, and my dog frisking round me -- when far ahead I discovered the form of a man, and I quickened my pace, desiring to overtake him. I gained upon the stranger sufficiently to observe that he wore a glazed hat and a brown coat, -- the former, at least, affording ground to believe that he must be a countryman; so I stepped out lustily, being elated by the prospect of finding a pleasant companion with whom to converse by the way. The stranger however, was evidently suspicious: he looked behind, and seeing me stride out, he began to stride also, thus increasing rather than diminishing the space that was between us. It was in vain that I sent on my dog, or that the animal, trotting from the one to the other, strove, as it were, to bring us together: the stranger held his pace, and I soon found that the hope of overtaking him, unless some check should occur, was idle.

The chase was thus continued, till a town or large village appeared in the distance, in passing through which I felt sure that I should lose my man. Not willing, however, to abandon my own project so long as the faintest prospect of a different result appeared, I sent my dog forward, and desired him to keep the stranger in view till I should come up. I lost both man and beast at the entrance of the village; and not seeing either of them in the street, I made up my mind to pass on, even at the cost of my faithful poodle's company. But the dog thought differently: he suddenly showed himself at the head of a street, lane, or alley, and having, as it were, invited me to follow, turned round and waited for me. By these means, I was led to a public-house, in the taproom of which, sure enough, and ensconced behind the buttress of a large chimney, I beheld my man. He made every possible effort to hold aloof from me: I addressed him in German -- he could not answer; I spoke to him in French, and received a reply in a wretched patois; after which I held out my hand and called him countryman, desiring him to keep a good heart, and not to shiver. He looked up like one who has received a reprieve on the gallows. He had mistaken me, it appeared, for a gendarme, and being like myself a liberated prisoner, trembled at the anticipation of a recapture. As may be imagined, we became excellent friends in a moment; and both having our faces turned towards Holland, we resolved to prosecute the journey together.

My new acquaintance represented himself to me as captain and part owner of a brig from Halifax: he had been ten years in a French prison, and having effected his escape with but a slender stock of money in his pocket, his means of getting refreshment by the way were quite exhausted. These tidings only made me the more desirous of accepting his companionship during my progress: I compassionated his sufferings, and told him he should share the contents of my purse -- he giving me, in return, repeated assurances that my outlay would be more than made good, so soon as we reached Rotterdam; and as I could not for a moment doubt either his inclination or his ability to perform the promise, I made him heartily welcome to the best at each stage where we halted.

It is not worth while to describe at length the little adventures that befel us during our progress to Nimeguen. They were such as fall to the lot of pedestrians in general, with this solitary exception, that at Nimeguen, my companion not being provided with a passport, would have found it impossible to obtain admission into the place, had I not interceded for him. But the commandant, a good-natured old gentleman, no sooner heard the particulars of our story, than he gave orders that both should be accommodated with apartments, and be permitted to rest in the town three whole days. We then took a trackschuyt, which in three days more conveyed us to Rotterdam, where, on one of the quays, at the sign of the Dolphin, we fixed our head-quarters. But my money -- not very abundant at the outset -- was by this time beginning to run short, and certain very awkward suspicions of my companion's honesty would rise in spite of me, seeing that he made no effort at all to replenish the purse. Still I hoped the best. I even went with him to the English Consul's house -- Mr. Ferrier's -- of whom we together begged a supply, but who told us frankly, that though he could procure us a passage to England, he had no money at his disposal for us or for any body. Accordingly, we were fain to accept letters to the naval officer in command at Helvoetsluys, and, in company with two or three more Englishmen, pushed off in one of the packet-boats for the mouth of the Maese.

In the course of this voyage, as well as during our sojourn at Helvoetsluys, I was very much indebted to the kindness of one of our fellow-passengers, a groom in the employment of the Prince Regent, who had been sent to Holland with a present of two fine horses for the Prince of Orange. That individual, being flush of money, insisted on acting as paymaster throughout, and used his best endeavours to get me away from the society of the captain, whom he never particularly admired. But, partly because I was not willing to wrong a fellow-prisoner, partly because I believed that, being honest, he would pay his debts, and otherwise befriend me on our arrival in England, I resisted all the groom's suggestions, and, taking my passage in the same ship with the captain, was conveyed safely to Harwich. As we messed in different parts of the ship, the captain boarding with the lieutenants, and I living with the petty officers, we had comparatively little intercourse during the voyage; and, when I came to land, I found that my friend had got the start of me by an hour. I was both provoked and mortified; and, being determined at least to tell him my mind, I made all haste to the London coach-office. But in this particular, too, my labour proved vain; the coach had started about twenty minutes, and my friend having ensconced himself on the top, I never saw nor heard of him again.

The Kilkenny Militia happening at this time to be quartered in Harwich, I proceeded to report myself to the officer in command, and received orders to join one of the messes of the corps till arrangements could be made for forwarding me to my own regiment. I went to the room allotted to me; but the miserable fare of the militia-men -- a red-herring and a bowl of potatoes -- agreed so little with my notions of comfort, that I at once made up my mind to have nothing more to say to them. I accordingly repaired to a public-house, where, with the last coin that adhered to the interior of my pocket -- an eighteen-pence token -- I treated myself, and a soldier whom I found there, to a noggin of English gin. Moreover, I found there an opportunity of befriending four foreigners, strangers at once to the language and the manners of our island, who had come over in the hope of getting a pension -- long ago granted to them by the Duke of York -- renewed. I ordered their supper for them, became their interpreter, went with them to the coach-office, and next morning saw them off ; -- trifling acts in themselves, doubtless, yet, by persons in their situation, felt and admitted to be grave favours. And now, being reduced to a few pence, yet resolute not to return to barracks, I pawned my watch to the landlord for five shillings, and sat down in a corner, with my pipe, not a little disconsolate.

I was thus circumstanced, when the door of the room opened, and there entered, with a shout, about a score of seamen, all rigged out in their best, and all bedizened with knots and streamers of ribbon. They instantly recognised me, for they were part of the crew of the frigate in which I had crossed from Holland; and, having informed me that they had received three months' pay, with three days ashore in which to spend it, they insisted on my casting in my lot with them. It will be readily imagined that I neither experienced nor expressed the smallest reluctance to become their guest. And, sure enough, for the entire space of time which they had at their command, ours was a life of revelry and joyance.

The first thing to be done was to provide a fiddler, and an adequate number of partners for a dance. These were soon procured, and supper, with an ample supply of grog, egg-flip, and other good things, being ordered, the ball began in a large outhouse attached to the inn. Nobody went to bed that night, and though the sailors ate less than might have been expected, the consumption of liquor was something quite unparalleled. Next day, hackney-coaches were procured, and, the fiddler playing all the way, we made an excursion, partners and all, into the country. There, too, a convenient house of entertainment was found, where, as in the town, dancing and frolic chased the hours away till evening. A dinner followed, and we returned to Harwich, with frequent halts by the way, in order that the crews of the different vehicles might refresh themselves; and, that nothing might be wanting to complete the farce, we did not compass our journey without a fight. One of our party happening to quiz a negro belonging to the band of the militia, the latter grew restive, and Jack and he had a regular set-to, from which Jack came off victorious. But why continue these details? -- the seamen kept up the fun till the hour arrived when their lieutenant came to inform them that their time was expended, after which they returned cheerfully on board of ship, and I was once more left to my solitude.

I was not altogether easy, in consequence of the breach of discipline of which I had been guilty, in absenting myself without leave from the barracks, and had made up my mind to return, when a corporal entered the room where I was sitting, and asked eagerly of the landlord whether or not he had seen me. I made myself known to the corporal at once, and was much relieved when he informed me that orders had arrived to forward me to my regiment, and that he was already in possession of my marching-money. The watch which I had pawned was redeemed, my little bundle packed, and at an early hour on the following morning I began my march towards London.

Chapter 15

Our first march carried us to Colchester, a distance of twenty miles, which -- I can scarcely tell why -- tried my powers of endurance severely. The second day we reached Romford, and on the third I found myself in my mother's arms. I had written from Harwich, to acquaint her of my safety, and to announce the time when she might expect to see me; and I was welcomed, in consequence, not by her alone, but by as many of our friends and relatives as she could get together. A very happy day was that, as were two others which succeeded it, during which the corporal was our guest, and by every member of the family treated with great kindness; and then, having bidden them all farewell, I set out for Hampton Court, where a detachment from the 11th was on duty, and to the officer commanding which I reported myself. Mr. Gould was an old acquaintance, who welcomed me back to the corps with great kindness; and I spent a day or two with the detachment very much to my own satisfaction, and not, I am inclined to think, disagreeably to others.

I joined my regiment at Hounslow, where, to my inexpressible delight, I found the man who, in former years, used to be my comrade. The greeting was on both sides the more hearty, that in our own troop there was not one in ten whom I could recognise. Indeed, I do not think that out of the five hundred men, from whom the fortune of war had separated me three years previously, one hundred continued to wear the uniform of the 11th Light Dragoons. Among the officers, likewise, great changes had occurred, though of them a considerable portion remained. Yet they all received me as if I had had some personal claim upon their attentions, and gave me every indulgence which I could reasonably desire. I was here equipped in new clothing, -- I got a fresh charger assigned me, -- and, in due time, found myself once more engaged in the common routine of military life.

At the period of which I now speak England was rejoicing, in all her towns and villages, over the restoration of peace. In London, the Prince Regent kept open house for the monarchs and great warriors of Europe; whilst, at Windsor, Queen Charlotte feasted the poor on the fat of the land. As I happened to be present at one of these noble festivals, -- for noble they certainly were, at least, in design, -- it may not, perhaps, prove altogether uninteresting to the reader, if I treat him to a description of what passed under my own observation.

Having spent so much time in private service, I became, as was to be expected, a sort of marked man in the corps, and soon found that among the officers there was considerable competition as to which should get me. It ended in my joining my fortunes to that of a young lieutenant, who, possessing a handsome income, and being besides a man of family, was, during this season of universal jubilee, permitted to do pretty much as he liked. Him I accompanied to Windsor; and, as he was much more in the metropolis than present with the corps, my time became to a great degree my own property. It happened, one day, that I strolled in my fustian undress, into the old guard-room of the castle, where tables were spread for two thousand persons at the least. They literally groaned under a profusion of choice morsels, such as haunches and saddles of mutton, sirloins of beef, fillets of veal, hams and tongues, rounds, barons, and I know not all what, -- with vegetables, salads, bread, and plum-pudding in proportion. I was amazingly struck, as may easily be conceived; and, having formed a strong wish to become a sharer in the festivities, I laid myself out -- as the result proved, not unsuccessfully -- to carry my point.

There were a variety of little offices or closets, adjoining the guard-room, in which women busily employed themselves in working tickets for the favoured individuals who were to be admitted to the dinner. Into one of these I wandered, just, as it happened, when the lady on duty had expended her entire stock save one, and of that one I was immediately rendered the possessor. I stuck it in my hat forthwith, -- the men carried the badges there, the women and children on the breasts of their robes, -- and soon found myself seated at a table, which accommodated, besides myself, fifty-nine diners. I came, however, under circumstances far more unfavourable than those around me; for they, one and all, brought with them their knives, forks, and drinking-cups, -- whereas, I not having so much as read any of the handbills which set forth the programme of the day's entertainment, sat down profoundly ignorant that any such precautionary measures had been requisite. This was a source to me partly of vexation, partly of extreme amusement. The vexation arose from the natural pressure of appetite, which I was not without apprehension I might find myself unable to appease; the amusement was furnished by the behaviour of my next neighbour, who seemed determined to make the most of the opportunity that was presented to him. The individual in question followed the respectable calling of an itinerant fiddler. Many a penny I had given the rogue; yet he was dressed on this occasion so smartly, that I knew him not, at least till after his excessive predilection for number one induced me to scan him closely. But that was the least of it.

We had all been seated perhaps a couple of minutes -- every eye being turned keenly towards the viands, that spoke to more senses than one; and my musical neighbour had sneered at my lack of preparation, and more than insinuated that I had no business where I was, when a flourish of trumpets announced the approach of royalty, and we all stood up to welcome the queen and the courtly cortège that attended her. She walked, followed by her train, along the several tables, the company greeting her with repeated cheers, and then, after expressing at each a hope that we would do justice to the cheer provided, she withdrew. Then followed the "Roast Beef of Old England," from a band that was appointed to attend; and then such an onslaught as in modern times has rarely, on any one given spot of earth, been witnessed. For my own part, having neither knife, nor fork, nor cup, I felt for a brief space as if I were destined to be a mere spectator. But my cross-grained fiddler supplied me with an opportunity of playing my own part in the game, and I did not fail to take advantage of it.

"I wish you would cut me a good slice of that fillet of veal," said he. "It is too far for me to reach, and lies handy to you."

"By all means," was my reply, "but you must lend me your knife and fork."

He did so; and I very coolly helped myself, taking care to cut up the morsel into pieces, and keep them ready for consumption by the hand. I shall never forget the rage of my right hand neighbour while this process was going on; neither did the enormous extent to which I proceeded to help him quite allay it. And by-and-by, when he gave me his jug, that I might fill it with beer for his use, and I, instead of handing it back, drank out of it, and drank to his health, I really thought the minstrel would have gone mad. Nevertheless, in the end, he and I became excellent friends. I plied him, especially with strong beer, to such a degree that he did not know whether his head or his heels were uppermost; and if he did not die of absolute repletion, the fault was neither mine who loaded his trencher, nor his, who most voraciously cleared it.

If the progress of the dinner astonished as well as amused me, much more amusing, as well as astonishing, was the scene with which it terminated. The queen, it appeared, had given orders that not a fragment of that enormous feast should fall to the share of any others than those who partook in it; and the consequence was that, on a second roll of the drums, such a scramble began as I have never witnessed either before or since. The women, having provided themselves with capacious aprons, came for the most part best off in that mêlée. They swept whole joints -- with puddings, potatoes, and Lord knows all what besides -- into their laps, while the men hastened to stuff their pouches to an extent which was truly marvellous. Among others, my musical neighbour used his best exertions to possess himself of a plentiful share; but the strong beer had so effectually filled his stomach, and clouded his brain, that in attempting to stretch across the table for something which excited his cupidity, the equilibrium failed, and he rolled on the floor, smashing into a confused mass all that he had previously gathered, and mixing the whole with fragments of his quart jug, which, somehow or another, had found its way into a wallet that hung by his side. I plead guilty to the charge of having tossed him with my foot twice or thrice through the mess, and then, amid shouts of laughter, I escaped, not knowing which to admire the most, the hospitality of my royal mistress, or the strange uses to which by her uncouth guests it had been turned. Before I conclude this story I may as well state that I met my fiddler a day or two afterwards, plying his trade in his every-day attire, and at his usual corners. We had a little bandying of half angry, half jocular words, which I cut short by tossing him a penny; and I do not know that we ever met afterwards.

Our next move was to Hampton Court and Twickenham, where similar scenes were repeated -- oxen being roasted whole, and all who chose partaking in them; but I need not pause to relate the effect which they produced upon myself. It will be more to the purpose if I state, that being so near London, I found frequent opportunities both of entertaining my relatives at the quarters of the regiment, and of visiting them in their own homes; during the latter of which occurrences an adventure once befel me, which, as it was rather a curious one, may be deserving of a brief notice. I had supped at the house of one of my aunts, and having rather overstaid my time, (for I was for duty at Whitehall on the following morning,) I was hurrying through Piccadilly, in order to reach my quarters, when at the corner of a street I was startled by the sound of fire-arms, accompanied by a noise as of the smashing of glass. A man passed me at the same moment, running, and holding up the skirts of a long surtout, and almost

134

immediately afterwards a second appeared, with a stream of blood flowing from his mouth. He made towards me, put a hand on each of my shoulders, and endeavouring vainly to articulate, deluged me in a moment with gore. There was a lamp close to us, by the light of which I could distinguish that he was a mere youth; but I had no time to do more, for instantly a voice shouted "Watch," and the wounded man, as if alarmed, hurried away, and endeavoured to mount the box of a hackney-coach which drove furiously past. The coachman, however, repulsed him, and he staggered across the street, marking his progress by the sanguine tide which flowed from him. And now the watch began to assemble, who, seeing me covered with blood, demanded whether I were not wounded, while the same voice which had summoned them desired to be informed whether any one were shot. I answered in the affirmative, and, pointing to the track, desired the guardians of the night to follow it up; for I was not the wounded man, as they would find if they made good use of their senses. Away they ran in pursuit, whereupon I, not caring to get further involved in the business, took to my heels, and reached my quarters without molestation. But the issue of the adventure was the most extraordinary of all. Being on guard next day, at Whitehall, a young man happened to pass the Horse Guards, whom I instantly recognised as the individual whom I had seen the night before fleeing with his hands upon his pockets. I stopped him, charged him with the fact, and was answered by a frank confession, accompanied, however, with an earnest entreaty that I would not betray him. It appeared that he was the son of a respectable innkeeper -- that he had fallen into bad company, and been persuaded to assist that night in a burglary at the shop of a linen-draper. But the linendraper, either because it was his wont, or having got some intimation of the design, was on the look-out to defeat it, and fired a pistol just as the leading burglar was removing the shutter, and about to cut a pane in the window. I did not disclose what I knew to any one; for the father of the young delinquent was an acquaintance of my own, and I am happy to say that the promises of amendment which he gave were never broken. But his companion, I afterwards discovered, did not live to have his moral principle put to the test. He died of the wound which the linen-draper inflicted, and was buried, I cannot tell where, but very quietly, by his associates.

We remained in the neighbourhood of London about six months, at the termination of which period we marched to Canterbury, where, and at Deal, the back pay was given to such of our men as had been like myself, prisoners of war. Of this the Jews first, and ultimately the publicans, reaped the principal benefit -- for, next to a sailor, a soldier is, of all living men, the least regardful of his money. But other work than this was already cut out for us, and Buonaparte's unexpected return from Elba sent us to the place where we were destined to perform it. I never shall forget the effect which the intelligence had upon us. It reached us one morning, and in two hours after came the rout to march for Dover, where transports lay to receive us; and by four o'clock on the following afternoon we were busily engaged swimming our horses ashore, towards the beach at Ostend.

It was about eight o'clock on a summer's evening when our disembarkation was effected. The process had been tedious, inasmuch as the transports were too heavily laden to approach within half-a-mile of the beach; and to swim horses through so wide a waste of waters is an operation that occupies a good deal of time. Nevertheless the regiment formed up as soon as circumstances would allow, and began its march the same evening to Nieuport. It was now that I found my knowledge of the German language greatly avail me. Being sent, with a comrade, to quarter in a farm-house about a mile beyond the town, I so entirely won the hearts of the family, by speaking so as to be understood, that they vied with one another in their eagerness to make us comfortable; and themselves undertaking to clean and fodder the horses, they kept us -- no reluctant guests -- all night at the supper-table. But this was not the only piece of good fortune that befel me, which I was justified in attributing to my long residence in the Count's family. I was instantly promoted to the office of billet-master for the corps; and, besides obtaining temporary rank as a serjeant, I came in for sundry perquisites, such as the French had taught the Belgians to pay as often as orders were issued for the supply of bread, or meat, or wine, to bodies of troops upon the march.

From Nieuport we proceeded to Bruges, where we halted an entire day, of which I made the best use, by visiting as many of the sights of the place as the opportunities at my command would allow. Our next point was Ghent, a noble city, where we witnessed the entrance of Louis XVIII., for the second time a fugitive from Paris. But as he came without parade, so during the whole of his sojourn there we heard little of him, except that he was a regular attendant at mass. Meanwhile fresh regiments were continually arriving, and we were in consequence carried, on the breast of the living tide, first to Merbeck, and ultimately to Goyek. We were at this latter place on the 29th of

May, when the Duke of Wellington reviewed the whole of his cavalry, and a finer military spectacle was never, I venture to assert, submitted to the admiring gaze of the Netherlanders. Unless my memory deceive me, twenty regiments formed in two lines that day, flanked and supported by a force of horse-artillery, such as all Europe besides could not match; and as the horses were in admirable condition, and the men young, healthy, and well-appointed, it is very little to be wondered at if both men and officers experienced but one feeling -- an earnest desire to be led against the enemy, and a perfect assurance of success.

We were well supplied both with forage and provisions; yet, somehow or another, money was scarce -- for no pay had been issued since we quitted England, and some corps were full three months in arrear. Now a soldier cannot get on -- at least in a civilized country, without a little silver in his purse. His allowance of grog or wine by no means contents him; and he cannot hear the sound of the pipe and tabor without desiring to dance. As usually happens in like cases, we were immediately put to our shifts; and the following was the expedient on which we lighted -- for a season with marvellous success. There are two coins used in this city, of which the dies are precisely alike; though the one, having a slight intermixture of silver with the copper, passes current for about threepence half-penny -- whereas the other is valued at half a farthing. Some ingenious fellow among us discovered, that by rubbing the latter with mercurial ointment it assumed at once the appearance of the former; and many a pint of gin, I grieve to say, was paid for with the half farthing. I can offer no justification of a procedure which was certainly dishonest -- unless, indeed, the exorbitancy of the prices demanded from us can be received as such. But I know that we laughed very heartily when the trick began to be discovered; and were the more free of our mirth that the very same day we quitted Merberk, never to return to it again.

Chapter 16

All this while we were in profound ignorance as to the state of things, both in France or elsewhere. We knew, indeed, that Buonaparte had made a triumphant entrance into Paris; and we heard from various quarters that the armies of the northern powers were moving. But how soon a struggle might be expected, or whether it would first occur with ourselves, was a point which we had no means to determine. We were thus circumstanced, my troop occupying quarters in a village palled Vione, when, on the morning of the 16th of June, the alarm was suddenly given. We had mustered for field exercise, ourselves in undress, and the saddles strapped -- as the expression is when we ride them without cloaks or valises -- when an orderly dragoon was observed approaching at speed, and making straight for the officer in command. He was the bearer of intelligence that the French, on the previous day, had attacked and defeated the Prussians at Ligne; and that Napoleon, with the bulk of his army, was in full march to attack the positions of the English. In an instant we received the word to gallop horses, pack up, and accoutre; and in an incredibly short space of time the whole regiment mustered beside its alarm-post, in every respect prepared for action. Let me not forget to mention that, like an old soldier as I was, I took care not to move without a stock of provisions for myself as well as for my charger. All the men carried their nose-bags filled with corn, and a supply of hay behind them, sufficient for four-and-twenty hours; but the young hands forgot that men, as well as horses, are little fit for work when they are starving. I had a lump of bacon and a loaf of bread in my haversack, of which not many hours elapsed ere I experienced the great benefit.

The line being formed, and wheeled into column by threes, we set forward at a good round trot; and, after compassing about fourteen miles, heard what the excessive heat of the weather induced us to believe was the rolling of thunder at a distance. Another half-hour's progress, however, set that notion aside; for then we could distinguish the smoke as it curled over the woods of Quatre Bras, and were no longer at a loss to tell that artillery was firing sharply. These sights and sounds had no tendency to repress our ardour; we gave the jaded horses the spur, and kept them on the trot till full five-and-twenty miles were compassed. It would have been both cruel and useless to urge them further without a rest, so we dismounted and loosened girths without feeding. But the halt was not prolonged beyond the interval which was absolutely necessary, and in a quarter of an hour we were once more in the saddle. And now, as we drew nearer to the scene of action, the evidences of deadly strife multiplied upon us. The cannonade became louder, and mixed with it was the short sharp rattle of musketry; while, by-and-by, a quantity of waggons, laden with ammunition and stores of every sort, were passed in one of the small towns. Finally, groups of persons were seen approaching, whom, on our nearing one another, we recognised to be the wounded, some of whom appeared to be suffering much, though all bore themselves nobly under their pain. Poor fellows, they drew to one side that we might pass, and cheered lustily. "Push on, push on," was their cry, "you are very much wanted; for there is no cavalry up." And we did push on as fast as our now jaded animals would go; but all our efforts failed to bring us to the field in time to take part in the action.

We had ridden, I conceive, about forty miles, and the sun was long set, when the red flashes of musketry and cannon greeted us. "Halt!" was the word given; "cut away forage, and draw swords." The hay was cut loose, our swords flashed in the air, and at the signal, "Quick trot," away we went again. But, as I have already said, we did not reach the field till the firing had ceased. We formed line, however, and riding over numbers of the dead, if not of the dying, approached our own troops, which lay upon their arms; whence in a few minutes we received orders to fall back, and to picket our horses for the night in a place that was convenient for them.

Throughout the whole of that night there was a dropping fire of musketry kept up in the woods to the right and left of our bivouac. The outposts of infantry chose to skirmish instead of sleep, and we were in consequence kept constantly on the alert. But this was not the only, nor, perhaps, the greatest grievance to which our position subjected us. The horses had not tasted water since the march began, and the darkness was such as, combined with their extreme weariness, hindered our men in general from going in search of it. Again the habits of the old soldier prevailed with me; and knowing that on the efficiency of my horse my own depended, I resolved, at all hazards, to fetch him some water. Accordingly I proposed to my comrade that we should steal away together; and he consented the more readily on my putting him in mind that the very same process which won refreshment for our chargers might insure a good supper for ourselves; and that the most zealous martinet would never blame us, if in seeking for the one we should chance to stumble on the other.

Armed each with a pistol, and carrying a sack and leathern bucket in our hands, my comrade and I stole from the bivouac; and having previously noticed a village about a mile distant, we made directly for it. We entered, and found the stillness of the grave; but, by-and-by, observing a light in the window of one of the houses, I knocked at the door, and we were admitted. My astonishment may be conceived, when the first object that met my gaze was a French grenadier, fully accoutred, and seated in the chimney corner. It was no time for hesitation, so I cocked my pistol; when up he rose, welcomed us with perfect self-possession; and pointing to his knee, informed us that he was wounded. Perceiving that he spoke the truth, I desired him to sit down again, adding an assurance that he had nothing to fear; and he, coolly taking me at my word, and smoking his pipe, I next addressed myself to the master of the house. It was to no purpose, however, that I demanded food and drink. The French, he replied, had taken every thing from him; which was not exactly the case; for my companion, having instituted a search in the cellar, soon returned, bringing with him part of a ham, a loaf of bread, and some butter. With these we judged it expedient to be content; so, wishing both our host and the wounded man a good night, we passed the threshold, and hurried back to the camp.

Before reaching the lines, we fortunately came upon a ditch full of water, in which we filled our buckets, greatly to the satisfaction of our weary chargers. Our horses were not, however, the only animals who benefited by this discovery. Having informed the rest where the water lay, they also provided enough for the wants of themselves and their cattle: and the night in consequence passed more agreeably than either by man or beast bad been anticipated. But as far as the means of satisfying other wants of nature were affected, I and my comrade stood, I believe, alone. We made a hearty supper of our ham and bread, and regretted only that it was impossible to share the morsel with others.

Day dawned at length, and exhibited to us some strange spectacles calculated as well to raise the spirits as to depress them. We could now observe that the whole surface of the country over which yesterday's fighting had occurred, was covered with the slain; while in our rear and on either flank, a prodigious force of cavalry and light artillery which had arrived during the night, was in position. The latter made a brave show, especially in the eyes of our gallant infantry, who, few in number, had sustained repeated shocks from the enemy's horse, and uniformly repulsed them. But it soon appeared, that let the decisive battle occur when it might, we were not on this ground to measure ourselves again with the enemy. By degrees the infantry began to march to the rear. The cavalry and artillery stood fast to cover them, when they, in their turn slowly withdrew, as if reluctant to yield a foot of ground without fighting for it. Strange to say, the enemy did not appear for some time to be aware of what was going on in our ranks. The infantry was well to the rear, so were the heavy cavalry, ere they made a movement in pursuit; indeed, it must have been full three o'clock in the afternoon ere we found ourselves under the necessity of throwing out skirmishers, so as to check the advance, which was then pushed with considerable ardour.

There was a good deal of carbine practice, and prancing here and there, for about half an hour, at the close of which, the artillery began on both sides to open; while a mass of black clouds, which had been gathering all the day, broke at the concussion, and the rain descended in torrents. It is curious to observe how, even in such warfare as this, a heavy fall of rain operates as a sedative on animal courage. The skirmishing ceased as if by common consent; and the fighting was confined to an occasional dash of one of the enemy's leading squadrons against ours, which covered the rear; when sword-cuts were exchanged, and men and horses went down, as well from among us, as from among the assailants. Once in particular we had rather a sharp bout of it, for the enemy contrived, I know not how, to interpose between the plain on which we were moving, and a narrow road that led out of it, and no alternative remained except to cut our way through them. We rode at them with loosened reins, and soon opened a way for ourselves, cutting to pieces, among others, a French General, and leaving not above half-a-dozen of our own men behind.

We halted that night behind the crest of the rising ground which is still pointed out to the curious traveller as the Duke of Wellington's position on the great day of Waterloo. The rain, which fell in torrents, and had done so for hours ere our arrival, soon reduced the face of the country to a state of swamp; and as our bivouac was formed in a ploughed field, the comparative comforts of our situation require no poet's art to describe them. At every step which you took, you sank to the knees, and your foot, when you dragged it to the surface again, came loaded with some twenty pounds of clay. Moreover, fuel, with which to make fires, was wanting; till in despair some of us ran to a village about a mile in the rear, and came back laden with various articles of furniture, the whole of which were committed to the flames. Then again as to food -- if I except a single biscuit and a glass of spirits -- none had been served out since daybreak, and none came throughout the whole of that dreary night, either to officers or to men. I cannot say that our martial ardour was such as to render us either insensible of, or indifferent to, the desagrémens of our situation; yet I am bound to record, that we sustained them with wonderful equanimity, comforted by the knowledge that the night, which was short, would soon pass away, and that the morrow would in some shape or another obviate the necessity of passing many more in a similar manner.

Before the morning broke, we were in our saddles: -- and immediately the horizon put on the hue of coming day, we shifted our ground to the brow of the hill, and there watered our horses. That done we dismounted; and removing the remnant of our fuel to the new parade ground we again lighted fires, and dried as well as we could, both our clothes and accoutrements. The Commissary, however, was slow in making his appearance; so, entertaining serious misgivings both as to my own powers of endurance, and those of my steed, which had been tried well nigh to the uttermost, I determined, let come what might, to find a breakfast for both. I looked round, and saw in the rear a village, to which straggling parties of the Foot Guards were continually passing. I ran thither, but looked about vainly, in every house, for those things of which I was in want. At last, just as I had come to the conclusion that further search would be useless, and that I had best return, I entered an apartment, where, in the middle of the floor, sat a solitary Yorkshireman, with a brown jar between his legs. He laughed, begged me to come in, and offered to share with me what he had: it was bread and sour cream, out of which both he and I contrived to make a capital breakfast. After which, I mounted by a trap-ladder to a loft, where, to my great delight, stores both of oats and peas were deposited. I filled my handkerchief, which was a large one; and having contrived, over and above, to get possession of half-a-dozen canteens of beer, I ran back, well pleased with the results of my adventure, to the front. My gallant steed fared well; and he repaid me for the care I took of him by the pliability and vigour of his movements throughout the day.

When I reached the ground, my companions were all busily engaged rubbing down their horses and cleaning their accoutrements. I took care to feed my charger first, and then groomed him; nor had I finished buckling up the neatly rolled cloak, when a gun was discharged from some point near us, and, in an instant, the whole face of affairs underwent a change. Drums beat, trumpets brayed, while salvoes of artillery from either side told of a battle begun; and, while we mounted and closed our ranks, peal after peal of musketry warned us that ere long their consistency would be tried. By-and-by an order arrived to take ground to the right, where we enrolled ourselves in brigade with the 12th and 16th; and, forming close columns of regiments, waited till the moment should arrive when to us, also, the honour should be awarded of striking a few blows for Old England and victory.

The place where we were directed to execute this formation chanced to be particularly favourable for obtaining a view over the whole field of battle, as well as the overnight positions of the two armies. And never have these eyes of mine rested on a more imposing scene than, for a brief space, was spread out before them. As far as the eye could reach I beheld endless columns of the French -- the infantry in front interlaced, as it were, with artillery; while in the rear were masses of cavalry, in comparison with which, as far as numbers go, we appeared as nothing. Then, again, on our side, I beheld horse, foot, and guns, all in admirable order, hidden in some degree from the enemy by the swell of the ground, yet all, as their attitudes denoted, thoroughly on the alert: while, both on our side and that of the French, staff officers in groups, and orderlies one by one, were galloping hither and thither, as if they had been the veritable messengers of fate. But the vision was like that which the sleeper obtains when, for a moment, the gates of Fairy-land are opened before him. From the hundreds of cannon, which sent forth death on each side, such a cloud of smoke arose as soon tendered objects indistinct; and when the musketry began to play, every living and dead thing on the earth's surface was shrouded under a canopy of gray mist.

It were idle in one filling the humble situation which I did to attempt any thing like the description of a great battle, especially such a battle as that of Waterloo. From the instant that the firing became general, all was to me dark and obscure beyond the distance of a few hundred yards from the spot on which I stood; indeed, it was only by the ceaseless roar, or the whistling of shot and shell around me, that

I knew at times that I and those near me were playing a part in the grave game of life and death. For the cavalry, unlike the infantry, come into play only by fits and starts, and they have patiently to sustain the fury of a cannonade, to which they can offer no resistance, and out of the range of which they are not permitted to move. Neither was the brigade to which I belonged left long in ignorance touching both the peril and extreme discomfort of this species of inaction. For the French, perceiving us, opened upon our columns a battery of howitzers and light mortars, one shell from which falling into the very centre of the 16th, created terrible havock. But as if to hinder us from getting unsteady, an aide-de-camp rode up at this moment, and two squadrons, one from the 12th, another from our regiment, were ordered to drive back some lancers which had threatened certain of our guns. We went at them with good will, but not, perhaps, with perfect judgment. We did not consider that, when the ground is soft and heavy, a charge down hill is, of all operations to which cavalry can be put, the most unsafe; and the consequence was, that rushing over the ridge at speed, very many of our horses came down, and we lost all order. The result need hardly be stated. The squadron of the 12th, which led, was almost cut to pieces, and we, with difficulty and in great disorder, recovered the brigade.

This was not satisfactory, yet we believed that we could account for it, and finding ourselves again in our proper places, we desired nothing more than a repetition of the experiment. But, during the remainder of the day, little else fell to our share than to sustain, as we best might, the heavy fire of cannon which the enemy continued to direct against us. At each discharge, men and horses went down: yet we suffered less than a regiment of Nassau Hussars, which, keeping ground in our rear, served to catch every ball that passed over us. Nor was it the least disagreeable attendant on our position, that we stood exactly on such a spot as enabled us to behold the last struggles of the wounded, whose strength sufficed only to carry them a few yards to the rear. There was a long sort of ditch, or drain, some way behind us, towards which these poor fellows betook themselves by scores; and ere three hours had passed, it was absolutely choked up with the bodies of those who lay down there only that they might die. Then, again the wounded horses, of which multitudes wandered all over the field, troubled us. They would come back, some with broken legs, others trailing after them their entrails, which the round-shot had knocked out, and forcing themselves between our files, seemed to solicit the aid which no one had time to afford, and which, if afforded, would have been useless.

We were beginning to get tired of this state of things, when an order reached us to form line and move off to the left. "Now then," thought we, "a charge is before us;" but it was not so. A square of Brunswick Infantry had, it appeared, begun to waver, and, as a failure on that point might have proved fatal, we were brought up to stop it if we could. We drew our swords, cheered, made our horses prance, and the desired end was gained. The Brunswickers perceiving that there was support at hand, took up their arms, which some of them had thrown away, and they throughout the remainder of the action behaved with all the gallantry for which their countrymen have in every age and country been remarkable.

Having effected this object, we were directed to fall back, and to dismount, that our horses might in some measure recruit their strength. Many wounded men passed us while thus resting; but of the case of only one I shall make mention, because it struck me at the moment as being a remarkable one. An infantry soldier approached, and asked me for a cup of water. I saw that he was wounded; and, recollecting that a canteen of beer was at my back, out of which I had been too much engaged to drink myself, I handed it to him and desired him to quench his thirst without scruple. The poor fellow drank, thanked me heartily, told me that almost all his regiment -- the 28th -- was destroyed; and then, lifting himself from my horse, on which he had been leaning, tottered towards the rear. I watched him, and saw that he had not gone twelve yards when he fell. Almost immediately afterwards his limbs gave a convulsive stretch, and he was a corpse. I went up to him, and saw where the fatal ball had taken its course, just above the hip-bone. Yet he seemed to die easily; and his voice, not three minutes ere the soul quitted the body, gave scarcely the smallest sign of weakness.

By this time the dusk was closing fast; and, as the battle continued to rage with unabated fury, the magnificence of the scene received, from minute to minute, a perpetual increase to its intensity. Over the surface of the ground, shells, with their burning fuses, rolled, bursting here and there with terrible effect. From the mouths of the cannon fire seemed to be poured, while the ceaseless glare of the musketry, as the opposing lines fought muzzle to muzzle, was terrific. By degrees, however, the sounds and sight of fire-arms began to be distinguishable where neither had before been observed; and the rumour ran from rank to rank among us, that the Prussians were come, and had fallen upon the right and rear of the enemy. Moreover, that the news was not without foundation, was soon apparent, from the altered state of things both near us and far away. Our infantry, which up to this moment had fought in squares, formed all at once into line. There was a heart-stirring cheer begun, I know not where, but very soon audible over the whole of our front; and we, too, were ordered to leap into the saddle and move forward. How can I pretend to describe what followed! On we went at a gallop, dashing past the weary yet gallant footmen, and, shouting as we went, drove fiercely and without check up to the very muzzles of a hostile battery. A furious discharge of grape met us, and thinned our ranks. Before it man and horse went down; but the survivors, never pulling bridle or pausing to look back, scattered the gunners to the winds, and the cannon were our own. Just at this moment, Serjeant Emmet of the 11th, whom I covered, received a shot in the groin, which made him reel in his saddle, from which he would have fallen, had I not caught him; while at the same time a ball struck me on the knee, the bone of which was saved by the interposition of my unrolled cloak. For in the morning I had not found time to pack it in its place; and it hung before me in loose folds, through most of which the bullet made its way, terribly bruising, yet not disabling, the limb. I was glad to save my serjeant, for he was a good and a brave man. Yet I own that I felt bitter mortification when the tide of war swept past us, and I felt myself cut off from sharing in the general triumph. Accordingly, perceiving a corporal near, I called him to lend his assistance, and no sooner saw him seize the serjeant by the other arm, than I loosed my hold. "One whole man," thought I, "is enough to take care of a wounded one;" and then I plyed my spurs into my horse's sides, and flew to the front. But by this time it was too dark to distinguish one corps from another. I therefore attached myself to the first body of horse which I overtook, and in three minutes found myself in the middle of the enemy.

There was a momentary check, during which the men demanded one of another, what regiment this was. I do not know how the discovery of their own absolute intermingling might have operated, had not an officer called aloud, "Never mind your regiments, men, but follow me." In an instant I sprang to his side, and, seeing a mass of infantry close upon us, who, by the blaze of the musketry, we at once recognised to be French, he shouted out "Charge!" and nobly led the way. We rushed on: the enemy fired, and eight of our number fell, among whom was our gallant leader. A musket-ball pierced his heart: he sprang out of his saddle, and fell dead to the ground.

Another check was the consequence, and almost instinctively we recoiled: neither, indeed, was the movement inopportune, for the impetuosity of a mere handful of men had carried them into the middle of a retreating column, and their destruction, had they lingered there must have been inevitable. For myself, having gazed hastily round, and noticed that the field was thickly studded with dung-heaps, I scoured off in search of my own regiment, with which, when it had halted, a good way off, I succeeded in coming up. But I was determined, as soon as a halt should occur, to return to the spot, and find the body of the slain; and, some hours afterwards, when the word was passed to dismount and rest, I carried my resolution into force.

Chapter 17

It was pitch dark when the acceptable order was issued, of which I have just spoken. It came too at a time when we found ourselves in the very heart of the camp which the French army had occupied on the morning of this eventful day, and very much struck were we by the ingenuity which these brave men had exhibited in their endeavours to render the lodging even of a single night commodious. With wonderful skill they had run up huts formed of the boughs of trees; the closely-interwoven leaves and branches of which were wellnigh weather proof; while within, raw meat of every description, -- beef, pork, and mutton, lay scattered about in absolute profusion. So beaten about was it, however, in the hurry of the strife, and in many instances so vilely dressed, -- the very hair being left on the morsels of the carcasses, and these but indifferently bled, -- that faint as we were for lack of food, we could not bring ourselves to touch it. We flung it from us in disgust, and refused to dress it. But the cravings of hunger are not to be stifled; and not a few wandered away from the ranks which they had been ordered to preserve, in the search after food both for themselves and their horses. Among others, I and my comrade went forth upon a cruise; and judging that the means of conveyance might be unattainable if we went on foot, we quietly drew the girths so soon as a convenient opportunity offered, and rode away. I never shall forget, so long as memory remains by me, the adventures of that extraordinary night. In the first place, the ground withersoever we went, was literally strewed with the wreck of the mighty battle. Arms of every kind, -- cuirasses, muskets, cannon, tumbrils, and drums, which seemed innumerable, cumbered the very face of the earth. Intermingled with these were the carcases of the slain, not lying about in groups of four or six, but so wedged together, that we found it, in many instances, impossible to avoid trampling them where they lay under our horses' hoofs. Then, again, the knapsacks, either cast loose or still adhering to their owners, were countless. I confess that we opened many of these latter, hoping to find in them money, or articles of value, but not one -- which I at least examined -- contained more than the coarse shirts and shoes that had belonged to the dead owners, with here and there a little package of tobacco, and a bag of salt. And what was worst of all, when we dismounted to institute this search, our spurs for ever caught in the garments of the slain, and more than once we tripped up, and fell over them.

It was indeed a ghastly spectacle, which the feeble light of a young moon rendered, if possible, more hideous than it would have been, if looked upon under the full glory of a meridian sun. For there is something frightful in the association of darkness with the dwelling of the dead; and here the dead lay so thick and so crowded together, that by-and-by it seemed to us as if we alone had survived to make mention of their destiny.

There are those, I doubt not, who will shudder when I acknowledge, that men circumstanced as we were at that moment, know little or nothing of the magnanimous feelings which in more peaceful hours take up their dwelling in the human heart. It is one of the worst results of a life of violence, that it renders such as follow it selfish and mercenary: at least, it would be ridiculous to conceal that when the bloody work of the day is over, the survivor's first wish is to secure, in the shape of plunder, some recompence for the risks which he has run and the exertions which he has made. Neither does it enter into the mind of the plunderer to consider whether it is the dead body of a friend or of a foe from which he is seeking his booty. I may be blamed, but I should deserve a double portion of censure were I to deny that my thoughts were fixed mainly on the brave man whom I saw fall, as has been described in the previous chapter; and that my object in seeking him out was to possess myself of his watch and gold seals -- the latter of which I had seen glance in the twilight when he dropped. I had made what I conceived an accurate memorandum of the field in which he struck his last blow, and raised his last war-cry, and finding that the crowds near at hand offered nothing worth our acceptance, I suggested to my companion that we should seek him out. Accordingly, we mounted and rode off, and in due time arrived where heaps of manure were piled up, beside one of which I knew that he was lying. I had not deceived myself: close beside the bodies of eight common troopers we found him. But other marauders had been on the prowl before us, for he was stripped to the very skin. Poor fellow! I saw where the ball had entered -- exactly in the middle of the chest; and I own that I then experienced something like relief from the thought that I had been saved the sin -- for such I now conceive that it would have been -- of robbing him.

Sobered, if not disheartened, by this disappointment, we at once turned our faces homewards. But though it had been easy to quit the camp, we now found that it would be a more difficult operation to regain it; for we lost our way, and were soon wandering we knew not whither, though still through a very crowd of slaughtered men. At last we halted in despair, and, picketing our horses, lay down upon the earth and fell asleep. But the instinct of soldiers is remarkable: at early dawn we woke again; and then, being really anxious that our jaded animals might obtain some refreshment, we looked eagerly round, in the hope that we might be able to discover some traces of a peaceful dwelling. We were not disappointed in this: at a considerable distance to the left, we discovered a house, which, having been set on fire the day previous, was still burning, and towards it, as fast as the nature of the ground would allow, we directed our steps. How frightful the whole scene! It was, indeed, a field of carnage over which we passed; and the smell of blood, as it rose upon the morning air, well nigh sickened us.

The house of which I am speaking, stood upon what had been the right of the position of the French army, and marked the point where the Prussians first fell in, when late in the evening they arrived to support us. The road which ran near it was blocked up with the cannon which, in the hurry of the flight, the enemy had abandoned; and round them, and before and behind, were heaps of slain -- some of which had fallen under the fire of the Prussians, others by the hands of our own men, who met them in their retreat and cut them down. With some difficulty we passed these wrecks of the battle, and entering the farmyard, found it crowded with wounded wretches -- some of whom had evidently received their hurts where they now lay, while others seemed to have dragged themselves thither in the hope of shelter. We could not shut our ears to their frightful cries, yet we were powerless to aid them; and what was to the full as mortifying, nothing of which we were in search lay here. We could not find so much as a drop of water wherewith to moisten our own lips or those of our horses, so we soon abandoned it, and made for another habitation, which stood at no great distance off. Here we trusted that we should be more fortunate, for the tide of war seemed to have spared this dwelling, and though multitudes of persons went and came from about its doors, we still hoped that we might be in time to secure something. Accordingly, we pushed on, passing under the Observatory, as it has since been called, whence Napoleon is said to have viewed the battle and directed the movements of his columns;

and great was our delight to find that not yet had the house or the premises round been thoroughly gutted. To be sure plenty of people were there -- some of them, too, peasants of the country, who were helping themselves to sheep, pigs, and bullocks -- a whole drove of which we found, to our extreme surprise, penned up in a sort of yard, adjoining to the farmstead. These live animals did not constitute the booty of which we were in search: we wanted corn and water, and food fit for immediate use; and corn and water, to our extreme satisfaction, we found, with both of which we plentifully regaled our now famishing chargers.

Leaving the horses to take full advantage of the piece of good fortune which had thus fallen to their share, we entered the house -- but neither bread nor any other necessary of life was there. Busy hands had been before ours, for over the floors of the different rooms all manner of wearing apparel was scattered, and drawers broken and ransacked, gave token of the manner in which they had employed themselves. At last I came by chance upon a cupboard which gave no signs of having been rifled, and forcing it open, I saw that it contained some valuable china and cut glass. The sight of these articles recalled to my remembrance that, on the evening previous to the battle, an officer of my troop had been so lucky as to stumble somewhere upon a bottle of wine, and that in proceeding to drink, when no cup was at hand, he had been obliged to break off the neck, and in so doing lost half of his treasure. I determined to convey to him both a glass and a service of china, and, with this view, made a small selection, which I packed up in a basket. But I was not permitted to carry my good intentions into effect, for, on returning to the stable, we found two Belgian dragoons there, who invited us to partake of a ham which they had discovered; and my appetite being exceedingly sharp, I laid down the basket in order to appease it. Some marauder observed this, and instantly snatched it up; nor had I time to pursue him, for just as I had risen to do so, a general officer galloped into the farm-yard, and instantly there was a cry from all quarters, "Escape as you best can." The general was loud in his denunciation of the plunderers he told us that the provost was at hand, and we leaped into the saddle, resolved, if possible, to escape him. And well was it that we did so; for we had not passed from the gateway many roods, ere he and his guard made their appearance, after which nothing remained for us but to make the best of our way at our briskest speed to the camp.

The intelligence which we brought as to the cattle and sheep which we had seen at the farm-house was not thrown away. Party after party sallied out, and in half an hour there was mutton enough in our lines to furnish all with a substantial meal. In a trice the cooks went to work, and by-and-by might be seen officers and men devouring the half-dressed food like cannibals. Neither were any questions asked concerning the sources from which a supply so acceptable came: all were anxious to partake of it, and all, when the repast was ended, looked and felt as if each were worth at least half a dozen of what he had been two hours previously.

The first wants of nature being thus satisfied, parties were sent out, under non-commissioned officers, to search for and bring in such wounded men as might have fallen in the woods, or on broken ground, where they could not easily be discovered. Scores of human beings, who but for this humane proceeding must have perished, were thus snatched from the jaws of death -- among whom were not a few mere boys, the whole of whom appeared to entertain of us, and especially of the surgeons, the most pitiable dread. It required, indeed, in several instances, two or three of us to hold the patient while the balls were extracted from his wounds and his hurts dressed; and then the gratitude of the unfortunate beings became as vehement as previously to the completion of the operation their fears had been ludicrous. Neither did we find it easy for some time afterwards to shake ourselves free from these convalescents. Though told they were at liberty to return to their homes, they would not leave us, and even contrived to crawl after us for a march or two, in order, as they said, to avoid the danger of falling into the hands of the Prussians.

It was noon ere the commissary arrived, bringing with him corn, biscuits, salt meat, and an allowance of spirits, the receipt of which proved eminently acceptable both to man and beast; after discussing which we received orders to fall in and march to the front. As we rose the hill an excellent opportunity was afforded of viewing, at a single glance, the whole theatre of these desperate operations. I have already spoken of the particular sights which, in the course of my wanderings over the field, met me; and I have now only to record that the effect of a grand coup d'œil was neither less astounding nor less awful than any which had been produced by the examination of individual objects near at hand. We saw, too, that if the slaughter among the French had been terrible, our gallant army had not come off unscathed. There, on the ground where they had fought, large heaps of English soldiers were scattered, covering, for the most part, the face of their own posi-

tion, and retaining to a certain extent the very order of their forma-
tions; and here, on either side of the road which we were traversing,
the pride of the gallant heavy brigade lay low: for the Life Guards, the
Royals, and the Greys had been carried by their impetuosity far into
the heart of the French lines, and though more than victorious in the
charge, were wellnigh cut to pieces. But why continue these details a
hundred abler pens than mine have told the story of their prowess and
their suffering. I cannot add to the amount of information already
possessed by the public -- so let me change my subject.

Chapter 18

We marched that day some distance on the road to Nivelle, and arriving towards dark at a very pretty village, we halted for the night in an orchard. There we remained the whole of the next day, cleaning our swords and accoutrements, which were covered with rust, and giving to our horses the rest and refreshment of which they stood sorely in need. As to our clothing, that was completely spoiled, and our boots we were obliged to cut from our legs, ere we could get them off. But four-and-twenty hours of repose and good feeding did wonders for us, and on the 20th we resumed our progress, in high spirits and very tolerable order. A succession of easy stages carried us to Catieaux, where we established ourselves in a pleasant grove, waiting for the arrival of the pontoons and heavy artillery, which might be required to reduce the fortresses that lay in our front; and I am forced to say that the three days which we spent there were not wasted. Not far from our encampment lay a large village, which, on reconnoitring it, we found to be abandoned; and, as the foolish people had left all their effects behind them, we saw no reason why we should not save the camp-followers some trouble, by appropriating them to our own use. The consequence was, that our meals were not only abundant but sumptuous; -- fowls, geese, turkeys, ducks, pigs, rabbits, and flour and garden-stuff in abundance, furnished forth, with wine and beer, our daily tables; and it would be injustice to all parties did I not add, that we dealt with them as those are wont to do who, having known what it is to fast by compulsion, take care, when the opportunity offers, to feast with hearty good will.

It was my especial delight to wander through the woods adjoining our encampment alone; on one of which occasions I encountered the adjutant, who, after telling me that he had looked for me for some time, asked whether I could speak French. I was not without apprehension that something might have gone wrong, so I answered in the negative. Upon which he replied, "Don't you think you could get out a few words in that language, if you were paid an extra franc a day?" "I dare say I could, sir," replied I, smiling. "Oh, I thought so," was the answer; "so come along with me." I followed the adjutant accordingly, and found that I had been selected to act as serjeant in a mounted staff corps, of which it would be the duty to protect the country people from ill usage, and to repress, along the route of the army, every thing like plundering and violence. From each regiment in the brigade three men were chosen, over whom I was set; and the orders which I received were, that I should detach six, three on each flank, during the march, and myself bring up the rear with the remaining three. We were not to act as executioners, nor yet as a provost guard, but simply as a military police; that is to say, we were to arrest all persons whom we might find marauding, and to hand them over to the provost for punishment. And in order to make us known, as well as to ensure for us the respect of our fellow-soldiers, each man was supplied with a scarlet belt, which he was desired to pass over his right shoulder, and to regard as a badge of honourable distinction.

It will readily be believed that I accepted the distinction thus proffered to me, thankfully, the more so as I found that it carried an addition of two francs daily to my pay, and one franc to each of the men who were placed under me. Neither had I any cause to repent of the arrangement. On the contrary, I more than once found myself in a position to render essential service to the helpless, at the same time that I hindered my own people from doing wrong; and of the first instance in which I came to exercise my authority, it may be as well if I give a brief account.

The day after I received my appointment we marched; and I, obeying the instructions that had been communicated to me, dispersed two of my threes on each flank, and with the remaining triad brought up the rear. It might be about noon when we approached a house by the roadside from which lamentable cries, as of people in distress, proceeded. "Serjeant!" exclaimed the colonel, who rode near me, "do you hear that? Go and see what is the matter." In an instant I called my men, and desiring them to dismount, left one in charge of the horses, while with the other two, sword in hand, I entered. The house was full of Belgian dragoons, who had been plundering and ill-treating the people at a great rate. I told them what my duty was, called upon them to surrender, compelled them to restore to the inhabitants the effects which they had taken, and made a dozen of them prisoners. The remainder fled through the back door, and we saw them no more. I cannot undertake to describe the gratitude of the poor people, whose property, and in some instances more than their property, we thus preserved. Neither have I power to tell how astonished the Belgians were, when they found themselves handed over to a sort of power which was marvellously rapid in the administration of justice. The whole of them were stripped on the instant, and received a dozen each -- a salutary example -- which taught the allies that they, not less than the English, would not by our wise and noble commander be allowed to perpetrate, with impunity, wrongs upon the innocent inhabitants of France, purely because with the French government their own happened to be at war.

We halted that day about noon, not far from a gentleman's house, which I was ordered to protect, and where, with my comrades, I spent the night. Next morning, as a matter of course, the march was resumed. But except that we were joined at a large village, or rather town, through which we passed, by Louis XVIII. and his suite, there occurred nothing of which it is worth while to take especial notice. To be sure, the manner in which the people of the town received the king, whom but a few weeks previously they had driven into banishment, was exceedingly characteristic. Triumphal arches and green boughs were erected at the head of the principal streets. Beside them stood the magistrates and leading men of the place, as well as a number of gaily-dressed maidens, who strewed flowers in the way of the royal party, and offered bouquets; while the air was rent with discordant shouts, from which no more could be gathered, than that the parties shouting were disposed to make the most of passing events as they occurred. But I must not omit to describe a scene which befel in the same town, and in which I was myself an actor. I have often thought of it since with amazement, and possibly my readers may think with me, that it was at least a strange one.

The brigade halted in this town for the night; and I received a billet on a particular house, to which, as may be supposed -- accompanied by my comrade -- I immediately repaired. We knocked at the front door, but nobody answered; whereupon we made our way round to the rear, where, trying the latch, we ascertained that it was not fastened, and immediately entered. We found ourselves in a passage, from which, on the right and left, two doorways diverged. One of these -- that on the left -- we tried, and were ushered into a small apartment, where, before a table literally covered with gold coins and bags of money, sat a man engaged, as it seemed, in reckoning up the amount of his treasure. The creaking of the door upon its hinges seemed to have disturbed him, for he instantly looked behind; and the expressions of astonishment, fear, agony, and horror which passed in rapid succession over his countenance, I shall never forget. He threw himself at once flat upon the table, stretching out his arms in the vain effort to conceal his wealth; and then, in a tone of voice, which bespoke the extent of his alarm, desired to be informed as to our wishes. I hastened to assure him that he had nothing to apprehend from us. I told him that we were English, not Prussians; and the announcement at once relieved him so far, that he was able to demand the cause of our intrusion; and on my informing him, he hastened to tell us that we were heartily welcome. He entreated us to go to the kitchen, where his housekeeper would take charge of us; and without so much as pausing to ascertain the amount of his exposed treasure, we at once obeyed. He was a monstrous lucky fellow in having fallen into our hands rather than into those of any of the gallant allies that co-operated with us. We got a good supper, and an excellent bed; but he retained his Napoleons, which, had some of Blucher's dragoons seen them, would have made their way probably to Prussia, at all events to Paris or its environs.

Up to the present point the British army seemed to have followed a route of its own. Our march of the next day brought us upon the track of the Prussians; and the contrast between our discipline and theirs was curious in the extreme. Our column passed, for example, about noon, a large château, with a village attached; and I and my men were sent, as a matter of course, to protect both. Alas! we came too late. The Prussians had been here before us, and the skill and industry with which they seemed to have carried on the work of devastation I have no language to describe. In the château there was not one article of furniture, from the costly pier-glass down to the common coffee-cup, which they had not smashed to atoms. The flour-mill, likewise, attached to the mansion, was all gutted, the sacks cut to pieces, and the flour wantonly scattered over the road. Stables, cow-sheds, poultry-houses, and gardens, seemed to have been, with infinite care, rendered useless; and as to living things there was none -- not so much as a half-starved pigeon -- to be seen about the premises. In like manner, the village was one wide scene of devastation. Its inhabitants appeared, indeed, to have escaped, for we came upon no human being, nor the corpse of any; but furniture, doors, windows, and here and there roofs, all seemed to have passed through the merciless hands of the spoilers. I never beheld such a specimen of war, conducted in a spirit of ferocious hostility. I was half ashamed of the connexion that subsisted between ourselves and the Prussians, when I looked upon the horrid work which they had perpetrated.

Having wandered over this wretched place, and ascertained that our presence was altogether useless, we mounted again, and rode on. Our route lay somewhat apart from that of the column, and carried us towards a wood, on approaching which we were challenged by a peasant, armed with a musket, and determined, as his bearing showed, to dispute our farther progress. I told him what we were; upon which he instantly recovered his arms, and entreated us to come forward. He became, indeed, our guide, and conducted us to an open space in the forest, wherein were collected the unfortunate fugitives from the very place which we had just abandoned. There they were, men, women, and children, established in a sort of bivouac, whither they had escaped with such little fragments of their property as the alarm of a moment had enabled them to carry off. Poor things! they clustered round our saddle-bows, as if we had been guardian angels sent to protect them from further violence. They offered us all that they had, which, of course, we refused to accept, and gratefully listened to our declarations that, for the present at least, danger had passed away. I have the satisfaction of remembering that, at my suggestion, they gathered up their effects on the instant, and went back to reoccupy the houses from which our somewhat ferocious friends had driven them. -- We rode on, and in due time reached an eminence, just beyond which the column had been directed to halt for the night. We pulled up on the summit to look round us, and saw, a little way removed from the line of march, another village, in which the process of marauding was going on in full vigour. Multitudes of stragglers had broken in upon the inhabitants, who were fleeing in every direction, pursued by their enemies. It was a shocking spectacle; and, as in duty bound, I resolved, as far as my means went, to give to it a different character. I accordingly commanded my party to draw swords, and down we went at full speed into the heart of the village. The effect of our charge was marvellous: the plunderers dropped their booty and fled in all directions. We rode after them, belabouring them with the flats of our swords, and in five minutes had the satisfaction of knowing that order was entirely restored. It is an old aphorism, the truth of which all experience confirms, that good actions invariably bring their own reward. We were not only thanked by the authorities of the place, but feasted and fêted at the principal inn; and we spent the night among these poor people as merrily as those are wont to do whom their entertainers regard as special benefactors.

In this manner I continued my march, giving protection, wherever

I and my party arrived, to the persons and property of all orders of Frenchmen, by whom we were uniformly treated as friends and preservers. Such services were not always unattended with personal risk; and once, in particular, we owed our preservation at least as much to our ingenuity, or presence of mind, as to the badges which we carried. We had observed a large mansion, removed by a considerable space from the road, and judging that it would be regarded as a prize by the marauders, we put spurs to our horses, and happily reached it ere any stragglers from the army could come up. I knocked at the door, which we found closed, but nobody answered: I knocked again, but still the signal was disregarded; on which, having previously observed that all the stables were empty, and that not a living thing was to be seen on the premises, I came to the conclusion that the place was abandoned. Under this impression, I had already directed my men to remount for the purpose of proceeding elsewhere, when one of the upper windows opened, and a man, putting his head through, desired to be informed who we were. I replied that we were "English police:" upon which he immediately entreated me to wait, and in a few seconds opened the door for our reception. He was an old gentleman, very venerable in his appearance, and full of alarm -- as he well might be -- on account of his family and effects, and for his wife and two daughters, who were in the house with him; for he not unnaturally mistook us for Prussians, of whose mode of dealing, wherever they went, the rumour had already reached him. Finding, however, that our business was to protect, not to fleece him, his gratitude set my powers of expression at defiance; and the ladies, who soon joined us, were to the full as lavish of their thanks as he.

We had scarcely passed his threshold, when a whole swarm of Belgians made their appearance, flocking up from a village which they had just plundered, and hastening to effect the same end at the château. I determined at once to resist them; so, planting one of my men as a sentry at the door, I drew the rest under cover, and quietly waited to meet the issue, be it what it might. On came the marauders as fast as they could run; and very angry as well as greatly surprised were they to find their further progress disputed by my sentinel. They peremptorily desired to know what our business was there; and some officers -- of whom a good many bore them company -- seemed resolute, in spite of the vidette, to force an entrance. Upon this I went out, and told them that we had been sent by the commander-in-chief to take possession of the quarter, and that his arrival there, with the

Staff of the Army, was every moment to be expected. The effect upon these gentlemen was electrical: they repeated my tale to the men; gave the word to fall in; were obeyed with marvellous celerity, and marched off without doing the slightest damage to any thing. Their departure relieved the old gentleman at once from all his anxiety, and induced him to cast every thing like disguise aside. About twenty peasants, well armed, accordingly came forth from their hiding-places. Horses, cattle, poultry, were in like manner released; and, in ten minutes, the château, with all the out-buildings attached to it, gave signs of ample vitality and very great abundance. We, of course, and our horses, were treated to our hearts' content -- besides receiving a warm invitation to visit the family again as often as opportunities might offer; and, finally, we did not quit the place till a thousand proofs had been afforded that, in the faithful discharge of the duties assigned to us, we had done real service to those who needed it.

In this manner I continued my march, day by day gladdened by the thought that I had been the means of preserving many an innocent family from wrong, and many a village as well as château from total destruction. At last, the head-quarters of the army reached Neuilly, where and around which an extensive encampment was formed. It was from the high grounds near the village that I obtained my first view of Paris; and its gilded domes and spires, and innumerable minarets, impressed me, as well as the prodigious extent of its area, with sensations of profound admiration. I acknowledge, too, that I thought, not without pity, of the state of public feeling as it must have then operated in the city -- where, from hour to hour, the advance of hostile columns was anticipated, and men could count on no other result than that their streets would become the scenes of strife. Yet the halt which we made appeared to promise better things, and the going and coming of frequent flags of truce told a tale of negotiations in progress. To be sure, the horizon seemed at one time entirely overcast; for a corps of French troops, which occupied Montmartre, refused to fall back when required to do so, and were instantly attacked and driven from their positions by a portion of our infantry. But except on that occasion, no fighting took place, though the outposts of the hostile armies wellnigh touched one another, and on both sides the extreme of vigilance was by night and day exhibited.

While we lay in this place, which, being of limited extent, afforded but inadequate accommodation even to the head-quarter staff,

I found myself involved in a little adventure, of which, because of the interest which it excited in me at the moment, I may as well give some account.

I was late of reaching Neuilly -- so late, indeed, that when I came up the place was crowded. I reported myself to the commanding officer, showing that all was right, and received from him directions to pass the night in the streets -- unless, indeed, I should prefer crossing to a town which lay on the farther side of the river. There would, however, be some risk attendant on this move, because the tricolour still floated from one of its public buildings, and the impression was that the French had not yet withdrawn from the place. Not relishing, however, the prospects of a night spent in fasting and the open air, I proposed to four of my people -- Germans, belonging to an hussar regiment -- that we should reconnoitre the town together. I found them quite ready to share the enterprise with me, and towards the river-side we accordingly proceeded.

We found that the bridge was barricaded on both sides; though in both barricades openings had been made sufficiently large to admit of the passing of a man and horse. We therefore rode through, when, leaving two of the men to keep guard at the farther side, I took the remaining two with myself, and advanced with great caution and deliberation towards the town. The first object that met our eyes, on approaching the main street, was a huge tricoloured flag, which waved over the barracks of the Chasseurs of the National Guard on an eminence hard by. As may be supposed, the vision had not the effect of rendering us less cautious; nevertheless, on we went -- neither seeing nor hearing any thing. In fact, the town was deserted. We rode quite through -- passing up one street and returning by another -- and then trotted off to make our comrades aware of how matters stood, and to join them with ourselves in our search after novelties.

We looked out for some respectable cabaret, having made up our minds to establish there our head-quarters; and had not gone far ere the well-known sign of the Bush informed us that our object was attainable. We knocked, but the signal was not regarded: we entered, and saw that the house was as desolate as the street. A fire was burning on the hearth -- the clock continued to go -- on the counter there stood a jug half filled with wine -- and in a cupboard we found a loin of mutton cooked, with a well-dressed salad, both ready to be served up. We next examined the cellars, which were abundantly stocked with casks, all, as we ascertained by sounding them, full of wine. In a word, it was precisely the sort of domicile of which we were in search, and we made up our minds not to look farther.

The next thing to be thought of was the accommodation of our horses, for which we were not slow in ascertaining that the cabaret could do nothing. I accordingly proceeded to the house adjoining, in the rear of which I found a stable, which, on examination, proved to be fitted up with half a dozen stalls, and abundantly stocked both with forage and litter. I threw the bridle over my mare's neck, and led her towards the door; but she snorted, tossed up her head, and, in spite both of coaxing and punishment, refused to enter. "There must be something uncommon here," exclaimed I, as I seized a fork and ran in. To toss the litter about was but to obey the impulse of the moment, and there sure enough we found beneath the straw a French soldier, shot through the heart, dead as a stone, but fully accoutred. How he could have come there we were at a loss to conjecture. But a practical acquaintance with the events of war has a marvellous effect in stifling men's sympathies on occasions like the present. We lifted the body in our arms, cast it into the river, and having made our horses comfortable in the stalls which they no longer refused to occupy, we returned to the cabaret, nowise indisposed to act with the same praiseworthy consideration towards ourselves.

We ate and drank merrily that night, but committed no excess: indeed, we could not divest ourselves of the suspicion that, after all, a snare might have been laid for us, and the same feeling of half anxiety which hindered us from lying down, operated, among other causes, to keep us sober. Once or twice, moreover, we went abroad, examining the houses near, and loitering at the corners of streets; but not one sign of human life could we discover: the place was evidently deserted. Accordingly, when dawn came in, I rode across to Neuilly, where many of my comrades met me, and it was agreed among us that we should return in a body, and spend that day as I and my former companions had spent the last. I have nothing to relate of events that befel till towards dusk, when, from my place beside the board, and surrounded by a dozen or more of the 11th, I saw a man peep in at the front door and instantly withdraw again. I sprang up, without speaking a word, and found a poor Frenchman hovering about the threshold, who, not without manifest indications of alarm, told me that he was the master of the house. A sort of general explanation immediately followed. We offered to pay for the provisions which we had taken: he positively refused to accept a sou; and telling us that his wife and daughter, and, indeed, all the rest of the inhabitants, were concealed in the woods, whither they had fled, be went away at our request to assure them that we were English, not Prussians, and that they might return without scruple to their houses. A happy family was that, so soon as its several members found themselves settled once more under the shadow of their own roof, and the invaders, from whom they had fled, anxious rather to apologize for what was past than to inflict upon them or their property fresh injuries. Indeed, the entire place appeared to change its character as house after house became tenanted, and the light-hearted owners betook themselves to their ordinary occupations. Nor can I pass on to other subjects without recording that the mutual good will which sprang up among us at the outset never suffered a moment's interruption. Throughout a space of nearly twelve months which I spent in or near Paris, I was always to my friend of the cabaret a welcome guest; and I quitted him and his amiable wife and daughter, at last, not without marks of unaffected sorrow on both sides.

Chapter 19

On the 7th of July intelligence reached us that Paris had capitulated, and shortly afterwards the order arrived to march in the direction of the capital. It was not, however, my fortune to witness or participate in the triumphal entrance which our columns made, for, with twenty-seven more mounted men -- of all nations, and belonging to all corps -- I was detached to protect the château of Bagatelle, in the Bois de Boulogne, where the Duke de Berri resided. It was a charming place, with a park, gardens, terraces, a sheet of water, a Venetian bridge, artificial rocks and grottoes, and hermitages innumerable. Neither, except on the score of hard duty had we much to complain of, seeing that the duke allowed for our daily use twelve bottles of Burgundy, besides giving us a kitchen-garden, whence at pleasure we might supply our table with vegetables and fruit. But as the rations both for men and horses were distributed only in Paris, the fatigue of fetching them from a point so distant proved often trying enough, especially as our duty required us every evening to patrol by reliefs round the grounds, from sunset till after sunrise on the following morning. Nor, indeed, were these precautions unnecessary. A large encampment had been formed in the wood, from which marauders came forth at all hours, whom nothing except the display of our scarlet belts hindered from reducing the duke's well-kept pleasure-grounds, to the state of a howling wilderness.

I shall never forget the impression that was made upon me the first time I visited Paris. Such a spectacle as the French capital exhibited then, will not, in all human probability come, at least for a while, under the observation of my readers; wherefore I would gladly describe it in detail, could I hope by any power of language to do justice to the subject, but that I feel to be impossible. Of the Champs Elysées, with its noble avenues, its stately trees, and its triumphal arch, I need not say any thing. They, as well as the Palace of the Tuileries, the Place de Concorde, and all the streets and squares adjacent were, I dare say, pretty much what the traveller who visits Paris in 1844 will find them. But the interminable encampments and bivouacs which overspread them -- the countless rows of huts which everywhere crowded upon the eye -- the unceasing noise of drums, trumpets, clarions, and other musical instruments -- the hubbub of voices which assailed you, as men of all nations conversed or sported together: these things together with the passing and repassing of thousands of men and women, as if some huge ant-hill had been disturbed, and instead of ants human beings came forth from its recesses, created altogether such a scene as cannot be conceived, unless it has been seen, and is never seen twice in any man's lifetime. For myself I was perfectly astounded, and rode on, with difficulty persuading myself that the whole was other than a dream.

We found the Parisians, particularly the women, civil and even friendly, to the greatest degree. They chaffered with us, flirted with us, sold their wares, and took our money with the best grace possible, and gave us in return a plentiful supply of indifferent brandy, served out in marvellously small glasses. We never, however, had much time to spend among them; for the way was long, and our burdens of forage and provisions weighty. Still a trip to Paris became one of our favourite recreations; and I, as holding rank in my party, found more than one opportunity of going thither when not on duty. For the most part, however, my time was pretty much occupied in attending to the conduct of my men, more than one of whom, as soon as the fruit began to ripen, I caught in the act of plundering. But the Duke de Berri, to do him justice, was extremely considerate on all such occasions, so that the delinquent generally escaped with a few hours incarceration.

While employed on this service, I had more than once the satisfaction of spending a day with my friends at the cabaret near Neuilly. My regiment was quartered in that town, and as often as leisure would permit, I rode over to see them; on which occasions I never failed of meeting from the good people of the house, the most hearty and affectionate reception. Neither did fortune fail of throwing in my way new acquaintances, from whose gratitude, the means which I possessed of serving them drew forth many solid tokens of regard. I need not tell those who have visited the French capital, that the banks of the Seine, to a great extent below Paris, are covered with vineyards; and probably there will be needed no direct statement from me to make my readers in general believe, that as the fruit began to ripen, the cultivators found it no easy matter to save their harvests from the rapacious hands of the foreign soldiers that were established among them. To such a height, indeed, was the practice of marauding carried, that guards were granted to such townships as applied for them, to protect the vineyards; and even these did not always succeed in hindering serious damage from being done to the property of the industrious cultivators. It chanced, that immediately opposite to Bagatelle, though separated from the duke's grounds by the river, lay some very extensive vine-farms. Over and over again they had been invaded, and as much damage done by treading down the vines, as by carrying off the fruit, when the representatives of the village came across and entreated that I would spare some of my men for their protection. I told them, what was true, that I had detached so many in other directions that no more could be spared. But I offered to accompany them to Paris, and to become their spokesman in representing the case to the proper authorities.

To Paris we accordingly went, -- the mayor, one or two other functionaries, and myself, -- and proceeding direct to the colonel's quarters, I made the circumstances of the case known, and received from him an order to detach two of my men, for the protection of the parties for whom I had interceded. This was immediately done. I went with the men, gave them their orders, namely to keep watch by turns from dawn to dark, by occupying an eminence whence the country for miles round could be reconnoitred; and to leave it to the peasants themselves to set their armed guards so soon as the night should set in. On the other hand I received from the authorities an assurance, that my men should be well cared for, plenty of good victuals provided for them, and their horses supplied with forage; while, over and above, it was intimated to me, that a cover would be laid for myself every day at the chief auberge in the place; and that whenever I felt disposed to go across, I should partake of the good things which it afforded. All this was very fair; and never once, from the beginning to the end of the harvest weeks, had I or my men the most distant occasion to complain that our villagers had grown slack in their attentions. On the contrary, as the red band effectually served its purpose, the people's gratitude grew so, that I and my people sometimes found it difficult to reject the favours which they pressed upon us.

At last, however, the harvest was got in, snugly and to as good purpose, as if the foot of the stranger had never defiled the soil of France; and I had already given orders for my people to return, when a deputation from the commune waited upon me to request that I would honour them with my company at the little fête, wherewith it was their custom to celebrate their harvest-home.

I accepted the invitation, as may be supposed, and do not remember having been present, in any part of the world, at a series of entertainments which more interested or amused me. We began with a public breakfast at eight in the morning, to which about fifty persons, young and old, sat down; after which, on the green, and to the sound of their own band, the lads and lasses danced till two. Then followed a dinner, sumptuous, abundant, and well served up, over which the mayor presided, where the great subject of rivalry, among all who were present, appeared to be how we, the strangers, should be most honoured. There was no lack of excellent wine, nor any disposition to stay the bottle in its progress; indeed we did not rise from table till past five, and many well-applauded toasts had been given. But the pledge of the day was the health of the three English cavaliers, to whom the kind-hearted peasants declared that they were indebted for preservation from famine. Nor was this all: the mayor, after proposing the toast, in terms highly gratifying to us, handed to me three paper packets, which he requested me to divide with the soldiers under my command, in testimony of the high sense which was entertained in the commune of our services. It was in vain that I besought him not to press upon us favours which were far beyond both our merits and our expectations. We had done no more than our duty, and were glad that we had been instrumental in preserving the property of persons who had given such manifold proofs of their excellence. But the mayor was resolute. He showed, indeed, that my persisting in the rejection of his bounty would have occasioned to him and his townspeople serious annoyance; I was obliged, therefore, to accept the packets, which contained just sixty francs apiece.

Of the habits of the Duke of Berri I have little to record, except that he lived a life of great seclusion, and was, and knew that he was, to the last degree unpopular among his countrymen. He never went from home except at night, and always returned again with as much privacy as possible, about the same hour on the night following. Why he should have been thus distasteful to the French I cannot conjecture. He has repeatedly honoured me with a few minutes' conversation, and I always found him affable, frank, and condescending; but it is certain that the French people hated him, and that the columns of the newspapers were crowded with stories and assertions to his disadvantage. Of the fate of that unfortunate prince I need not now speak. Even at the period to which my present narrative refers, the probable occurrence of such an event might have been safely predicted; and so fully did the Duke himself appear to be convinced of the fact, that he dwelt, as I have just said, in the strictest and most guarded privacy.

In the course of this autumn there occurred for the amusement of the Allied Sovereigns several grand reviews, at all of which I was present, rather as a spectator than as an actor. It was my duty, as one of the cavalry staff, to keep the ground, or attend on the officers commanding; and the opportunities thereby afforded me of seeing all that passed were very great. I remember that on one occasion above 8000 British cavalry, and cavalry in British pay, were paraded together. I think that the whole world could produce no such imposing spectacle as they presented; and the heavy brigades in particular, -- the Life Guards, the Blues, the Royals, and the Greys, drew forth bursts of spontaneous applause, even from the French populace. Yet there occurred an event which, though ludicrous in the extreme, threatened to produce some serious results, and out of which I am by no means sure that serious results did not here and there arise. The order of the day was to present the semblance of a cavalry action, in which a body of Brunswick horse were posted on one of the roads, to represent the enemy. These stood in front of as dense a crowd of civilians as Paris, and the towns and villages near, may be supposed to have sent forth, while everywhere carriages had taken up their stands, so that the whole area was thronged. The heavy brigade was ordered to dislodge them. They came on at first steadily, covered by their skirmishers; by-and-by they formed line, and the trumpets sounded to trot. Then came the signal to gallop, and to charge; and it was obeyed with such a show of vigour, as fairly upset the common sense of the Brunswickers. A panic seized them: they imagined that they were going to be ridden down; and suddenly wheeling round, they scampered off in all directions, making a way for themselves, without respect of persons, through the middle of the crowd. I defy a stoic to retain his gravity, if he had witnessed the scenes that followed. There were the people shrieking and running for their lives: there the Brunswickers spurring as if a legion of fiends had been in pursuit of them, and casting over their shoulders, from time to time, looks of the most abject terror. And, finally, there was the heavy brigade, grave as judges, till the trumpet sounded a halt, when, as if an irresistible impulse had come on them, they all burst into a roar of laughter. I never saw such a scene of mirth as that parade ground presented; and unless my memory deceive me, among the heartiest laughers of all were the Duke himself and the Emperor of Russia.

In the month of September of this year I bade adieu to the château of Bagatelle, and moved with my little detachment into Paris. I got a billet on a gentleman of the name of Vandamme, an apothecary in large practice, who resided in the Rue St. Honoré, and proceeding to deliver it was informed that there was no room in the house for my accommodation. My host, however, offered terms in lieu of what the law allowed me, which I did not think that it would be judicious to refuse. He gave me five francs a day, wherewith to provide board and lodging; and the lodging being furnished with an excellent stable, in which my horse was put up, I managed, out of my daily allowance, to fare sumptuously at one of the restaurants.

I am not going to describe Paris, or its endless places of public amusement. Were the subject fresh, instead of being absolutely stale, I could not flatter myself with possessing skill enough to bring the strange picture vividly before the reader's eye; and such a picture, if not vividly painted, had better not be painted at all. Every body knows how matters are managed within the precincts of the Palais Royal, -- how vice walks abroad undisguised and unblushing-how the gaming-tables are thronged, and other scenes enacted, of which even to speak in English society would cover the cheek with blushes. Again, the Louvre, with its treasures, gathered from every nation under heaven, was, in the days of which I now speak, a spectacle such as the eye of man will never, in all probability, look upon again. To be sure the splendour of this scene did not long continue after it had become to me an object of daily admiration. Each of the nations of continental Europe claimed the treasures of which the French had despoiled them; and by the Allied Sovereigns and Chiefs orders were issued to restore to the several claimants the masterpieces to the possession of which they could establish their right. The French were excessively annoyed by the promulgation of these orders; so much so, indeed, that resistance to their execution was anticipated, and an overwhelming force of all arms was warned to be in readiness, for the purpose of putting down the first movement towards sedition. But not a finger was stirred. Multitudes of anciens militaires walked to and fro about the streets, chafing and giving vent to their wrath in impotent "sacres," but the feeblest attempt to create a disturbance was never offered, and paintings and statues departed from Paris with much less of ostentation than had marked their entrance. I believe that I was John Bull enough somewhat to chuckle over this consummation of a war begun for the purpose of subjugating Old England; and yet I am not sure now that the impulse was a wise one which caused me to triumph. For the purposes of art such a variety of models can never again be collected into one place. Possibly it may be a matter to be regretted that, even for the sake of wounding the vanity of the French, they were ever dispersed again.

It is not, however, to be supposed that I, a poor non-commissioned officer, sought for amusement only in the visits which I paid to the Palais Royal and the Louvre. The theatres, one after another, were by me frequented, and many a place of public amusement besides, of which my reader, were I to attempt any thing like a description, might be apt to think that I should have acted more prudently had I held aloof from it. But I must not forget to mention that at these haunts of vice numerous quarrels sprang up between the English officers and the officers of the reduced French army. The consequences of these were almost always duels, in which many lives were lost; till, in the end, the grievance became so heavy that both the Duke of Wellington and the French government interfered to put a stop to it.

On more than one occasion during my residence in Paris, I found that my knowledge of the French language -- the result of my three years' captivity -- served me in excellent stead. For example, having been removed from my pleasant dependence upon Mr. Vandamme, I was introduced into the family of a silk-merchant, whose wife, by the by, was an Englishwoman, and where I was treated throughout with the most marked attention. From these good people I learned much, which I should have never known otherwise, concerning the state in which the inhabitants of the capital were kept, while as yet authentic information concerning the issues of the Waterloo campaign failed to reach them. At first, it appeared, two despatches were received from Napoleon's headquarters, which gave an account of the battle of Ligné, and the total overthrow of the Prussian army. These were greeted by a general illumination, and such displays of rejoicing, as set all the Parisians, whether of high or humble rank, agog. By and by came accounts of the affair of Quatre Bras, which described the English as totally annihilated; and stated that, in two days from the date of the communication, the emperor expected to establish his head-quarters at Brussels. Next day came a third despatch, full, as the former had been, of promise, though speaking, strangely enough, of a second meeting with the obstinate islanders. And here followed a pause, of the agonizing nature of which my informants assured me that it was impossible for human language to convey an adequate idea. After this all was trepidation, anxiety, and distrust. Hour by hour, and minute by minute, crowds assembled at the post-office, and at every point where it was supposed that information might be obtained; and when none came, their spirits sank in a degree altogether proportionate to the height to which they had previously been raised. Finally, stragglers and fugitives began to pour in: and then such a revulsion of feeling took place, as those alone can conceive who have found themselves denizens of a great city, which having seen a mighty army march forth from its walls full of dreams of conquest, find themselves suddenly bereft of all protection, and expect from one minute to another the arrival among them of a cruel and vindictive enemy, flushed with conquest, and thirsting for revenge and for plunder.

Having remained here some little time, I was sent to Marli, for the purpose of protecting the royal game in the park, with which, it appeared, that both officers and men of the Allied Armies made abundantly free. I was again put in charge of a party; and at the house of the steward, a M. Perron, -- a relative, and not very remote, I believe, of the famous Indian general, -- I spent some weeks greatly to my own satisfaction. Nothing could exceed the liberality with which our table was served: indeed, we ate our meals every day with the family; and when seasons of rejoicing came round -- such as Christmas and New-year's-day -- we entered heartily into all their amusements. Of Christmas I have little to observe, for it seemed to me to be spent somewhat gravely; but New-year's-day was, in every sense of the term, a festival. Then all the domestics dined at the same table with the master and mistress; and enormous as the amount of viands was, the whole were cleared away ere the company rose. Next followed a game, somewhat similar to our Twelfth-night gambols, during which a king and queen were chosen, and treated with all conceivable deference; while waltzes, quadrilles, and dances of every kind, kept all ranks, degrees, and ages, astir till daylight. I must confess that the terms of easy yet respectful familiarity, on which the upper and lower classes in that well-regulated family lived, struck me as being delightful. Perhaps we could not, consistently with the order of our education and manners, transplant it without risk into this country; yet, I deceive myself, if any right-minded Englishman has ever looked upon a scene of the kind, without wishing that its occurrence were as habitual here as in the land where he may be sojourning as a visiter.

It is not worth while to describe the adventures which befel me while acting in the capacity of gamekeeper to the royal family of France. I have had strange meetings with men of all ranks, English as well as foreigners; and, by steadily yet respectfully doing my duty, I am not aware that I made any of them my enemies. Neither shall I speak at large of an affair which threatened at one time to lead to serious consequences, when some French park-keepers shot a dog belonging to the First Dragoon Guards, which they found one day poaching, as was his wont, in their rabbit-burrow. The dog, it appeared, belonged to no one in particular. He had followed the regiment from England, -- was a prodigious favourite, -- had gone through the battle of Waterloo, charging uniformly in front of the line, and, after the battle was over, made his appearance as usual beside the fire of the main-guard, where he was welcomed as a highly-favoured guest. He followed his own regiment, of course, to St. Germain's; and, being of the lurcher breed, was in the habit of running down both hares and rabbits, which he uniformly carried home for the use of the men, who fed him. I need scarcely say how furious the regiment was when intelligence of the death of poor Soldier reached them; or how, with one consent, the troopers vowed to take vengeance on the murderer, to whom, by some chance or another, they had obtained a clue. I do not know how long they might have watched for their opportunity, but at last they found it; and sure enough the unfortunate wretch was set upon in the streets, and very severely beaten. But as good fortune would have it, I happened to come up at the time. I instantly ran among them; assured them that he was not the man; got him out of their hands, though not till after he had suffered severely, and escorted him home. If I had been a favourite with the steward before this, I rose by many degrees higher in his good graces afterwards. Indeed, the whole corps of foresters treated me henceforth as a brother; and many a merry evening I spent, in consequence, at their several lodges.

Once, while I lay here, there arrived from Paris a royal shooting-party, which consisted of the Duke de Berri, the Duke d'Angouleme, Monsieur the Comte d'Artois, and about a score besides of the chief nobles and grandees of France. The order of the day's sport, though now familiar enough in this country, struck us Englishmen as being curious; for the sportsmen took no trouble, being content to post themselves in the centre of a wood, where an open space had been created by felling the trees, and towards which, from the surrounding copses, several rides or broad paths conducted. Meanwhile a multitude of beaters drove up the game all round, which, as the poor animals ran into the open space, were shot down with great diligence. I observed that the distinguished tirailleurs did not so much as take the trouble to load their own pieces: each was attended by a servant, who charged a reserve gun, and handed it to his master, so that the firing was continued, and the slaughter very great. Among other animals killed that day were two wild boars. Of the total number I can say no more than that they loaded several light wagons.

Chapter 20

It was now the spring of 1816, by which time France had submitted to the terms which the Allies proposed; and, among other arrangements, it was agreed upon that Paris and its immediate environs should be evacuated. A strong army was, indeed, to remain, for the purpose of securing the fulfilment of the conditions of peace, and consolidating the throne for the Bourbons; but its divisions were to find their quarters in towns nearer to the frontiers, so as to leave the interior of France free to the exercise of its own usages. In accordance with these arrangements, I one day received my route, so suddenly that there was not time so much as to see and bid farewell to my kind host, who chanced to be from home; but I took a last meal with his wife and family, in great affection, if not in the highest spirits; and parted from them, when it was over, amid many, and I believe sincere, protestations of regret on both sides.

I rejoined my regiment the evening previous to the commencement of the march of the whole English army towards their quarters. I was left, however, behind, with two men, to see the last of the baggage packed, and to escort it all the way to Cambray, where the head-quarters of the corps were to be established. Two waggons were placed at our disposal, one of which we loaded early in the day, while the other, by reason of the non-arrival of some of the officers' traps, continued to stand empty. Had the waggoner merely murmured I could not have blamed him. The delay was provoking enough for him as well as for us; but when he avowed his determination to draw off, I knew my duty too well to permit it; so I told him, in peremptory language, that he must wait my orders. Being anxious, nevertheless, to save both him and myself trouble, I resolved to go in search of the missing articles, and, mounting my horse, placed one of my men as a sort of sentry over the waggoner, with strict orders not on any account to permit his escape.

I had not been long gone ere our friend, Jean Crapot, began to give signs of a vehement disposition to escape. He flogged his horses and moved forward, whereupon my trusty vidette, after vainly protesting against the move, drew his sword, and commanded the deserter to halt. The screams of the waggoner, who no sooner beheld the flash of the steel than he shrieked out, soon drew a crowd around them. The crowd called loudly for the municipal guard, and in five minutes my friend Billy Duff, a little old man belonging to the 8th Hussars, was surrounded by some dozen or two of armed men, who pointed their weapons towards him, and covered him with a very choice shower of French abuse. At the same time the officer commanding this party drew his sword and attacked Billy, who, to do him justice, behaved with admirable coolness, being content to parry, without returning, the thrusts that were made at him. I shrewdly suspect, however, that honest Billy, would have practised that day his last trick of fence had I not opportunely arrived to his assistance. I instantly desired him to lower his weapon, well knowing that resistance from both of us would have been useless; and the rascally Frenchmen sprang upon him forthwith, wrested his sword from him, and made him their prisoner.

I was very indignant, as may be easily believed, and protested against the proceeding; but no one paid the least regard to me. The cowards knew that the English army was gone, and they resolved to have their spite out against the few stragglers that remained. Accordingly Billy was dragged off, amid their yells and execrations, to the guard-house, where he was by-and-by conveyed as a prisoner before the French field-officer of the day. I confess that I was at my wits' end. On the one hand I did not know where to turn for help, on the other, I was resolved that Billy should not be deserted; so, buckling on my sword, which I had heretofore left in my quarters, I ran where I knew were the adjutant's lodgings, scarcely venturing to hope that I should have the good fortune to find him. As sometimes happens, however, in cases of emergency, Fortune stood my friend. He was in the very act of mounting his horse when I arrived, and at once agreed to go with me to the municipal guard. I have no language sufficiently strong wherewith to describe the insolence of the crew that were on duty there. They led us through a long passage, flourishing Billy's sword over their heads, as if it had been a standard taken in some general action, and introduced us into the presence of the commanding officer, in terms to which his own insolent manner entirely responded. It was to no purpose that the adjutant demanded the release of the man. They would not give him up till he should have been led as a prisoner before the commandant of the town, and his crime regularly entered in the black book. For poor Billy's crime, according to their showing, was that he had drawn his sword against a peaceable citizen; whereas he had simply done his duty, by using the means which every sentinel is supposed to have at his disposal, for hindering his post from being violated, or a prisoner put under his charge from escaping.

Having come to the determination of laying a charge against Billy before the English authorities, the officer of the guard put his prisoner under the escort of a serjeant and six men, and gave orders that he should be marched to the quarters of Colonel Kelly, who had been nominated military commandant of Paris. I went with my comrade, as in duty bound, and came in for my own share of the insults and threats with which a crowd, accumulating from street to street, seemed anxious to overwhelm us. Neither were they content to cover us with abuse; they closed in upon the escort, made a snatch at my sword, which with much difficulty I retained, spat upon us, and repeatedly exclaimed that we ought to be put to death. In a word, our progress was one not merely of vexation but of imminent hazard throughout. Neither were our prospects much brighter when we attained to the end of our journey. For, though Colonel Kelly's baggage crowded the courtyard, he himself had quitted his apartments, and it seemed more than probable that we should be left, after all, to the tender mercies of the French people. From such a fate, which must have been a trying one, our better angel saved us. As we were marching back to the guard-house I observed in one of the cross-streets a carriage standing, which I knew to be Colonel Kelly's; and by-and-by he came, with his lady, from a shop, and was about to enter. I called out to him. We were led up. The written charge was handed in, read, signed, returned with a smile; after which he told the escort they might go, and he would look after the prisoners. "Now, my lads," said he, as soon as the Frenchmen had departed, "get back to your stables as fast as you can, and make your escape out of the city. The troops are all on the march; I will not be answerable for your safety here." We needed no second bidding. Making choice of all manner of by-lanes, we reached our billet unobserved; and the horses being saddled and the baggage gone, we instantly mounted. In less than an hour we were clear of Paris, and on the evening of the sixth day overtook the regiment at Cambray.

I had begun by this time to grow weary of service in the staff corps, I therefore applied for and obtained permission to rejoin my regiment, which occupied Bergen, in Dutch Flanders, and the villages round, and lived on the best and most friendly terms with the natives. It was here that the Waterloo medal was served out to us, -- which the colonel graced with a long and eloquent speech, besides granting us three days of entire exemption from duty, and himself, with the rest of the officers, presenting us with a very handsome gratuity in money. It is scarcely worth while to relate how the money went, or after what fashion the days of fête were expended. The Flemings are nowise backward in their cans, -- as all who know them will testify; but I suspect they never beheld such wassailing as gave a character to the three days in question. Still the results were by no means injurious either to them or to us. We feasted them all, gave dances to their wives and daughters, and won their hearts by our liberality. I am sure, at least, that from that time forth we lived together on the most friendly terms, -- and that when we quitted them they deplored our removal as if ties of close consanguinity had united us.

There occurred while we lay here two adventures -- both of them serious, one fatal -- of which I may as well make mention.

We were a good deal scattered about, in small parties, and under numerous commands -- forage being, as it seemed, scarce; or, if not, the Duke being naturally desirous to press as lightly as possible, in its exaction, on the inhabitants. I was one of fourteen who, under one Serjeant Ford, occupied the village of Morqueon; and there was another detachment at a place called Fellay, near Arras, of which a corporal had charge. One day Serjeant Ford received a letter from Fellay, to inform him that the men stationed there were extremely uncomfortable, and to request that he would ride over, and endeavour, by his influence with the mayor, to obtain for them better treatment. I volunteered to accompany the serjeant, and away we went.

A few hours' ride carried us to the village; and, on inquiring for the house where the English troops were quartered, it was immediately shown to us. We entered, and found the whole party seated round a table, on which stood several flasks of brandy, and glasses in proportion, while the landlord seemed bent on making them drink their fill -- he, by the way, sedulously setting the example. This was by no means the sort of spectacle by which we expected to be greeted, and we stared at one another not a little astounded, which the landlord no sooner observed than he addressed to us marks of his most particular attention. He assured us that everybody then within his gates drank at his expense; that we could not oblige him more than by making the most of his good cheer; and that he should not be contented till we had drained his cellar, which he should take care to replenish whenever the convenient moment came. Soldiers are seldom backward in doing honour to an invitation such as this; so down we sat in the chairs pulled out for us, and I am bound to add that, for a couple of hours, the scene was as curious, yet as sociable and merry, as mortal eye need rest upon.

Our comrades of the corporal's party, who appeared to have had nearly enough ere we arrived, filed off by degrees, one after another, to their beds: the serjeant likewise retired; but our host, whose thirst seemed to be unquenchable, kept his place, and insisted upon it that I should not leave him. At length, however, the liquor took such effect upon him that he became quite mad. All of a sudden he seized a burning beam, and made a blow at my head, which with some difficulty I eluded. I disarmed him instantly; upon which he sprang up, ran to a closet, and, snatching a pistol, began to load it. Happily for me, one of my brother-soldiers still dozed upon his chair; and he, on my shouting out, rushed upon the madman, and wrenched the weapon from his hold. But he was bent upon mischief: he armed himself with a heavy brazen candlestick, and striking me a blow on the forehead, laid me senseless on the floor. It is not worth while to continue the relation of a mere -- yet a desperate -- riot. It ended in the man of the house escaping, we could not tell where, -- and I having been put to bed, all seemed over.

It was not so, however: Serjeant Ford, annoyed at what had occurred, and apprehending that a false tale might reach head-quarters, got out of bed, and lodged a complaint against the landlord at the police-office. He was arrested, brought to trial, and sentenced to three months' imprisonment, besides paying a fine of seven hundred francs to the Crown. But the most curious piece of the business remains to be told: not only did he bear me no ill-will, but both he and his wife, when I saw them again some time after his release, thanked me for all that had happened; for the effect of his punishment was to cure him of his propensity to drinking, and he became from that time a respectable and sober man. So much for the administration of justice in Dutch Flanders. I never saw a criminal prosecution more fairly and honestly conducted: I never heard, except in this particular instance, of punishment being followed by effects so beneficial.

The other adventure, of which I have to speak, was by many degrees more tragical; for it ended in the death of one of the finest young men in the 11th Light Dragoons. Serjeant Tongue, connected, I believe, with a highly-respectable family, and himself singularly handsome and of a good address, was yet the slave of a temper so violent and ungovernable, that he ceased, when irritated, to be, to a great extent, at least, master of himself. He had formed an attachment to a very pretty girl, the daughter of the mayor of Moul; and the young lady made no secret in any quarter that she returned his love. It happened once upon a time that a fête was to take place in the village; and Tongue, having engaged his lady-love to be his partner in the dance, looked forward with great eagerness to the accomplishment of his wishes. Unfortunately for him, he was detained in his quarters beyond the hour at which the dancing was to begin, and when he entered the ball-room, he beheld to his unspeakable chagrin, that his partner had given her hand to another. This was a French hussar, the son of the publican at whose house the fête was held -- a fine, gay, well-dressed youth -- who, with a comrade, had come over from a neighbouring village where they were quartered, and seeing the mayor's daughters sitting by, claimed the right to dance with them. I was told that their doing so was quite in agreement with the usages of the country, neither do I doubt the truth of the statement; but Tongue saw the matter in a different light. He stood, with folded arms, watching them as they swept round. He observed, or fancied, that the hussar used freedoms with the maiden, such as his English sense of decorum could not tolerate, and he lost all self-command. He ran home to his quarters, loaded a pistol with two blank cartridges, and, bidding me and another man put on our swords, rushed back to the ball-room.

We followed him, of course, scarce knowing what was meant; but the moment I observed the situation of his partner, my mind misgave me. I would have interfered, and done my best to lead him away; but ere I could make a step in advance, the music ceased, and Tongue, springing forward, seized the French hussar by the collar. A frightful scene followed: he did not fire, but, holding the pistol cocked, he struck the young man some severe blows with the muzzle, and dragged him through the room, looking all the while more like a maniac than a sane person. It was to no purpose that the farmers, by whom he was greatly beloved, tried to appease him. He continued to strike and drag the unfortunate Frenchman through the room, till one of the company, unfortunately, threw his arms round Tongue's neck, and endeavoured to extricate the hussar from his grasp. It was an unwise act: during the scuffle that ensued, the pistol exploded, and the young hussar fell to the ground terribly wounded.

As Providence would have it, the muzzle had turned obliquely from its object when the explosion took place. The consequence was, that the powder made no breach in his body, but it burned his clothes, scorched the whole side of his abdomen, and appeared to all the lookers-on to have killed him. In an instant, Tongue's senses seemed to return: he was overwhelmed with anguish and remorse; and though the generous young hussar assured him that, come what would, no more should ever be said about the matter, he never smiled afterwards. The wounded man was conveyed to bed, and medical assistance sent for. The villagers, with whom Tongue was an especial favourite, entreated him to think no more about the matter; and the mayor himself was the first to put his name to a paper, in which the circumstance of the wound was attributed entirely to accident: but Serjeant Tongue continued inconsolable. At last, one day when the serjeant-major came to visit us, and Tongue with myself was attending him in his inspection of the men's quarters, our poor comrade, pretending sudden illness, ran home to his own quarters. We did not suspect any thing -- at least the serjeant-major did not -- neither had I the most remote idea of what was really intended; wherefore our horror may be conceived, when, on repairing to his billet, we found a letter, addressed to the serjeant-major, on his table. It contained a statement of the mental agony which for many days the writer had experienced, and ended with a declaration that he meant to destroy himself. We ran to the stables, and there learned from one of the men that he had gone into the orchard, carrying both his pistols with him, as if for the purpose of shooting sparrows. We followed him thither, and saw him sitting in a dry ditch, and the pistols beside him. Instantly, on perceiving us, he sprang up, and presenting one of the pistols at us, charged us, as we valued our lives, not to advance a step nearer. The serjeant-major, who was a feeling and humane man, threw himself on his knees, and entreated Tongue to cast the weapons from him, and to listen to reason; but the poor fellow only shook his head and smiled bitterly. One of the pistols he did fling away; he then planted his back against a tree, and placing the muzzle of the other in his own mouth, blew his head to pieces.

I shall never forget the horror of that scene, nor the deep and universal mourning that followed. For the young French hussar was by this time recovering fast, and never uttered one word of reproach, far less of threatening, against his rival. But the deed was done; so there remained for us only the painful duty of giving the rites of sepulture to his remains -- which we did, Lieutenant Wood reading the service over him, and the whole detachment attending as sincere, though not as formal, mourners.

Chapter 21

Our next station was in and around Arras; during our occupation of which, there occurred a grand review, or sham-battle, on the plains of Valenciennes. Of the great plain in question I need scarcely speak. While the summer crops cover its surface it is not destitute of beauty, for vegetation is abundant; and vegetation, look on it where you may, is always beautiful; but a more miserable scene than it offers to the eye after the crops are gathered in, I have seldom had the misfortune to behold. There are no cheerful villages looking forth from the woods that embower them -- no healthful and merry peasantry moving about -- but far and wide, beyond the reach of the sense of vision, lies one huge waste, where the very roads, so soon as the rains set in, cease in a great measure to be discernible. It was there, for the amusement of the Allied Sovereigns and Chiefs, that, one day in the month of November, a large army assembled; and the various evolutions which mark the progress of a mighty battle were gallantly executed. I confess that my recollections of that brilliant affair are too little mixed up with enjoyment to cause my lingering over them. We marched from our quarters at one in the morning under a torrent of rain. We formed the line about eight, and continued till nearly dark charging, wheeling, changing ground, and careering about, till both men and horses were thoroughly spent; and we returned to our billets more jaded by many degrees than I, at least, had ever been before -- not even excepting on the 18th of June, when the pride of Napoleon and of France fell beneath us.

From Arras we proceeded the morning after the review to Hazebrook, where our regiment lay in barracks throughout the remainder of .the winter. Of these, however, we did not take possession, till some delay had occurred, of which, as I myself was, to a certain extent, the cause, it becomes me to speak somewhat more at length. The circumstances were these: -- I was sent on with a party to take over the barracks from the Queen's Bays, and to make them ready for the reception of the regiment. I proceeded accordingly; but on arriving at the station, I found the rooms in such a state that I positively refused to take possession. They were not only filthy in the extreme, but the miasmata proceeding from them was horrible; and to add to the evil, I

181

discovered in an apartment, the door of which I was obliged to force, the corpse of a dead man. How he died, or why his comrades had thus abandoned him, we were never able to ascertain; but the effect of my report, first upon the surgeon, and afterwards upon the commanding officer, was such, that the latter refused to introduce his men into a place of which the air seemed to be putrid. The consequence was, that for several weeks we occupied billets in the town; nor were we removed into the station originally intended for us till every room in the place, as well as the stables attached to them, had undergone a complete fumigation.

While we occupied this station, it was my fortune to witness one of those shocking exhibitions from which every feeling of humanity urges us to shrink but on which a curiosity, which is almost always resistless, compels us to attend; I mean the public execution of several persons, whom the law had condemned to die by the guillotine. There were in all four victims to offended justice: three of whom had been concerned in a burglary, attended by circumstances of gross cruelty; while the fourth stood convicted of the offence of arson, for which, in France as well as in England, death was in those days the penalty. The miserable men were conducted on foot from the prison to the scaffold, which stood in the great square or centre of the town; and being without shirts, and having their hair closely cropped behind, they looked, with their pale faces, ghastly enough. When they arrived at the appointed place, round which an enormous crowd was collected, three of them were halted, while the fourth, mounting by a ladder, was received at the top by two executioners. These men, a father and son, wearing dark red frocks, but not otherwise disguised, took their victim and bound him, belly downwards, upon a board, which they thrust forward in such a way, that his head passed through a groove in a broad upright beam, and lay over a bag, which was suspended there to receive it. In the groove was the knife, which, on a signal being given by the elder of the two, fell, and ere we could so much as draw a breath, the head was severed from the body. It dropped at once into the bag, whereupon the executioners untying the trunk, cast it through a trapdoor into a hole beneath; and then scattering sawdust over their horrid platform, made ready to deal in like manner with the next that should come. I shall never forget the sense of faintness which came over me, when I beheld the blood pour like water out of a pipe, from the palpitating trunk; yet, if any judgment might be formed from the ceaseless chattering of the people round us, none except my countrymen shared in the feeling. Moreover, it horrified me to observe, that here, as is said to be the case in London, a large portion of the spectators were women. How extraordinary it is, that they, the most delicate of nature's handiwork, should thrust themselves into situations of such frightful interest. I declare that their conduct throughout altogether shocked me: they never ceased to chatter, no, not at the moment when the knife was falling; and so soon as one dead body had been committed to its temporary hiding place, they appeared impatient till another should be stretched out before them.

In this place we spent the winter, miserably enough. The weather was cold, with much rain; the convent in which we were quartered was in a state of great dilapidation; fuel proved to be both scarce and bad; and provisions of all kinds were wretched. But these, though serious drawbacks to our comforts, did not constitute the worst evil of which we had to complain. A reduction in the army having taken place, volunteers from the disbanded corps were permitted to enlist in the 11th Light Dragoons; and these, most of whom came from the corps of Artillery Drivers, proved to be, in point of character, of the worst description. The consequence was that our regiment, which, up to the date of this unhappy occurrence, had maintained an excellent name, now fell off, both in morals and reputation, and a system of pilfering arose, such as compelled the commanding officer, however naturally averse to the proceeding, to tighten the cords of his discipline exceedingly. There were more punishments in the regiment during four months after the volunteers joined us than I had ever seen in all the years during which I had been a member of it; and I am reluctantly forced to admit that they were all richly merited.

Out of the very worst of these recruits two separate troops were formed; and to one of the two, which had its quarters at an inconsiderable village on the great chaussée of Lisle, I found myself attached. It was a source of extreme annoyance to me, for I knew none of the men; and, besides that, the quarter was a bad one, the whole country being flat, was laid under water, as if it had been a lake instead of a plain. Indeed, there was no passing from one farm-house to another (and it was among the farm-houses that we were distributed), except by the aid of huge stepping-stones, each of which measured not less than from five to six feet in height, though its top barely surmounted the surface of the inundation. Now, though the natives, from long practice, found it easy enough to pass to and fro, the operation proved for awhile exceedingly hazardous to us; and to the last there needed great self-possession, and a state of brain perfectly clear, to carry us through. Fate so ordered it that I should be one of those to whom the difficulty of the passage should be rendered experimentally manifest; and the circumstances under which my mishap befel were these:

I had learned that, in a farm-house some way removed from mine, a serjeant lay, with whom, as well as with his wife, I had long been acquainted. As may be imagined, the intelligence gave me great delight, and I resolved that no delay should occur ere I paid them a visit. Accordingly I proceeded one day to their quarters, and, being there informed that they had crossed the inundation to a village not far off, I followed them thither. The meeting was affectionate on all sides, and led to an adjournment into the back parlour of a linen-draper's house, the master of which dealt in contraband as well as in exciseable articles, and was famous for his well-flavoured and potent eau de vie. We chatted over old times, drank largely, and by-and-by became musical as well as talkative. The lady, in particular, favoured us with a ditty, in the chorus of which we were expected to join; and, as the children of the family slept in cribs round the room, the effect, as our music grew momentarily louder and louder, was somewhat ludicrous. First, the little urchins opened their eyes, and lifted their heads with a curious look over their cradles. Next, they began to scream, as if to increase the melody of our canzonette; and, finally, they sprang out of bed with one accord, and ran, as if the spirit of evil had pursued them, calling aloud for their mother. For myself, I was in fits of laughter; for the mother came presently, to entreat that we would be quiet; and the whole of her little troop, accounting themselves safe only beside her apron-string, bore her company. Never was a more ludicrous scene presented. The landlady now coaxed, now remonstrated for silence: the serjeant's wife continued to pour forth her song, till it reached the twenty-sixth stanza; while the serjeant, on whom the liquor had taken considerable effect, beat time with amazing energy on the table, and the children, whimpering all the while that the solo was in progress, broke out into perfect yells so soon as the chorus began. I must confess that I was never more amused in the whole course of my life; for there was terror mixed up with our landlady's indignation, which gave to it a very comical turn; and though I knew that her alarm was not groundless, I confess that I saw nothing in it that did not savour of the grotesque.

At last, however, my friend the serjeant's wife fairly broke down.

She could not recollect the twenty-seventh stanza of her canzonette; and, as the night was wearing apace, and roll-call near at hand, we judged it expedient to depart. And now came the thought, how were we, in our existing state of brain, and in a dark and stormy night, -- for the wind blew a hurricane, -- to cross the swamp? I confess that, as far as I was myself concerned, I made up my mind to a ducking; but my friends took a different view of the case; so away we set in high glee, the lady jeeringly telling me to keep close to her, and she would guide me through all difficulties. The event proved, that in this, as in many other instances, there may be excess of hardihood as well as its opposite. We got, indeed, as far as the point where the water was well known to be deepest, -- the serjeant in front, carrying a paper lantern in his hand, his wife following, and I bringing up the rear; but there we came to a stand-still: the lady's courage failed her; she stopped short -- declared that she could go no further -- and our situation became as pitiable as can well be imagined. At last we each gave her a hand, but neither entreaty nor objurgation could prevail upon her to take another step. "Stoop down," cried I, "and make the attempt to scramble from stone to stone:" she tried to do so; but the effort proved fatal, for her foot slipped, and down she fell, dragging both her supporters into the water. As a matter of course, we were all soused overhead, yet there our troubles ended. By sheer strength of arm I contrived to keep her mouth clear of the flood, while her husband, who was a tall man, dragged her forward: and thus, at the expense of a severe wetting from top to toe, we managed in the end to reach their quarters. A change of habiliments was here given to me: supper too was provided; and, by the help of a little more brandy, we managed to pass the night merrily enough. Nor was the slightest inconvenience experienced either then or afterwards by any of the party in consequence of the rash attempt and its ludicrous, though most uncomfortable issue.

It is not worth while to continue a detailed narration of the many little adventures that befel me during the remainder of our sojourn in France. They were precisely such as those who understand what a soldier's life is will be able to conceive for themselves, while, to the mere civilian, I feel that it would be impossible to convey any accurate notion of them. For example, I was on one occasion quartered with a party of harum-scarum youths, at a farm-house near Lisle, of which the owners appeared to have made up their minds to treat us with as little regard to our comfort as possible. They not only never offered to share with us any of the petty luxuries which they themselves enjoyed, but they made a point of refusing us the accommodation of their cooking utensils, and never failed to extinguish the fire in the kitchen, as soon as they themselves were done with it. For all this, my wild scapegraces took care to pay them off to their heart's content. In the first place, a hot loaf would disappear from the oven, no human being could tell how; then a lump of butter made its way in some mysterious manner from the larder, though the good woman had taken care to lock the door and put the key in her pocket. The honest man's clover, too, which he had stowed away with infinite care in the loft, made its way somehow or other into our horses' racks, and the animals grew fat and sleek in consequence, even while the allowance of forage served out to them by the legitimate authorities was admitted to be inadequate to their necessities. All this both astonished and chafed our hosts, who never could bring home a charge of pilfering against any one, and came at last to the conclusion that we were in league with the enemy of mankind. But the circumstance which brought these curmudgeons at last to their senses was this.

It is the custom in that part of France for the women to keep themselves warm by placing under their garments, while they sit at their needlework, pots filled with the ashes of charcoal. Nobody would have noticed this, had our landlady afforded us the comfort of a fire in the grate; but this, as I have said, she regularly raked out after dinner, and if any of us complained of cold, she contented herself by remarking "that she could not sympathize with his distress." One day she had, as usual, sneered at our want of hardihood, when all at once an explosion took place beneath her, and she jumped up, unhurt, it is true, but the very image of rage and consternation. The fact is, that one of my lads had tied a small quantity of gunpowder very tightly in a worsted bag, and contrived dexterously to bury it in the hot ashes just as she drew her feu-pot towards her. Some time was, of course, required to burn through the flannel, during the progress of which my lady sat in her glory; but no sooner was the train fired, than all her courage forsook her. From that instant both she and her husband were subdued: they expressed great regret to me at the line which they had previously taken; they promised, in case we would cease to molest them, that they would change their bearing towards us; and as we really did not desire at their hands more than we conceived to be reasonable, I engaged, on the part of my comrades, that all tricks and annoyances should cease. The farmer and his wife kept their word, and so did we, of which the result was, that during the remainder of our sojourn beneath their roof there was the best understanding between us.

Another little frolic in which we indulged greatly astonished the good people of Baillieul and its vicinity. The 5th of November over-taking us here, we resolved to burn a Guy Fawkes, after the manner of our boyish days at home. A man of straw was soon made, dressed up, and duly painted, which, with a bag of gunpowder in his interior, we mounted upon a little cart, and dragged with much laughter through the place. At first the inhabitants seemed totally at a loss what to make of our proceedings; but, by-and-by, having stumbled upon an itiner-ant Flemish fiddler, and persuaded him, by dint of large potations, to mount the car beside our Guy, the sound of his music, and the ludi-crous grimaces which he made, drew a crowd of delighted natives to follow in our train. It would be tedious to speak of the antics which were played off -- all of them laughable at the moment, though un-worthy of description, -- till in the end an adequate number of fagots was collected, and the last scene alone remained to be enacted. Our intention was to burn our Guy in the little square or place of the town; but the mayor, apprehensive lest the thatched roofs might be ignited by sparks from the bonfire, entreated us to remove into a field of his own, a little way off. We complied with his request at once; and a dark night having happily set in, we proceeded, by the light of half-a-dozen torches, to erect the gallows and to suspend Guy, with his fagots gathered round him. There was great shouting and merriment all this while; the fiddler played as if he had possessed the power of twenty fiddlers; men, and women, and children danced to his strains; and when the torches were applied, and the fagots began to blaze, the mirth of all classes among the lookers-on seemed only to increase. So it was till the flames reached the mine which the man of straw bore about with him in his stomach. But the effect of the explosion I shall never forget. Nothing of the sort had been anticipated by the French people; the catastrophe seemed to come upon them like some convulsion of nature; for they uttered a wild scream, took to their heels one and all, and never stopped to look about till they found themselves safe in their respective domiciles. This was, of course, the very point of the joke to us; and as no human being suffered from it further than by the fright at the moment, it did not interrupt the excellent terms on which we had hitherto lived with our hosts.

Besides these frolics, peculiar to our calling and situation, we found entertainment, as well as instruction, in several grand reviews; camps being formed during the summer months, in which the troops of England and her allies were assembled. Moreover, we were yet in France when the Waterloo prize-money was issued to us; -- and as it certainly went further there than it could have done at home, so were French shopkeepers and publicans principally the gainers by it. -- We had also our fairs, our races, our fox-hunts, and other manly sports; some of which appeared to irritate, and all to astonish, the people among whom they were enacted yet let me do them justice, -- except in a very few instances they exhibited no disposition to pick quarrels, or molest us, though a regard to truth compels me to acknowledge that we were not on all occasions over-careful to study either their prejudices or their customs.

At last, however, the period came when the army of occupation was to be broken up. We were stationed in and around Cambray when the order to this effect arrived, and we received our route to march upon Calais; which we reached, unless my memory be at fault, early in November of 1818, and not long afterwards embarked for England. A joyous day it was to all when once again we found ourselves, amid a crowd of our countrymen, forming in the streets of Ramsgate. We landed there on the 20th, were billeted for the night, and proceeded next day to Canterbury. But ours was destined to be no more than a passing visit to the beloved land of our birth; and the reader, if he think fit to pursue my narrative further, will find whither it was that the fortune of war next carried us.

Chapter 22

Before we quitted France a report had somehow got into circulation that the 11th Light Dragoons would be sent to India, and the 21st, which had served there some time, return home, and be reduced. We had not long occupied the barracks at Canterbury ere the truth of this rumour was confirmed. It was announced to us officially that early in the coming year the embarkation would take place; and leave to visit their friends was accordingly granted to such of the men as chose to apply for it. I was in the number of those who considered it expedient not to refuse the indulgence. A furlough of fourteen days was in consequence conceded to me; and I spent the brief season very happily among my relatives in London; several of whom, -- my mother being included in the list, -- I was destined never to see again.

Late in the month of January, 1819, we marched from Canterbury to Chatham, where our horses were taken from us, and our saddlery and arms carefully packed for a long voyage. We lingered here about a week, at the termination of which the route arrived; and an easy journey of eight miles carried us to Gravesend. There lay two fine Indiamen, the "Atlas," of 1200 tons, and the "Streatham," of 800; on board of which we were appointed to take our passage: and soon after midday on the 7th of February we were all, with our baggage, embarked. I need not describe the scene of discomfort and confusion which greeted us.

Even when she is not the bearer of troops, an Indiaman, making her last preparations for the outward trip, is, of all sea-going craft, the least inviting; and when to her ordinary lumber is added the presence of several hundred soldiers and their effects, the confusion is increased fourfold. Nevertheless, in the present, as in other instances, the inconveniences to which we were subjected soon passed away; and a considerate captain, and abundance of good cheer, rendered us not merely contented but merry.

I am not going to entertain my readers with a transcript from the ship's log; nor yet to describe what has been described a thousand times already, -- the order of a landsman's life while voyaging from Gravesend to Calcutta. We had the usual alternations of foul and fair weather, and we had -- or believed that we had -- more than one narrow escape from foundering; once by reason of some neglect in stopping the hause-holes, through which the sea broke with resistless violence, and again, when in the tropics, we were taken aback in a heavy squall. At the crossing of the line Neptune and his train paid us their accustomed visit. Then was the ceremony of shaving gone through. Then were fire-engine, water-buckets, and slush-barrels brought into play. Then were men's tempers tried, -- without in any case failing them, -- and mirth and revelry kept the ship for a season in an uproar. Moreover, flocks of Mother Carey's pretty little chickens followed us round the Cape, -- the huge albatross did not disdain to visit us, -- and a bird called the booby, lighting on our yards, permitted himself to be knocked down with a stick or with the hand. Why should I speak of sharks, flying-fish, or dolphins, -- why try to convey to such as have not looked upon the scene something like an idea of the tropical ocean, as well when it is calm and quiet in its might, as when the hurricane sweeps over it? All these are matters on which I cannot think of touching, -- partly because they have no novelty about them, -- partly because to be rightly understood they must be made the objects of men's outward senses; not offered as material on which the imagination may employ itself.

Neither is it worth while to go into a minute detail of the little accidents which befel in the course of our voyage; or the sports and amusements by which we cheated it of its tedium. We had men fall overboard and get drowned. We had one case of suicide, -- where the victim of her own headstrong temper was a woman. We had a death or two, followed by the committal of the bodies to the deep; and we were all much solemnized as we watched their downward progress. On the other hand, the ship being supplied with a very fair band, it was our custom of an afternoon to get up a sort of universal ball to the sound of its playing. On these occasions the officers and other passengers, of whom several were ladies, used to dance on the quarter-deck; the ship's company did the same thing on the forecastle, and the soldiers and their wives footed it away merrily in the waist. On the whole, therefore, we got on pleasantly enough. Nor let me forget to mention the degree of respect which was invariably paid to the Lord's Day. As often as Sunday came round all hands, -- seamen as well as soldiers, arrayed themselves in their best. They then assembled, at a given hour, upon the quarter-deck, -- the soldiers occupying one side, the women and children the other, the seamen standing towards the booms, and the cabin passengers close to the cuddy, that they might accompany the captain, who, with great solemnity and reverence, read the morning service of the church. Neither did our sense of what was due to God's Sabbath end there. The day was a day of rest, -- as much so, at least, as the nature of our situation would allow; for no more work was imposed upon the seamen than was absolutely necessary; and we were universally left to our own meditations.

In this manner a certain number of months ran their course, during the progress of which we not only never planted foot on shore, but never once cast anchor. It would be contrary to truth, therefore, were I not to acknowledge that we were getting heartily tired of our confinement on board of ship, when one day a voice from the masthead gave the joyous announcement of land on the starboard bow. There was an immediate rush to that side of the vessel, and hundreds of eyes wearied themselves in the endeavour to realize the promise which the look-out man had given. But the coast of Bengal, especially about the mouth of the Hoogley, is, as all the world knows, flat as well as barren; and though the breeze blew in our favour, and we steadily moved along, a good hour elapsed ere from the deck symptoms of what we sought could be discovered. At last, however, the glitter of a gilded pagoda in the sun attracted our attention. A loud and joyful shout rent the air; we heartily congratulated one another on the prospect of a speedy deliverance, and walked the deck for the remainder of the day in the highest state of excitement.

The anchor was dropped that night off the Pagodas, for the first time since our gallant crew had heaved it in Portsmouth harbour. By early dawn next morning we started again, and tiding along, found ourselves by-and-by abreast of the wild and tangled island of Saugor. How shall I describe the succession of wonders which from that time forth put in claims upon our attention? In the first place, every object on which the eye fell, the herbage, the buildings, the boats, and the people that manned them, had about them a character to which the mere power of novelty gave an indescribable interest. The first boat that boarded us contained four men, all black as ebony, and naked, except that a girdle was round their waists. These were regarded as persons of a very humble class, and we were right; but the next cargo that arrived bore themselves with so much dignity, that we felt as if we were in the presence of some native princes. They wore long loose robes of very white cotton, large turbans begilded and otherwise adorned, and moved about with a step so slow and measured, that it

191

was impossible to divest oneself of a feeling of restraint, as often as one stood near them. My astonishment may therefore be conceived, when I saw one of the ship's officers seat himself on a gun-carriage forward, and a native prince produce an enormous razor and set about the process of shaving him. Neither did the matter end there. The same grave and reverend personage, after completing this process with the third mate, offered, with a profound salam, to give me a specimen of his skill, to which, with a laugh, I submitted. I had never been so well or so pleasantly shaved before, and I stuck to my original barber for several years afterwards.

The Hoogley becomes at a short distance from its mouth so beset with shoals and sandbanks that the large Indiamen are compelled to cast anchor; the passengers and goods being transferred to vessels of more inconsiderable bulk, are in them conveyed as far as Fort William. It was on the third day from our arrival off the Pagodas, that we got into a couple of brigs, which, taking advantage of every turn of the tide, bore us slowly on our way. Nothing could be more delicious than that voyage. The river becoming narrow as we receded from its mouth, introduced us to a succession of exquisite landscapes, every feature in which was to us as captivating as it was novel. Here embowered beneath the branches of the clustering banyan, over which would rise the stately stem of the cocoa-nut, might be seen some mosque or pagoda, or it might be the country-house of a native of rank; there a cluster of huts overshadowed by rich foliage, which was all strange to us, and therefore beautiful. Then again the country, though universally flat, was clothed in a livery of the freshest green; for we reached our destination in the very middle of the rains, and the verdure of the East, during the rainy season, is exquisite. But I must not continue these details; Indian scenery, like the scenery of other regions, must be seen, either in reality, or on the canvass, to be estimated aright. All the descriptions in the world would not excite in the reader's mind one distinct idea, wherefore I cease to weary him and myself by any further efforts to accomplish an impossibility.

There is nothing so tempting nor so dangerous to the European on his first arrival in the country as the fruit which is pressed upon him by the native dealers. A long confinement on board of ship, during the larger portion of which no luxury of the sort has come before him, gives additional value to the odoriferous poison in his eyes; and unless he shall have been forewarned against it, and possess over and above a large share of self-control, he is sure to eat in more than moderation, and to suffer. I ate, and I suffered; for the day before we reached the landing-place I was in a violent fever.

If you are ever taken ill in India, you are not, in cases like this, kept long in suspense as to the probable issue of your complaint. I was in bed with a raging fever one day, on the next I was sufficiently recovered to disembark with the baggage; and proceeded though not without a good deal of suffering, to take up my residence in Fort William. The fort itself is a magnificent structure, well defended with broad ditches, and covered by a succession of works, on which many heavy cannon are mounted. But the circumstance which attracts, in a principal degree, the stranger's admiration, is the exceeding care which is taken to keep it clean and well ventilated. Every day the sewers are washed out and sprinkled with quicklime; while, ere sunrise, the sweepers are at work, not only as often as occasion seems to require, but much more frequently. Moreover, the inmates of Fort William have other than human guardians of their health, so far, at least, as health is liable to be affected by the presence or removal of putrefying garbage. Every body has heard of the bird called the Adjutant, which walks about, respected, and therefore tame, and feeds upon carrion of every sort, from the body of the mouse up to the human frame, of which numerous specimens are, every tide, washed down the Ganges. A strange-looking creature he is -- that Adjutant -- with his bald head and his ashen-gray wings, and his portly form lifting his bald head nearly four feet above the surface of the earth. And then, when the heat of the day comes, away he goes into the skies, ascending so far that you can observe only the shadow of his form in the sunbeam.

The Adjutant is greatly respected by all classes of people, neither is he much of a plunderer; but this is more than can be said for a species of hawk which also frequents Fort William and its vicinity in great numbers. Nothing can escape the quickness and the daring of that depredator. If a cook pass from the cookhouse to the barracks, he will dart down upon the basket which the man carries on his head, and take possession at one swoop of its contents. Indeed I have seen a hawk fairly fasten upon a bone which a soldier was picking, and wrest it out of his hand and from between his teeth. Neither is the fort free from the visits of troops of jackals, which make their way through posterns and lower embrasures after nightfall, and break the sleep, besides awakening the fears of strangers, who have not become accustomed to them. The jackal, however, at least as we find hint here, is a very harmless and timid animal. He will run away with whatever morsels of animal food your own or your attendant's carelessness may have left in his way; but he never ventures to look man in the face, and flees from the barking of a watch-dog.

The buildings within the fort are very commodious and handsome. Besides some noble barracks, capable of containing at least 3000 men, and casemates where a like number may be lodged, there are the houses or apartments of all the functionaries, such as the governor, surgeons, storekeepers, chaplain, and so forth; with a church well-built and exceedingly commodious, an arsenal, and magazines out of number. I believe that the fort itself mounts, or is capable of mounting, 1000 pieces of cannon. It is likewise well stocked with small arms, shot, shells, powder, and other munitions of war; and is enriched, besides, with a very curious collection of native weapons, all of them taken during the progress of the struggles which raised the power of England in the East to the height which it now occupies. Then again the bazaar, portioned out into all manner of departments, and abounding in every article of which either native or European might be expected to stand in need; -- the vegetable market, the fruit market, the stalls on which clothing was spread forth, the tables of the money-changers, and the money-changers themselves calling out, from amid their bags of gold, silver, copper, and shells, invitations for the visiters to deal with them; all these sights and sounds, and many more which I have not now leisure to describe, even if I minutely recollected them, kept both the outward senses and the inward thoughts constantly employed, and sent me home, day after day, full of wonder.

Nor let me forget, while endeavouring to convey to others some idea of the sort of impressions which a first acquaintance with Calcutta produced upon myself, to make mention of the style in which we, private soldiers, lived, and the degree of deference that was paid to us by the natives. For example, having reached our quarters greatly fatigued, and seeing a number of cane-bottomed beds or sofas arranged round the room, I slipped off my clothes with all speed, and throwing myself on one of them, soon fell asleep. I did not awake till about four in the morning, when there was a great bustle in the place. For a whole troop of natives entered, swept and washed out the room, spread some tables with nice clean cloths, and by-and-by brought in breakfast. Meanwhile, I went in search of my clothes; but, lo! they were gone. I inquired for them eagerly, and was yet in considerable alarm, when an Hindoo stooping down, began to unlace my boots; and before I could well conceive what it was that he meant to effect, they were both stripped from my feet. Well, thought I, if we are to pay for all this attendance, the king's allowance will not go far to keep us; but as I saw that others resigned themselves freely to what seemed to be their fate, I too gave way, and the natives held their course. The result was, that without any trouble to ourselves, we found our clothing and accoutrements cleaned, a sumptuous breakfast spread forth, and nothing more required from us but that we should partake, at our ease, of the goods which the gods provided. Exactly as the clock struck eight a dozen cooks entered, followed by as many servants, all of them bearing on their heads baskets of savoury viands, and with stewed steaks, eggs, white loaves, butter, and coffee, before us, the fault would have been entirely our own, had we failed to fare sumptuously. So it was likewise at dinner time. We had no trouble -- no anxiety; for the same attentive natives once more covered our tables with every thing which in that climate is either usual, or accounted a luxury. I must confess, that my astonishment knew, at the outset, no bounds. Yet, it is marvellous how soon we become accustomed to usages, which, when first seen, surprise -- or, it may be, vex us. I had not continued long in India ere not these marks of attention alone, but others of a more equivocal nature, were received by me as a mere matter of course. Certainly the Indian soil is that in which luxurious habits grow with a rapidity unknown elsewhere.

We had not been long at Fort William, ere Lord Moira, then governor-general, reviewed us; and we received orders to proceed to Cawnpore, whither we were to be transported in boats. I had never been in perfect health since we first entered the Hoogley; and now the sickness broke out on me with such violence that I was removed by the Doctor's direction to the general hospital. For eight-and-twenty days I continued in such a state, that my life was despaired of; and the origin of the whole was my own imprudence in indulging too freely in the fruit of the country. Thanks to an excellent constitution, however, and the careful nursing which I received, the crisis of the fever passed, and I recovered; though not till my sufferings had taught me the lesson that the folly of an hour in matters affecting the body as well as the mind, not unfrequently lays up for him who is guilty of it, days, or months, or even years, of useless self-reproach.

I was still an invalid when the regiment embarked in the boats, which were to convey it by the channel of the Ganges to Cawnpore;

and being unable to move, the doctor caused me to be carried in a palankeen, and lodged with the sick in the hospital barge. Of the commencement of the voyage, and of the circumstances attending it, I am therefore unable to speak, except upon the report of others. But long before we reached Dinapore, which is accounted, I believe, the half-way station, my health came back, and great was my enjoyment in consequence. I have certainly not much to say in commendation of our transports, whether allusion be made to their seaworthiness, or to the extent of accommodation which they afforded. Wretched affairs they were, being, like the country boats in general, almost on a level in their deck with the stream, and in every pore pervious to the water; no pitch being used in caulking, the loose cotton is soon pushed aside, and then through all the seams the water makes its way, giving ample occupation to one man in baling, and to another in the fruitless endeavour to stop up the yawning chasms with fresh material.

The current of the Ganges is, during the rainy season, very strong. Whole fields -- do not mean the produce -- but the very soil of the flat country on either bank, are swept away by it; and if, as not unfrequently happens, the wind set in an opposite direction, the swell becomes tremendous, and the danger to the navigator is great. More than once it seemed to me that the destruction of the frail bark in which we had taken our passage, was inevitable. Yet the Bengalees are in their own way skilful navigators, and by some means or another they contrived to carry us through all our difficulties. Once, I remember, even they considered themselves in a very delicate plight. We arrived at an enormous lake, or inundation. The wind blew a hurricane -- the waters were white with foam, and the very means of making fast the boats were wanting. After a good deal of hesitation, our crew faced the danger, and their gallantry carried them through; but there were other barges there which would not venture to follow the example, and these suffered severely. Happily no lives were lost; and we all arrived the same night at Dinapore.

Chapter 23

Dinapore is a station for an infantry regiment; and were it not that lying low, it is, during the hot season, very unhealthy it would present many features of attraction even to the European. The country round is extremely rich and well wooded, while an excellent bazaar under the management of the quarter-master, as these military markets always are, supplies the troops with every article of consumption of which they can stand in need. The barracks, too, are commodious and well arranged, having a large grass plat in the centre of the square, and ample stabling attached to them; and though the distance from Calcutta be not less than five hundred miles, the accommodation afforded by a water conveyance appears materially to abridge it. It was in Dinapore that, for the first tinge, I encountered elephants holding their way through the narrow streets of the regimental bazaar, yet injuring no one; and as the spectacle surprised me very much, so the expression of my wonder drew forth from others, familiar with the animal's habits, many tales of their extreme sagacity, of which the following is one.

A particular elephant, which was pointed out to me, had been in the habit, as often as it passed a confectioner's stand, to receive from the keeper of the stand, in the very heart of the bazaar, a parcel of sweetmeats. The owner of the beast becoming aware of the custom gave the elephant's keeper money, and desired him not to restrict his charge in his recreation, but to pay for what the elephant got regularly once a week. The mohut, a dishonest man, kept the money to himself, in consequence of which the confectioner, who began to grow tired of feeding such a customer on credit, applied to him for payment; it was refused, and the confectioner, as a matter of course, protested that he would disburse no more sweetmeats. Well, it came to pass once upon a time, that the elephant arrived as usual in front of the stall; he held out his trunk, offered his accustomed salutation by grunting, yet received nothing. On the contrary, the baker loaded the mohut with abuse, and he and his gigantic charge by-and-by passed on; they proceeded to the tank, whither they were going to water, and the elephant drank as usual. They then returned -- but the elephant would stop again in front of the stall, and the confectioner again assailed him and his driver with the language of reproach. A summary punishment awaited him. The elephant, pointing his trunk with great accuracy, let fly among the pastry and sugar-plums before him such a shower of dirty water as soon reduced the whole to a state of absolute dissolution. As was to be expected, the confectioner complained to the owner of the beast, upon which all the facts of the case became known, and the poor artiste having been remunerated for all the losses which he had sustained, a fresh mohut was found to take care of his customer.

Nothing could exceed, on very many accounts, the degree of interest which attached to the remainder of our voyage after we quitted Dinapore. The farther we penetrated into the heart of the country the more were we struck with the peculiarity of the scenery and the strangeness, at least to us, of the customs of those who inhabited it. Beautiful villages lay here and there along the river's bank, all of them clustering round their own pagodas; and each having its baths, its oratories, and terraces by which the inhabitants approached to cast upon the sacred stream their votive offerings. The consequence was, that as often as we looked towards the shore we beheld little groups of both sexes at their devotions, while the very bows of our vessel were garlanded with the innumerable bouquets which, tossed in at places higher up, came floating down the stream to meet us. I have counted scores of these rich garlands, throughout which the queenly lotus always shone conspicuous, bespangling the surface of the water at the same time. Nor could I repress a feeling, almost of involuntary reverence, for the sort of religion, wild and extravagant as it is, which led its votaries to do honour to the Deity by so simple yet so elegant a custom.

In making a voyage up the Ganges you invariably bring-to at nightfall. The native boatmen have, indeed, no idea that it is possible to hold their course in the dark, and as their provisions, simple though they be, require cooking, it is at night that the process is invariably gone through. A very striking scene it consequently is after your cables are made fast, and under the trees, that grow to the water's edge, dozens of fires are lighted. Woe, however, to the European who approaches too near to these fires while the rice that is required for the evening meal may be undergoing the necessary preparation. If he disregard the shouts and signals of the natives, they throw both rice and their cooking utensils in the fire, and then, for the amount of remuneration, the transgressor is entirely at their mercy, for let the claim be what it may the officer is sure to allow it. But it was not the boatman's meal alone which was dressed at this hour. Our own native cooks chose the same season, as indeed necessity required, wherein to make ready for our use the rations of each morrow; and once the circumstance of their doing so was productive of a little adventure which was long after spoken of among us with much interest.

The case was this. We brought up one evening, as usual, and made first our boat to the roots of a large tree that grew close to the water's edge. We then landed, as our invariable custom was, and watched the cooks first light the fires, and then get the provisions in order for dressing. But instead of going on with that very necessary operation, they all, with one accord, fell upon their knees, and lifting up their hands, began, in a monotonous sort of howl, to pour out their prayers to the moon. At first we were astonished, then we became irritated; but by-and-by, on looking up, we saw that an eclipse had begun. It was in vain that some of us urged these devotees to leave the moon to herself, and to dress our supper. So long as the shadow was on the moon's disc, they remained on their knees, praying earnestly; and when at length she shone forth again in her glory, they rose, clapped their hands, and shouted vehemently. It was a striking sight that of these naked, yet robust men, all offering up their adorations to one of the host of heaven: neither was the issue less remarkable. They dressed our meal readily enough, which we consumed, and then went on board to sleep. But they spent the whole of the night in singing and dancing, as the best mode of expressing their joy at the moon's deliverance from her enemy.

Among other strange sights which greeted us while prosecuting that upward voyage, I must not forget to notice the alligators which lay among the shine on the river's bank, like so many logs of trees, and rolled themselves into the water only when we approached them. I had never seen the monster before, and was in consequence a good deal alarmed by him, especially after I had listened to sundry tales of his great ferocity and exceeding strength, both by land and water. But the only practical effect produced by this commencement of our acquaintance, was to put a stop to the evening baths, in which we had heretofore indulged. One of the brutes was wounded by Captain Elliot, of the 11th, and after a fierce struggle, secured by a party of natives; and a closer acquaintance with his huge jaws and sharp teeth, had no tendency, it must be confessed, to reconcile us to their proportions.

Onwards and onwards we went, the river narrowing slightly as we drew nearer to its source, and a novelty of some kind or other greeting us at every stage. One day we passed a huge rock, which rises upright out of the centre of the stream, and which the violence of the current has, in the course of ages, well nigh cut in twain. It is surmounted by a hut, in which dwells a Fakir, one of that class, half-mendicant, half-enthusiast, with which all parts of India abound, and whose habits are now familiar to every well-read person. How they levy contributions of rice and bread from door to door, I need not therefore tell, neither is it worth while to describe their voluntary penances -- their years of torture as they stand motionless, never sitting or lying down to rest, and often holding one or both arms in the air; their horrid exhibitions on the swing, when a rusty hook is driven through the skin of the back, and themselves are whirled round, shouting and apparently triumphant, for half an hour at a time. These matters are set forth so much at length in all manner of publications, that even this hasty allusion to them might well have been spared. But it is one thing to read of exhibitions so strange, and quite another to witness them; the subject may be stale to all the world besides, but it has still some interest for me.

While we were in the act of passing this rock, a numerous fleet of boats appeared in the offing, which as they approached, were seen to contain the relics of the 21st Dragoons. These men were on the passage to Calcutta, and a more miserable set of scarecrows it has never been my misfortune to behold. Climate and disease appeared to have made sad havoc with the whole of them. They were yellow and flesh-less; and a hasty attempt to open with them some conversation in passing, showed that their tempers not less than their animal moisture, had been dried up by the suns of India. For example, having fixed my eye upon a gaunt and currie-coloured serjeant, I hailed him, and proceeded to ask whether Cawnpore was a nice place, and things cheap there. "You'll find out all that for yourself," was his reply, as he turned upon me a ghastly look, "when Jack Morbus (meaning the cholera,) has brought down your buffalo hide to regulation pattern." There was something irresistibly comical in the expression of the speaker's countenance, as well as in the cankered and crabbed answer which he vouchsafed to a civil question. So we burst into a hearty laugh, and thus the two regiments passed one another.

In due time we reached Benares, the sacred city of the Hindoos, and were fortunate enough to arrive at a season when some great religious ceremony was going forward. The river was in consequence covered with votive garlands, and multitudes of both sexes were refreshing at once soul and body in the sacred stream. We did not bring-to, however, till we came opposite Ramghur -- a place of some note in this part of India, and the residence of a Raja; and there, according to custom, so soon as the boats were moored, I, with several more belonging to the detachment, landed.

There was something peculiarly delicious in these moonlight walks, as well because of the exquisite balminess of the air, as that they led us through fields of flowering cotton or luxuriant indigo, the bursting pods of which strew the pathways, and send forth a strong, yet not an overpowering, odour as you crush them under foot. On this night, however, our rambling propensities brought us into a situation of some danger, I verily believe, and certainly well calculated to alarm. I and my comrade were traversing a cotton plantation, when, looking to the right, we beheld a drove of black buffaloes feeding, by whom we were no sooner perceived than they tossed their heads into the air, and made a rush towards us. There was nothing for it but to take to our heels, so we ran as fast as our legs would carry us, till we reached a quickset hedge, through which, at some cost both to skin and garments, we managed to squeeze. We were thus saved from the buffaloes; but on advancing towards the entrance of the village, our horror may be conceived when we found ourselves suddenly within twenty yards of what we mistook for a tiger. The beast was lying on a sort of bamboo cot, and seemed to be asleep, on which I pulled my comrade by the sleeve, and we quietly but rapidly retreated. Our consternation, however, was almost immediately changed into pure wonder: we saw some natives approach the beast, pat him on the head, and walk on; and being thus encouraged, we drew near in like manner, and saluted the object of our terror. It was not a tiger, but a chita, or hunting leopard; nevertheless, he did not seem to acknowledge our acquaintance so freely as he had done that of the Hindoos; for he opened his eyes with an expression so suspicious that we were heartily glad to leave him to his own reflections. We accordingly pushed on to the Raja's palace, which we found to be a large brick building, surrounded by iron rails, and having gazed with wonder at the quantity of confectioners' shops that abutted upon it, we turned our faces back again towards the boats. A considerable detour carried us wide of the buffaloes, and we reached our sleeping berths in peace.

From Ramghur we proceeded to Allahabad -- the Holy City, or City of God -- beside which the Jumna pours its waters into the

Ganges, both, at the point of junction, possessing a character, of great sanctity. Here stands the tomb of the good and gallant Marquis Cornwallis; here, too, is an ancient fort, within the walls of which there used to be one of those sacred columns which the Hindoos adore, which was indeed standing when we reached the place, but has since been thrown down. It was here, after having the boats dragged with infinite difficulty over a long succession of shallows, that for the first time we encountered a tornado in the power of its might, from the overwhelming violence of which our frail craft escaped only through the foresight of the crews in mooring them after they had been fairly run on shore. I shall never forget the terrible effect of that whirlwind, which, had it endured another hour, must have shaken the whole country into chaos. The loftiest and strongest trees either bent before it like reeds or snapped asunder, and were then tossed into the air; while the clouds of dust and sand which it swept along its course, blinded our vision, and seriously incommoded our respiration. Happily for us and for all that lay within its influence, it did not continue more than half an hour, though for more than twice that space we could follow its onward progress, as it swept away from us in a straight line, carrying devastation and terror over a large extent of country.

We had a good many deaths during the passage, which lasted in all three months, and we buried our dead in deep graves which we dug along the river's edge. We might have saved ourselves the trouble. Our right wing, which preceded us a little way, had suffered in like manner, and they also deposited the remains of their comrades where the earth could cover them; but their graves, when we reached them, were all tenantless; the wolves and jackalls had dug the bodies up, and the scattered fragments of military clothing with which the sides of the different pits were covered, showed that the wild beasts had not left their lifeless owners to the tedious process of natural decay.

On the 28th of October, 1819, we arrived at the place of our destination, and disembarking at an early hour next morning, were marched forthwith into barracks. We found them extremely commodious and comfortable; and as great care had been taken to put them in order for our reception, we counted, not without reason, on spending our time here with much satisfaction; for Cawnpore contains a large garrison, and is besides the residence of many persons of distinction, of gentlemen in the civil service of the Company, of merchants and others, and these have provided for themselves every accessory to enjoyment, not forgetting either a handsome assembly-room or a neat theatre. But it was not so much about these things as with reference to the horses which the 21st had left for our use, that my curiosity was excited. I accordingly embraced the first opportunity of visiting, along with a volunteer from that regiment, the stables; and, sure enough, the spectacle that met us there was strange enough. It was feeding-time when we entered, and the horses, -- all of them entire, -- kept up such a screaming and pawing with their fore-feet upon the floor, that I could have fancied myself, not in a cavalry stable, but in a den of wild beasts. Neither, on inquiring into the characters of the individual chargers, was the impression produced by the first general survey effaced. One was a furious kicker, -- another would tear to pieces any one on whom it could lay hold, and had actually bitten two men to death, -- a third was accustomed to dance on his hind legs for ten minutes on a stretch, and to lash out with his fore feet as if he had been a trained boxer, -- a fourth took fits of sullenness, and standing stock-still would strike with his heels right and left, so as to throw an entire squadron into confusion. In a word, a set of brutes more vicious was represented never to have come together, and it is but fair to add that on first mounting we so found them. But a few sharp field-days, with a little stinting of corn, gradually tamed them. Several men received hurts, from bites, kicks, and falls, -- many were run away with, till horse and rider became accustomed to each other, -- but in the end we proved ourselves their masters. And then a very hardy, if not a very fleet, species of cattle we found them.

We reached Cawnpore at the most agreeable season of the year; and up to the month of March had little to complain of. To be sure the volunteers from the 21st, who joined our ranks, proved to be, as such persons usually are, troublesome, and in several instances not very worthy characters. Still we got along pretty well till the hot winds began to blow, and then restrictions to which it was judged expedient to subject us brought the true tempers of our seasoned comrades to the test. They murmured against the regulations of the regiment. They thwarted and interrupted the non-commissioned officers in the discharge of their duty, and took at last to stoning them as often as they visited the barracks after dark. The colonel would not suffer this; so he called them all together, and assured them that the very first who should be detected in an act of insubordination would find cause to repent it. There needed no more to make these bad men desperate. They laid the blame chiefly on one Corporal Irwin, -- and they swore among themselves that they would have their revenge.

Corporal Irwin might be a little sharp; but he was a just man in the execution of his duty: nor did he ever exact from others more than he was always ready to perform himself. For this he became a marked man; and one evening, after giving out the orders for the morrow, a scoundrel of the name of Hislop fired at him from behind a pillar, and desperately wounded him near the shoulder. The corporal fell, and the assassin endeavoured to escape; but he was instantly seized. For we, -- the old hands of the 11th, -- were much attached both to our regiment, considered as a body, and to the officers and non-commissioned officers belonging to it; and finding the turn which affairs had taken among these strangers, we were determined that they should be taught that they would receive no countenance from us. The corporal being carried to the hospital there lost his arm. He did not, however, die, -- at least, not immediately, -- but his constitution received such a shock, that after undergoing the amputation there was not vigour enough in him to accomplish a rally. He lingered several months, and then expired. With respect again to Hislop, his fate was sealed. Being put into double irons, he was handed over to the care of the principal jailer in the place; and having been in due time tried and found guilty of an attempt to murder, he was condemned to death. He was hanged, as he deserved to be, in the sight of the assembled garrison.

Chapter 24

It was now the season of the year when the maladies peculiar to this climate usually show themselves; and, in spite of all the precautions that were used to hinder it, fever and cholera both broke out among us. Terrible was the havoc which they made in our ranks. At breakfast-time, or on the early parade, ten men might appear in perfect health, -- within an hour half the number would be taken ill, and ere sunset the greater portion of them would die. The hospital became, as may be imagined, a scene of complicated horrors. Providence was kind to me, so that as a patient I had no cause to visit it; but hearing one day that my cousin had been carried thither in a raging fever, I proceeded to nurse him. I never saw such a sight. With respect to my poor relative, he was already insensible, and in less than half an hour he expired. But elsewhere objects that both shocked and harrowed met my gaze on every side. There stood the doctor, -- a kind and a skilful man, -- with his sleeves tucked up and his arms crimsoned. Several assistants were near with basins in their hands to receive the blood which he took from the sick men's veins, while of the sick themselves, some were raving mad, others gloomy and desponding, others wholly insensible -- the spark going out in these last, one after another. There could be little of order or regularity in disposing of the bodies of those who in such numbers, and so rapidly, paid the last debt of nature. Every morning a couple of carts came to the hospital, and in these the corpses were removed to the public cemetery, where not a few, attended only by the comrades who loved them most, went to the sleep which knows no waking. Let me not, however, dwell upon events, the remembrance of which will hair by me through life, and ever in sorrow; indeed, I will quit this subject altogether after I shall have described a little adventure which befel me, not unconnected with it, though partaking more of the ludicrous than the pathetic.

When sickness broke out our men became divided into two classes, one of which the thought of the precariousness of their position sobered, while in the other it produced diametrically the opposite effect. These last, in order to drown care, drank hard and lived merrily; and, strange as it may sound, it is nevertheless true, that of them nine out of ten escaped. To my shame be it spoken, the example of these reckless livers had more influence over me than that which the graver men set, and I drank, in consequence, harder during the prevalence of that epidemic than ever I did before or have ever done since; the result on one occasion was this.

There was a standing order from the surgeon, that whenever any of the men were observed to take to their beds, or lounge upon them at unbecoming seasons, the serjeant of the day should direct them to be removed at once to the hospital. It happened, once upon a time, that my comrade and I having gone together for the purpose, as I well remember, of purchasing a glass for my watch, we were asked by a native merchant whether or not we should like to be supplied with a bottle of superlatively good wine. Such a suggestion was not to be neglected, so we adjourned to his tent, and there, together with a little bread and cheese, consumed between us three bottles of Cape, which the honest old man sold to us for genuine Madeira. The wine proved too much for us. To walk home with it was out of the question, so we ordered a covered bullock-car, drawn by two animals, and jogged along in this clumsy vehicle towards the barracks. Arrived there, nothing would content us but a dram of arrack; and the vile spirit coming immediately upon the scarcely less deleterious wine, placed us at once hors de combat. We staggered to our beds and were both fast asleep in a moment.

How long I had lain in a state of unconsciousness I cannot tell; but a vivid dream, in which I saw that the regiment had marched, leaving me behind, at length awoke me. It was pitch dark. I sat up in my bed, rubbed my eyes, tried to collect my thoughts, but could not. One of my arms, moreover, being somewhat stiff, tended still more to confuse me. In a word, I was completely distracted. Accordingly I stretched my hand towards the wall, in order to ascertain whether boots, saddle, accoutrements, &c., continued to hang where it was my custom to arrange them. They were not there -- and the conviction became strong that it was no idle dream of which I was the victim, but that I had indeed been abandoned by my comrades. Full of alarm, I sprang out of bed; and determined to make my way to the apartment in which troop A used to be stationed, I rushed towards what I conceived to be the bolted door of my own room, and pressed the whole weight of my body against it.

A door it doubtless was which in this strange way I had encountered, and as it did not happen to be so much as on the latch, the result to myself was a roll heels over head. Not having sustained any injury, however, I immediately gathered myself up again, and in the very bitterness of grief shouted out, "Are you all gone?"

A feeble voice, the tones of which were not unfamiliar to me, replied by demanding, "Is that you, George?"

"To be sure it is," was my answer. "In the name of fortune where am I?"

"Don't you know?" was the reply.

"Know!" answered I, "how should I? Is the regiment gone, and are you and I left to die here together?"

"No, to be sure not, but you are in the hospital."

"In the what?"

"In the hospital -- you and your comrade were brought in yesterday afternoon, both labouring under apoplectic fits; and if you had done what was right and becoming, you would have been a dead man by this time."

In an instant the whole truth flashed across me, and the adventure appeared so ridiculous, that, hurrying back to my bed, I there indulged in a hearty fit of laughing. Neither was the disposition to be merry removed when daylight exhibited my comrade, lying on the opposite side of the room, and wondering, as I had done when I first awoke, where he was, or whether his identity had not changed. The result of the whole affair was, however, this. After learning that the serjeant on duty, a young and rash man, had ordered us to be carried into hospital, without so much as waking us to ascertain how we were, and that the surgeon took from each of us on the instant, thirty ounces of blood, the loss of which only caused us to sleep the more soundly, we were given to understand that we should again be visited in our turns by the medical staff, as well as by the colonel and adjutant of the regiment. Accordingly, at the fitting time, the whole of these gentlemen entered, and our cases were stated to the commandant, not, as I imagined, without a very quizzical expression in the countenance of him who reported upon us. We, too, were sorely puzzled to keep our gravity; but the mock examination ended in our being told to return to our quarters, and to take care how we put ourselves wantonly in the way of again being removed, as apoplectic subjects, into the hospital.

There died of the fever at this time not fewer than one hundred and twelve men, besides women and children, belonging to the 11th Dragoons. Our excellent surgeon also, Dr. O'Mally, fell a sacrifice to his indefatigable zeal and attention, and Captain Nowlan and the paymaster soon followed. Neither was the mortality confined to us; of the 87th infantry, as well as the Company's artillery, many sunk under the disease, and the deaths among the native troops were to the full as numerous. At last, however, the monsoons set in, and with them came a complete relief from the pressure of the disease; occasionally a man would die, but the violence of the distemper had passed away, and we were enabled in consequence to enjoy ourselves both within doors and without, as far at least as a ceaseless fall of heavy rain would allow; and in truth the violence with which the floods came down surpassed every thing of which I could have formed an idea. I have seen the barrack-square converted in less than an hour into a tank or pond, in which there was a depth of two feet of water, through which swarms of small fish were swimming, very much, as may be imagined, to our astonishment, and greatly to the delight of the natives. Neither were we long left in doubt as to the causes of the phenomenon. One day I was suddenly invited to watch with my comrades the progress of a water-spout, the formation of which was going on at no great distance from the cantonments. I saw a column of water rise from a flooded meadow, and rush up, as it seemed, to meet a dense cloud that had gathered over it; the sun, too, happening to shine out at the moment, and to cast his rays obliquely upon the pillar, the effect was more beautiful than I have language to describe; and when in a few minutes afterwards the continuity of the pillar was broken, the spray from its lower portion fell over us as if it had been a shower of diamond sparks. It was not so with the heavily-laden cloud, which likewise in due time discharged its contents upon our heads. We read and hear of rain that resembles the pouring of water out of buckets: I never till that day was able to believe that there was any substantial truth in the simile. Nor was this all; with the rush of waters came down shoals of fish, some of them of a size sufficient to excite the cupidity of the natives, who, attacking them with nets and buckets, conveyed them to their houses, and speedily converted them into material for a delicate supper.

As long as the monsoons last, the whole surface of the country is under water, and for a little while after the floods abate, the sterility is excessive. But in process of time vegetation begins, and the grass springs up, and the flowers blow with a rapidity which to the European strangers seems well nigh miraculous. Neither can the salubrity of the climate, while this state of things continues, be surpassed in any part of the world. I never experienced a more delicious temperature than that to which we were generally subject, from the end of October to the beginning of March. I never beheld a scene more delicately luxuriant and rich than the fields and meadows and woods presented during a considerable portion of that interval.

At last the season of relief came round; and the 8th light dragoons having arrived from Meerut, we received orders to pack up and march, for the purpose of occupying the station which they had abandoned. To such as have not witnessed in India the march of a regiment of cavalry, it would be no easy task to convey an idea of the extraordinary spectacle which is presented by it. Let my readers bear in mind, that troops never move in our Eastern possessions without carrying their market and their market people along with them. The bazaar, indeed, is not attached to the station, but to the corps: and the dealers being all regularly enrolled, must either go with the regiment whithersoever it may proceed, or cease to hold their licences as merchants. Hence, the night preceding the day on which the corps is to set out, all the tents in the bazaar are struck. Away then proceeds the motley crew, bullocks, cows, camels, horses, and here and there elephants, transporting their goods; and as the site of each day's encampment is beforehand explained to them, they are generally ready to receive the troops when they arrive, and to provide them with the necessary refreshments. Meanwhile, at the first sound of the trumpet, the tents required to lodge the regiment on its march are packed upon the backs of camels and elephants. The former class of animals carries one tent, the latter two; and when the enormous size of the machine is taken into account, as well as the pegs, lines, and mallets required in pitching it, the strength of both beasts of burden -- especially of the elephant -- surpasses our power of computation. Moreover, as each baggage-animal has its company of attendants, each troop horse its native groom, and each man his servant, and each officer his half dozen at least, I am sure that I do not place the numbers too high when I say, that for one trooper there are at least fifteen followers in the camp. I cannot, indeed, compare the march of the eleventh to any thing more appropriate than the flight of the Israelites out of Egypt; for the column, though in point of numbers respectable enough, was absolutely obscured even on the line of march, by the swarms of men, women, children, and beasts of burden, that surrounded it.

The march which begins at an early hour in the morning, generally continues till about nine, when the tents are pitched, and other preparations made to pass both the day and night on the ground. It is astonishing to see the enormous extent of that encampment. Our single regiment, for example, covered much more than a square mile of country, for the horses are picketed at wide intervals from each other, and the tents of the several troops pitched so as to keep the horses of the one apart from those of the other. Some way in rear again, stand the officers' tents, all set up in a row, like the street of a town; while further back still, is the bazaar -- itself a town, and a very bustling town too, where every thing that is to be had in Calcutta may be purchased, though the corps be in the very heart of the jungle. Neither is the process by which we arrive at this state of order more akin to the operations of a mounted regiment in Europe, than the aspect of the Indian camp, resembles that of a camp in the western hemisphere. The word is no sooner given to halt, and dismount, than we hand over our charges to our native grooms. By them they are led to water, dressed, fed, and otherwise arranged, while we apply ourselves first to the business of breakfast, and then to the search after as many novelties, as the state of the bazaar may afford. But if we lead an easy life by day, it cannot be said that we enjoy much of quiet during the night: then all the brutes, whether horses or camels seem to break loose. There is a continual floundering over the tent-cords -- a continual shouting of people -- a continual neighing of steeds, insomuch that he who has self command enough to close an eye, or snatch an hour's sound sleep, need not distrust his own power of obtaining rest should he be thrown into any situation whatever.

I have neither the design nor the necessary qualifications to describe either the customs of the people, or the political condition of the country. Abler pens than mine have accomplished both tasks before me, -- neither have I any ambition to bring my poor talents into competition with those of the men who wielded them. But the incidents which befel myself, and the little adventures that occured to others, I am bound to relate, even at the risk of saying over again what others have said, far more pleasantly.

On the seventh day from the evacuation of Cawnpore, we reached Feruckabad, which we found occupied by a considerable garrison, consisting entirely of the Company's troops. It is a pleasant place, having a market, which is well supplied with vegetables, more especially with the potato, of which a short while previous to our visit, the natives had never seen a specimen; and being built upon one of the banks of the Ganges, it enjoys at the same time the means of easy and direct transit for its produce. We did not however linger here more than a few days. By easy stages we proceeded onwards; and on the 6th of December, arrived at the place of our destination.

Meerut, which lies beyond Cawnpore somewhere about two hundred and seventy-five miles, struck me as being by far the most desirable station which we had as yet occupied since we landed at Fort William. Situated on the edge of an extensive plain, over which the winds from every quarter sweep freely, it is, beyond all question, more congenial to the constitutions of Europeans than any of the towns or cantonments that lie nearer the sea. Moreover, it forms the headquarters of a large force, consisting of four troops of horse artillery, of one European, and one native cavalry regiment, of one regiment of European infantry, and two, if not three, of Sepoys. From among these, their wives and children, as well as because of the number of civilians that are also settled there, an extremely agreeable society is formed; and the habits of all classes being gregarious in the extreme, the intercourse kept up among them was of the closest. Then again on the plain we found ample space to manoeuvre and to exercise; and for other matters, whatever a man's tastes might be in reference to his out-door pursuits and athletic amusements, here ample opportunity was afforded of indulging them. We had cricket, long-ball, and rackets, -- there was capital angling in the tanks, all of which swarmed with fine fish. There was shooting of every description, -- not omitting to particularize that of the tiger itself -- and more than one magnificent carcase brought in testified to the skill and energy with which our officers pursued it. Indeed, I may sum up my commendations of the place by stating that I have no recollection that the time hung, throughout our sojourn there, heavy on our hands; and as to its influence upon our health, we soon began to wear again the same florid hues and filled-up frames that used to adorn us at home.

We had occupied these quarters some time, -- having been visited in the interval by Sir Edward Paget, -- when a rumour began to circulate that between the East India Company and the Rajah of Bhurtpore ground of dispute had arisen. The rajah in question, Doorjan Saal, had, as is well known, set aside his nephew, and, ascending the throne, began ere long to exhibit a disposition the reverse of friendly towards the English. Inhabiting a place which had never yet opened its gates to an enemy, and which, though thrice assaulted in Lord Lake's day, had thrice repulsed the assailants, he regarded himself, and was by the people of Hindostan in general regarded, as the only king throughout that vast continent who might be expected to counterbalance or hold in check the power of the strangers. Hence, having quarrelled, no matter about what, with the English government, he could not be prevailed upon, either by threats or remonstrances, to make the smallest concession; and on our part preparations began by degrees to be made towards curing him of his obstinacy, by depriving him at once of his fortress and his power.

It is no business of mine to remark on the steps which are taken by those high in power, and, as such, quite out of the sphere of a private soldier; but I only repeat what were the universal whispers in the army when I state that every necessary arrangement for carrying on the war with vigour was begun and completed by Sir Edward Paget. He was still in command of the troops in India when the necessity for war became apparent, and he it was who managed, in spite of the heavy drain occasioned by the operations that were in progress elsewhere, to draw an army together, and to supply it with such materiel as to render a failure under the walls of this famous citadel all but impossible. He did not, however, reap either the renown or the profit which attended the execution of plans which he had wisely laid. Just before active operations began, his successor arrived from England, and, with a generosity which was considered at the moment well nigh to overpass its legitimate limits, he instantly resigned the command. Now there was no necessity for this. It was noble, indeed, and chivalrous, because it enabled another to gather the crop which his wisdom had sown, matured, and brought to the very season of harvest, -- but I do not believe that the rules of the service required it; and I know that the issues were by all ranks among us greatly deplored. I have nothing to say against Lord Combermere. He was, and is, an excellent officer, and richly merits whatever good fortune may have attended him. But Sir Edward Paget's name stands at least as high, and the soldiers that served under him could not but lament that he threw into other hands the prize for which be had played, and which he had won. However, this is a subject with which I have no concern; so I return, without further preamble, to my own narrative.

Chapter 25

The cantonments of Meerut are separated from the lower ranges of the Himalaya mountains only by the plain of which I have already spoken, and on the edge of which they are planted. So close indeed are these inviting regions to the quarters of the force, that many civilians as well as officers of rank, purchase or erect for themselves country houses among the hills, and repair thither, as to a place of shelter, during the hottest of the months. More than once I accompanied the colonel thither in the capacity of orderly, and not in any quarter of the world have I beheld scenery more varied or more truly magnificent. Even the lower ranges introduce you to defiles and passes of surpassing grandeur; beneath and beyond which lie valleys, fertile in the extreme, while in the background -- up rise those giant ridges from which the snow is never withdrawn, and over which no human foot ever has passed, or in all probability ever will pass.

It was at the close of the monsoon, in the year 1825, that a small force, of which the 11th formed a part, assembled at Meerut, under General Ochterloney, and began its march towards the Jumna. Our immediate chief was an old and infirm man, as most of the Company's generals are. Nevertheless, we felt perfect confidence in ourselves, and our own regimental officers; so we pursued our journey, nothing doubting that it would terminate in results altogether satisfactory. A few days carried us to the brink of the river, on the opposite side of which stands Multoa; a town of considerable size and great note, inasmuch as it is the residence of some of the most distinguished of the Mahomedan families which claim India as their native country. There we halted, while the infantry bridging the Jumna, by means of boats, passed over, and took up their quarters in the town. It was to no purpose, however, that the General opened a communication with the Rajah of Bhurtpore, the towers and bastions of whose lordly residence were from this point distinctly visible. Either because he credited the declarations of his priests, who assured him that his nest was unassailable, or that he was aware of the inconsiderable amount of the force by which at that moment he was threatened, the Rajah turned to every proposal a deaf ear; and we being by far too weak to enter upon more active operations, were forced to maintain for some time an attitude of extreme watchfulness, while from other quarters troops were drawn together, and moved up to support us.

While we lay here an event befel of which I make mention, because of the deep interest which it created, not in the 11th Dragoons alone, but in every other corps attached to the expedition. There was in my troop a man named John Feathers, a native of London, and an extremely good soldier; between whom and myself, indeed, a close intimacy had long subsisted, and who was universally respected in the regiment. He was followed in the march by a little dog of the terrier breed, to which he became very much attached, and which seldom failed of showing itself at his heels, let him be where he might. One day, I think it was the second after our departure from Meerut, he and I had been drinking in the canteen, not so as to intoxicate, or even to inflame, but merely to refresh ourselves after the work of the morning, and the dog, as his custom was, lay down at his master's feet, where he either slept or seemed to sleep. By and by we rose to go out. We paid no heed to the dog, taking it for granted that he would observe our proceedings and follow, and had approached close to the tents of the regiment, when John discovered that he was not near us. He whistled, the animal came not; whereupon he went back, and I for company's sake went with him. We found the dog lying where we had left him; John called him, but he took no notice of the call, upon which his master being somewhat provoked, seized him by the neck and gave him a beating. The brute being frightened struggled, and at last bit his master slightly in the wrist; but the scar was so trifling, bringing scarcely any blood at all, that neither he nor I took much notice of it. As a measure of precaution I washed it for him with arrack, and after getting it tied up he went to sleep.

The dog was certainly not rabid, for he attended John's footsteps ever after, and during the weeks that we lay in the Jumna, exhibited no signs of hydrophobia. The case was different with his master. He came to me on a certain evening, and complained that he felt excessive pain in the wrist where the dog had bit him. Being alarmed -- I could scarce tell why -- I advised him to consult the surgeon, but this he refused to do, and went to bed at his usual hour. Next morning the pain had ascended as high as the shoulder, and when he entered my tent, I saw that the expression of his face was terribly altered. He complained also of great thirst, and when milk was given him, though he managed to swallow a little, he rejected the rest with every symptom of disgust. There was no disguising the sad truth from ourselves any longer. He was evidently suffering under a paroxysm of hydrophobia, and the surgeon being made acquainted with the circumstance, he was conveyed to the hospital tent. The utmost care was taken of him; but it availed nothing. He died that night at twelve o'clock, in a state of raving madness.

We were all grieved and sobered for a brief space by the fate of poor Feathers; but the grief of soldiers, like that of children, seldom lasts long; and in a day or two our attention was altogether devoted to the events and accidents of each day as it came round. As may be imagined, we did not fail to pay frequent visits to Multoa, which we found singularly clean and neat, especially in the region which lay nearest to the stream; for there each particular house had its flight of highly ornamented steps that led down to the water's edge, and conducted the bathers to the place appropriated for their ablutions, whether they might be male or female, upgrown persons or young children. Neither was this the whole, nor the most striking feature which arrested our attention in this place. I never shall forget the first day on which, with five of my comrades, I crossed the bridge of boats, and entered the town. There was no crowd of carriages or palanquins in the street, neither were the pedestrians numerous; but a multitude of baboons constantly gathered round us, and made as if they would oppose our further progress. The fact is that the Indians of this part of the country are singularly superstitious, and hold many kinds of creatures sacred. On shore we have the baboon, in the river there is the turtle, of which countless throngs come as regularly to be fed from the hands of their devotees as if they were indeed gods, though dependent on their votaries for nutriment. There was something well nigh ludicrous in the menacing attitudes which the baboons of Multoa assumed, so soon as they ascertained, which they were not slow in doing, that we were foreigners. But they did not show much fight, for when, after a moment's hesitation, a cry was raised "six dragoons must not be stopped by a crowd of monkeys," and we dashed among them with our bamboos, and began to lay about us, they took to their heels in all directions. They retreated, however, still retaining an attitude of hostility. For no sooner had they gained the tops of the houses than they began to chatter and show their teeth, and even to pelt us with the bits of mortar and stone, which they managed to break off for the purpose.

The people looked very grave at us when they beheld the sort of bearing which we put on towards their much venerated baboons. If they had been aware of the sort of treatment which we occasionally awarded to the turtles, they would have been a thousand times more indignant. The turtle, as I have just stated, is accounted sacred here; and to refuse food to one of the genus who might apply for it by lifting his head above the water, would involve the delinquent in a degree of guilt far more heavy than is incurred by the utmost extent of cruelty to a human being. Nevertheless, I acknowledge to having more than once baited my hook for these very same gods, and not without prodigious efforts brought more than one of them to the shore. The brutes weighed from seventy to one hundred pounds. They differed from the sea turtle chiefly in their extreme whiteness and in the delicacy of their flesh, but they were not to be despised as an article of food, and when dressed, with abundance of cayenne pepper and other spices, the epicures among us accounted them great delicacies.

At the further extremity of Multoa stood a ruined temple, by ascending one of the towers in which, at least two hundred feet high, we succeeded in obtaining an extensive and striking view over the whole face of the surrounding country. From this point I could distinctly perceive Bhurtpore and its gigantic fortifications, as well as the very inconsiderable camp, within the limits of which the whole of the force as yet brought up to reduce Bhurtpore was assembled; and it was impossible not to feel, while looking upon the relative strength of the hostile parties, that if this were all which England could bring against the Rajah, her game was desperate. The lapse of a little time, however, sufficed to show that these surmises and speculations were wholly groundless; but as it is not yet time to enter upon the serious business of the siege, I may as well disburden myself at once of the petty anecdotes and narratives which stand between me and that which constitutes after all, the main incident in my Indian adventures.

While we lay in the vicinity of Multoa a camp follower died who belonged to that caste or class of the native population, which always burn their dead. His body of course was set apart that it might be consumed; and being curious to behold a spectacle of the kind, I took care to attend. In the sloping bank of the Jumna the friends of the deceased dug out a convenient resting place for the pile. It was a sort of terrace, which measured perhaps six feet in length by four in breadth, and there, upon a couch, composed of a double row of very dry billets, the body of the wretched camp-follower was stretched. They covered him thickly with a coat of gie, that is of melted butter made of the milk of the buffalo, upon which they piled a quantity of dry grass with fagots, and light wood over all. As soon as the preparations were completed, several of the near relatives of the deceased approached to ascertain that all was in order, and immediately on their retiring the torches were applied, and the flame sprang upwards with amazing rapidity; I never looked upon a more disgusting sight. The pile burned furiously, so much so indeed, that several persons with long poles, were obliged from time to time to keep the half-consumed flesh from rolling out of the flames; and what was more horrible still, the hawks, of which I have elsewhere spoken, as infesting this hemisphere, succeeded more than once in setting both flames and poles at defiance. I saw several of these birds pounce down, seize a morsel of flesh while it was broiling and fly away with it. At last I grew perfectly sick; and returning to my tent, thanked God that I had been born in a land where such horrors were unknown.

We lingered on in this situation for a good many months, during the hottest of which, including March and April, we managed to render the tents habitable only by fitting to the doors on the weather side a sort of screen of grass, which was kept perpetually moist with water. By-and-by, however, the division broke up, and returned for the monsoon to Meerut, where poor old General Ochterlony died -- respected, yet scarcely regretted, by the troops that served under him. We returned, moreover, just in time to witness the consecration by the bishop of a handsome church, dedicated to St. John, which had been built by private subscription. Let me not omit to give the credit which is his due, to the pious and excellent pastor of that church, the Rev. K. Fisher. If ever man lived to discharge the duties of his station, Mr. Fisher was that man; and the consequence was that he won over many a profligate to repentance, besides securing the affections of the whole garrison, and making numerous converts from Heathenism to Christianity. I shall never, as long as I live, forget the tenor of the admonitions which I received from him, and some, I doubt not, out of the multitudes who then held the same language with myself, still survive to repeat it.

While we occupied our old cantonments at Meerut, a fire broke out in the stables, which was supposed, I cannot tell how truly, to have been occasioned by the wilful negligence of some of the natives. It cost us several valuable horses, besides many more so injured, that not till the expiration of many weeks were they fit to be ridden. And not the least provoking part of the business was, that the perpetrators of the crime played their cards so skilfully, that beyond a suspicion, nothing was ever brought home to them.

Thus passed several months, at the termination of which, the order reached us to advance once more into the immediate vicinity of the hostile city. We set out, as our custom was, at an early hour in the morning; -- yet even then, on passing the gate of Mr. Fisher's country-house, we saw the good man waiting to greet us; and fervent were the prayers which he put up for our wellbeing, whether we should ever behold him again or not. I assure my reader, that I am neither a hypocrite in matters of faith, nor a sickly sentimentalist; but I declare to him in all soberness and honesty, that I never was more deeply affected myself -- nor saw a regiment of soldiers more deeply affected, than we all were by the prayers and the blessings of one whom we so sincerely loved and respected. Neither let me fail to observe, that not in my poor judgment only, but in that of all the most intelligent of the members of the British army -- is there any thing which so much stands in need of reformation, as what I may venture to call the Chaplain's department in the service. Our superiors may think as they please, -- but we, who fill up the ranks of the British army, know that we have souls to be saved, and very grateful should we be were there always at hand those who could tell us how to proceed, in order to ensure their salvation; and I can attest -- in proof of this -- that there was not a man in the 11th Dragoons, nor indeed in the European garrison of Meerut, who would not have laid down his life for the Rev. Mr. Fisher, more cheerfully than for any officer under whom he immediately served.

Onwards we moved, not easily forgetting our kind friend, or his generous benedictions, till by-and-by we took up our old ground, on this side the Jumna, and opposite to the city of Multoa. I cannot tell why we should have expected to remain there, but we did not remain, for the very next morning we crossed the river; and pushing on to a range of heights, which in some sort, command the plain on which Bhurtpore is built, we there pitched our camp, waiting till the army should assemble, and the siege, of which nobody any longer doubted, should begin in real earnest.

From day to day, after our establishment in this camp, troops, stores, and cannon came up. The heavy guns which had been collected at Agra, were transported to the place of assembly by water, and the new commander-in-chief, Lord Combermere, making his appearance about the same time, the whole army was reviewed, and next day put in motion. It was the duty of the 11th, supported by some native cavalry to cover the advance, and many a formidable piece of ground we passed over. Not an enemy however showed himself, and about noon on the third day, the towers and bastions of Bhurtpore uprose in the centre of a huge plain, immediately before us. Nothing could exceed the carelessness, or the misplaced confidence of its ruler and his troops. Though they must have been long aware of our hostile designs, they took no precautions whatever to defeat or even to retard their accomplishment; indeed, we found that the very trenches which Lord Lake's people had dug were not filled in. Lord Combermere, as may well be imagined, made haste to prevent their remedying an error so gross and so palpable. The trenches were immediately occupied by the king's 34th regiment of foot, and much time, as well as a large amount of fatigue saved to the besieging army in consequence.

The town and fort of Bhurtpore are planted in the very heart of an enormous wood, of which the outskirts approach within five or six hundred yards of the defences of the place. The wood is intersected in all directions by roads or passes; and while the infantry worked in the trenches and pushed their saps, we, that is the cavalry, had it in charge, to guard these passes so as to prevent both ingress and egress to the garrison. We were not always permitted to effect this, or to do the ordinary duty of outline picket, without molestation, as well from the enemy's guns, as from attacks by their very active and vigilant cavalry. The former of these modes of annoyance cost us several lives, among which I must mention that of Colonel Faithful, chief engineer to the army. The latter did not often pass off without wounds both to men and horses on either side. One day in particular I well recollect that the arm of Mr. Gruer, who commanded our picket, was severely hurt by a thrust from a lance; while the charger of one of his men had his tail cut off close to the stump, as clean as if the operation had been performed by a surgeon.

The wood which surrounded Bhurtpore was so dense, that in spite of constant service at the outposts, a good while elapsed ere I succeeded in obtaining of the place such a view as could be said to allay my very natural curiosity. It was only, indeed, by riding to the far extremity of one of the avenues, that you could hope to see a yard beyond your own ground; and this, for some reason which was never explained to us, we were particularly cautioned from hazarding. But there is no repressing the laudable disposition which urges men in general to increase their knowledge. My comrade and I being on patrol one morning, determined to indulge the desire under which we had both for some time laboured; and finding all clear to the extent which we had been directed to reconnoitre, we pushed gallantly beyond it. Suddenly we found ourselves on the edge of the open country; and the formidable appearance of the place against which our operations were directed I shall not soon forget. There seemed to be no limits to the succession of redoubts and batteries which covered it on every side. Abbattis, too, had been felled and laid with consummate care, so as to obstruct the approaches, and expose columns in advance to the fire both of cannon and musketry; while, that a sharp look-out was kept by the garrison, and the parties detached from it, we had soon the best reason for knowing. Though there were but two of us, we scarce showed ourselves on the open plain, ere four or five guns were directed against us; and the precision with which the artillerists threw their shot, soon warned us to withdraw. We did so, well pleased to have seen so much; neither did we return empty-handed. The wood was full of animals of the chase -- of deer, buffaloes, hares, antelopes, and even of wild boars -- to the pursuit of which, when not engaged on duty, we were accustomed to devote many an hour; and this day my comrade having killed a wild hog by a pistol-shot, we gathered him up, and carried him triumphantly into camp.

It was, not, however, exclusively by reason of the stock of game which abounded there, that the woods around Bhurtpore proved fruitful to us of interesting occurrences. Numbers of Bhurtporeans -- by what motive instigated I cannot tell -- used to penetrate these thickets; and to pursue and make prisoners of these afforded us almost as much sport, as to chase the antelope, or run down the wild hog. Yet we never succeeded in extracting from them any valuable information. They would even deny that they belonged to the fort, or had any connexion with its inmates; nor could either promises or threatenings prevail upon them to alter their tone.

Meanwhile the besieging force set to work in good earnest, and pushing forward their approaches, threw up batteries, from which, in due time, a heavy fire was opened. Of the solidity of the walls, however, against which this cannonade was directed, it would be difficult for those who never looked upon them to form a conception. Though faced with common masonry, they were constructed within the shell out of huge trunks and limbs of trees, which, being arranged longitudinally, and having the intervals between them filled up with solid and well rammed clay, offered to the shot such resistance, as could have come from no other kind of fortification whatever. I have seen scores of balls strike and splinter the stone work close to the line of breach, without causing the slightest inclination of the rampart itself; indeed several days elapsed ere the feeblest commencement was made in the work, which breaching batteries are expected to accomplish in half that interval. Neither were our gunners permitted to have all the amusement to themselves. The enemy kept up a heavy fire from a large number of cannon -- not without some loss, and more annoyance to the besiegers; indeed the crashing among the branches, as often as the Bhurtporeans warmed to their work, was awful; and not a few of our people received wounds from the splinters which were thus scattered about.

In the labours of the siege we mounted men took no part. Our duties consisted in guarding against sorties, and hindering supplies from being thrown into the place; and in the execution of these services we came, as I have elsewhere related, more than once into collision with the enemy. But as I cannot recall to my remembrance any affair of which the details put in especial claim upon the reader's attention, I will not weary him by forced descriptions where there is, in truth, little or nothing to describe.

Chapter 26

So passed several weeks, the roar of artillery sounding continually in our ears, and casualties occurring from time to time, as if to remind us, that we were enacting not the semblance but the reality of war. Among these sounds there was one which became by degrees so familiar that we expected it as regularly as midnight came round; and, having heard it, became forthwith satisfied, that hostilities would not be renewed at least for an hour or two. There was an enormous gun on one of the bastions of the city, which the garrison were accustomed to discharge only at stated seasons -- or if some particular effect was desired to be produced. The report emitted by that discharge drowned every other noise for the moment, and if they never succeeded in doing any execution in the camp, the fault lay, not with the loading but with the pointing of the gun. From us it got the name of Sweet-lips, and the common remark used to be, "Oh, now Sweet-lips has spoken, we may go sleep." The gun of which I speak now ornaments the parade in St. James's Park. It is an extremely beautiful piece of mechanism, but considered as a weapon of war, was perfectly useless.

Time ran his course, and the publication of an order one day, in which volunteers from the cavalry were invited to share with their dismounted comrades the honour of the assault, informed us for the first time that a breach had been effected, and that it either was, or was expected soon to be, practicable. As there is never any backwardness among British troops to occupy the post of danger, when it is pointed out to them, so the publication of the order just alluded to was hailed with loud acclamations. Every man upon parade, indeed, hastened to give in his name, nor was it without occasioning much mortification to those whom he determined to keep with their standards, that the colonel finally made choice of ten men per troop for performing this novel service. But the joy of the favoured few, and the envy of the rejected many, proved in the end to have been equally misplaced. After we had paraded several times on foot by ourselves, and were now looking for the route from hour to hour, the arrival of a fresh European regiment in camp caused us to return to our horses. With three British regiments the general conceived that he was strong enough to storm a town, of which the garrison was understood not to fall short of fifteen thousand men; and with three British regiments, supported by a considerable body of sepoys, the assault was finally delivered.

I can give no account from my own personal observation of any thing that went on in the trenches, either during the process of digging and laying the mine by which it was proposed to enlarge the main breach, or just before the mine was sprung. It was reported in the camp, indeed, that a serious accident occurred: that the troops being formed for the assault edged too near to the loaded chamber of the mine, and that the explosion, though it tore the enemy's defences to pieces, was scarcely less fatal to us, by blowing up the leading company of the 14th regiment, and killing a good many men in the company that followed. These things may or may not have happened. All that I know on the subject is, that having been moved up on the day of the assault to the edge of the wood, we sat on horseback from an early hour in the morning, watching with breathless anxiety for the report which we were given to understand would at once open out the way for the advance of our comrades, and act as the signal for the rush.

It is marvellous with what a slow and heavy step the moments pass by when men are thus circumstanced. I thought that the clocks would never strike nine, and yet the hands were moving that day as they usually do, neither faster nor slower. We spoke to one another, too, in whispers, as if there had been risk of creating an alarm, which there was not; and vainly and eagerly we strove to catch so much as a glimpse of the scene of action, through the thick branches that interposed between us and the town. At last one of our officers, who had repeatedly consulted his watch, said aloud, as if speaking to himself, "We'll have it soon, for it is close upon the hour." He had scarcely uttered the words, when a far-off cheer was heard. A boom of cannon and a rattle of musketry, and then, and not till then, we heard the roar of an ignited mine, and we knew that the struggle was begun in earnest. I never looked upon an object with deeper and more breathless interest than upon the wreath of smoke, which like a vapour rose above the branches. It was the canopy beneath which brave men fought and died; it was the shroud in which not a few of them had been enwrapped ere to our eyes it became visible.

If I except the untimely explosion of the mine, of which, however, I can speak only on the authority of vague rumour, no arrangements could have been more judiciously entered into, or more skilfully carried out, than those which led the way to the storming of Bhurtpore, and aided in its capture. While the troops were moved over night into the trenches, and stood ready to spring forward at the appointed signal, all the drummers and musicians remained in camp; where, beating the reveillie, and executing the signals that were usual on days of perfect quiet, they did their best to prevent a suspicion from entering into the minds of the garrison, that the crisis of their fate was come. How far the device succeeded I cannot pretend to say. The heavy firing which followed the explosion of the mine showed, that never for an instant had the breaches been left unguarded; and the tenacity with which the defenders held them good, was vouched for by its long continuance.

We were deeply interested in a scene, of which we would have given worlds to become spectators, when the adjutant, who was employed to look out, suddenly reported that the British ensign waved upon the top of the ramparts. In a moment all was excitation and bustle. A loud long cheer, so soon as we felt ourselves firmly in the saddle, caused the glades and deeper recesses of the forest to ring, and away we went at full gallop, in order to intercept a body of horsemen, whom the adjutant had observed to emerge from one of the more distant gates of the fortress, almost as soon as the British standard began to wave from the summit of the breach. Not unobserved, however, by the garrison, albeit, sharply engaged with our infantry on their own ground, was this our forward movement. They turned upon us instantly some six or eight guns, the balls from which passed over, or in front, or on either side of us; yet, with two exceptions, all proved harmless, and we held our onward course unchecked. One man was cut in two close by my side. The other shot struck a horse, and sorely wounded his hinder-quarters; but these were the only instances in which the enemy's fire told, though it was both well-directed, and warmly sustained.

Being now within two or three hundred yards of the fort, our riflemen, of whom I was one, were sent out to skirmish. Away we dashed, ten of us keeping well together; and disregarding the shower of balls that fell round us, we succeeded in gaining the edge of a large pond or tank, the high banks of which, together with those of some salt-pans adjoining to it, rendered us tolerably safe from the artillery practice of the enemy. Here we extended our files, which we had scarcely done, ere I found myself opposite to some twenty or thirty horsemen, whom, judging from their long robes and magnificent turbans,

I put down in my own mind as nothing less than the Rajah himself, and some of his immediate attendants, endeavouring to effect their escape. I tried to pull up and get a shot at them; but ere I could do so, one of their body took deliberate aim at me, and his ball struck the ground just under the nose of my charger. I returned his fire, and saw him bend over his saddle-bow, at the instant that a ball from somebody else splashed into my cloak and lodged there. But the party, of whatever class of men it might consist, did not linger long where they first confronted us. The 59th having by this time won the ramparts in their rear, opened upon them a heavy fire of musketry. Whereupon they gave the spur to their steeds, and without so much as pausing to observe what might be in front, they galloped off towards the point where egress into the open country was most immediate.

The salt-pan lying between us and the fugitives, we could not dash in upon them; but away we flew, as fast as our horses would carry us, rounding that obstruction, and striving if possible to head them. At last we arrived, one by one, at a road which led directly to one of the gates of the city; and the scene of confusion which there opened on me I shall never forget. Forth from the gateway and over the drawbridge rushed multitudes of fugitives, whom our victorious infantry closely pursued; and the slaughter which was effected by the bayonet, by musketry, and by the crushing of man upon man, I have no language sufficiently frightful to describe. Neither were we without our incidents; the excitement attending which at the moment was very great. For example, the first objects that arrested my attention on rounding a corner of the road, were Serjeant Waldron, of our regiment, and a ferocious-looking Rajpoot, savagely confronting one another. The Serjeant having discharged his pistol, had his horse drawn up to a position wellnigh rampant, while the Rajpoot, who stood within six yards of him, was taking deliberate aim at him with his carabine. I saw that there was not a moment to be lost. I thrust both spurs into my horse's flanks, and, while in the act of advancing, I took aim, fired, and brought the Rajpoot dead to the ground.

Serjeant Waldron sprang forward to meet me, gave me his hand, and thanked me for his life; after which we drew our swords, and dashed into the midst of the fugitives. Numbers were cut down, some with arms, others without, till by-and-by the survivors lost all heart, and intreated us to spare them. We had no mind to kill men who offered no resistance; so, desiring them to throw down their arms one by one as they approached, we saw them gallop or scamper off, and never once troubled our heads to inquire whither they were going. Yet there was one little group in that miscellaneous crowd which I must claim credit for having saved from insult, and guarded to a place of safety. I saw two fine-looking women, whom a band, apparently of servants, followed, make one or two efforts to pass, yet continually shrink back again. Upon this I rode forward, and making myself understood by signs, rather than by words I volunteered to be their protector; they gratefully gave themselves up to my guidance, and I had the satisfaction to carry them uninjured through the throng, and to see them ride off in a direction where all was clear, after I had received from them the most gratifying acknowledgments.

Having seen them safe, I returned to my former station, time enough to witness the barbarity with which a corps of Sepoys cut down the fugitives by whole sections. Not having any particular delight in scenes like these, I rode aside, and going up to my Rajpoot, who lay where my ball had dropped him, I observed, to my surprise, that his carabine was of English manufacture, and that it bore, besides the common Tower mark, the number 1800. Meanwhile, however, my comrades had moved off in a different direction, so conceiving that I was bound to follow, I gave my horse the rein, and tried to trace them. In this effort I crossed several fields, in the far corner of one of which I came upon a single Rajpoot, who seemed to have posted himself there over a heap of loose armour, and who, on my calling to him to surrender, instantly placed himself in an attitude of defence. I rode at him, delivered a heavy blow on the top of his head, felt that the sword had made no impression, yet saw him fall. The fact is, that the weight of my blow stunned him, even while the solidity of his turban hindered the edge from penetrating. I did not stop to repeat the blow, which was clearly not mortal, inasmuch as he turned himself round as I passed, and spat at me; but I was too anxious to rejoin my regiment to think of avenging the insult, and therefore left him with a whole skin in the mud.

In prosecuting my search after my missing comrades I passed several spots of ground, which cumbered with dead men and horses, as well Europeans as native, besides broken arms, torn garments, caps, turbans, and so forth, exhibited manifold signs of a battle stoutly maintained. By and by I plunged into the wood; and there too, as I afterwards learned, a warm skirmish had occurred, many of the Bhurtporeans climbing up into the trees, and shooting our men from their perches. Of these almost all were put to death; yet in the heat of that wild affray a little incident occurred, of which, because of the merit due to Major Smith, the chief actor in the scene, and because of the evidence which it affords of the absence from modern warfare of all feelings that brutalize and degrade, I am bound to make mention. A poor native child, of singularly interesting appearance, had fled with his father from the fort. The party to which the father belonged, fell in with our people in the wood, and a warm struggle ensued. In the course of this skirmish the unfortunate man was killed; whereupon the child, throwing himself down beside the dead body of his father, wept bitterly in apparent regardlessness of the thousand deaths by which he was surrounded. Major Smith, of the 11th, being greatly touched at the scene, rode forward, and causing his native servant to interpret for him, promised to be a protector to the child. He faithfully redeemed the pledge. The child was removed from the field of slaughter to the major's tent, and was finally, at the major's expense, established in life.

The town was now our own, and the pursuit of the fugitives having been carried far enough, the trumpets and bugles sounded the recall, and we formed up in obedience to it. I shall never forget the shocking spectacles that greeted me, as I rode towards the ill-fated city, and still more after I had passed beneath the gateway. In every direction, along the road, beneath the arched gateway, strewed over the old city, under the ramparts and above them, the dead lay in hundreds; the mangled bodies of women, ay and of children too, being intermingled with the carcasses of slaughtered warriors. Of the wounded, moreover, not a few exhibited towards us the most malignant feelings. One man had been cut down as he was in the act of scattering over a narrow causeway, handfuls of crows-feet-a vile implement, which has three long sharp spikes, one of which always turns uppermost, inflicting painful and desperate wounds, both on men and horses. He was not dead when I passed him, and though his arm had lost its power to throw his horrid implement to any distance, he nevertheless strove to shove one under me, and spat at me in impotent fury. Others I beheld, whose garments had taken fire from the explosion of their own pouches. These not only rejected our assistance, but covered us with execrations when we advanced to proffer it. In a word, the spirit with which the garrison was embued, seemed to have been one of the wildest fanaticism; which needed but the guidance of some mind of higher order than that of the rajah, to render it irresistible.

The booty taken in Bhurtpore was, I have reason to believe, immense: a large portion of which went, I suspect, in indiscriminate pillage among the assailants and the followers; yet enough was secured to give to the commander-in-chief a very handsome donative, and to each private soldier, native as well as European, between 40 and 50 rupees. In the citadel, which held out one day after the town, little was found of value. Three deserters were, however, recovered; one of whom was tried, and the next day shot; while the remaining two were condemned to transportation for life, and an existence whether long or short in chains, hard labour, and close imprisonment.

Chapter 27

Such is a brief and necessarily imperfect narrative of the siege and capture of Bhurtpore, an event on the great political importance of which, it would be ridiculous for me to hazard an opinion. One fact, however, is not only certain in itself, but was felt and acknowledged at the moment throughout the whole of India, namely, that there existed among the native powers a sort of superstitious conviction that Bhurtpore would never yield to the force of British genius or British valour; and that so long as Bhurtpore continued to assert its independance, a rallying point would still be left to the native chiefs, whenever they might snake up their minds to rebel. That idle, yet not harmless delusion, the results of the siege in 1825, at once dispelled; and not till this day has the effect of so unlooked for a defeat ceased to operate upon the humbled spirits of all who witnessed it.

The siege being ended, and some of the principal fortifications blown up, one or two regiments of native infantry were left to complete the work of destruction; while the rest of the army drew off, and encamped at various points more or less distant from the trenches. Our encampment was not far removed from the citadel, nor had we occupied it long, ere a staff officer came in and desired that a troop might attend him, in pursuit of two or three loads of treasure which were understood to have escaped. It so happened that my troop was the first for duty; so away we went, carrying neither forage nor provisions along with us; and for two days and as many nights, our toil and privations were excessive. We penetrated through some tremendous passes, which a handful of resolute men might have held against an army, and more than once arrived at a village just in time to learn that the treasure with its escort had passed some hours previously, and was gone, nobody could tell where. The result was that after having been reluctantly compelled to pillage several villages, and to make free with the people's fodder, we returned to camp not more rich than when we set out; and had little else to show as a memorial of our wild expedition than horses more or less blemished, and ourselves jaded well nigh to death.

It was soon after the conclusion of this abortive excursion, that the deserter of whom I spoke a short time ago, was hung over one of the bastions, after which the fortifications of the place were one after another thrown down. This done, the troops received orders to fall back towards their ancient stations, and we in obeying it had an opportunity of visiting several places of great and deserved repute among the people of Hindoostan. Among others we passed through Agra, where I beheld the superb tomb of the Shah Jehan and his favourite wife, a structure so gorgeous, that any attempt to describe it even with the pencil would be preposterous. It stands upon a terrace confronting the river, the whole of which is paved in mosaic; and being itself composed entirely of beautiful white marble, offers, with its four minarets, and its noble stair of ascent, one of the most magnificent specimens of a very peculiar style of architecture that the imagination of man can conceive. Here too are the tombs of several ministers of state, scarcely less magnificent, though formed of different kinds of stone, some being red, others of a darker colour; yet all strikingly beautiful. But I must not dwell upon subjects with which I feel myself inadequate to deal. Rather let me return to my own personal narrative, of which little more remains to be told; inasmuch as life in India to a private soldier has for the most part too much of sameness in it to sanction any endeavour on his part to draw out its details beyond the narrowest limits.

On the 12th of March, 1826, we resumed our old quarters at Cawnpore, through which not long after our arrival, passed the ex-rajah of Bhurtpore, on his way as a state prisoner to Calcutta. And here I am reluctantly compelled to acknowledge that a disposition to carry to a terrible excess all the vices that appertain to this country, showed itself in our regiment, and especially among the remains of the volunteers from the 8th. The habit, indeed, of drunkenness, became so confirmed among us that there was no making head against it; and frequent attempts at assassination, not always, I grieve to say, abortive, were the consequence. I cannot in terms sufficiently strong caution my brother soldiers against the folly, as well as the wickedness of yielding themselves up to so terrible a vice.

Even if they be preserved from dipping their hands in the blood of their fellow-creatures they are sure, under the influence of its madness to be hurried into actions which must cover them with shame, and entail on them long years of fruitless remorse. But I know by experience how little the experience of others is, by giddy young men apt to be regarded. I can, therefore, serve them in nothing more effectually, than by expressing my earnest wish that they may buy the one, if buy it they must, at a rate less ruinous than it has been my fortune to see it purchased by others, whose prospects for the future were at one time bright as a morning in May.

If I except a visit which the Governor-general paid us, and the occurrence of a frightful fire, by which both barracks and stables were destroyed, there occurred throughout the remaining months of the year nothing of which I consider it necessary to make mention. The fire in question cost us, I remember, a good many of our horses; for besides that, several perished ere we could get them clear of the burning pile; not a few scampered off into the heart of the country and never came back to us again. My own brute was a perfect devil, and chanced to be among the number of those, which, finding themselves momentarily free from bit and halter, tried to regain their liberty: but to my extreme mortification the monster was one day brought back. He was a perfect scarecrow when he came, and I heartily regretted that I was ever so unfortunate as to see him again.

From Cawnpore we moved to Meerut, where, since we last occupied the station, the same accident had occurred which rendered ourselves, for a time, houseless. We were therefore agreeably surprised to find a range of new and commodious barracks thrown up for our reception. We made ourselves as comfortable in them as circumstances would allow, and became witnesses on one occasion to such a fall of hailstones, as I at least, never beheld in any part of Europe. The blocks of ice, for they were nothing less, measured, many of them, a full inch in length; and they fell with such violence, as not only to destroy the blossom and even the upper branches of the fruit trees, but seriously to injure the people that were abroad, and here and there to kill their cattle. I confess that as I gazed abroad upon the phenomenon, my thoughts reverted to the account which Moses gives of a similar judgment inflicted on the Egyptians long ago: and I could not but feel, that had this continued many hours longer, there would have been little left for the locusts to glean, had supreme power determined that they should come to complete the ruin which the elements had begun.

Our life in India was not, however, entirely a strange intermixture of military duty, and dissipation, and shere idleness. We had, both at Meerut and elsewhere, our more rational amusements also. For example, while we lay at Meerut, Mr. Wolf, the well-known missionary, paid us a visit, and his discourses, for he preached to us by the commandant's permission, were, if not very edifying, at all events

231

abundantly strange. He gave us a detailed account of his wanderings -- of the persecutions to which he had been subjected, and of the fragments of the scattered tribes which he had discovered in various places. Nay he was so imprudent as to venture into the field of prophecy itself, and to fix the year 1846, as that in which the restoration of Israel shall take place. We looked at one another, not knowing very well what to make of the speaker, so long as he confined himself to details like these. But when he proceeded to assure us that he had cast out devils, and to describe the very process by which the operation was carried through, we could not stand his palaver any longer. It is a rash thing in these days to assume the character either of a prophet, or a worker of miracles.

Again the country round Meerut abounding with game, we were permitted, from time to time, to go out in quest of it; and in parties of six or eight, we passed many a pleasant day, and even week in the jungle. But with me, as well as with many more, the season of enjoyment passed rapidly away, and dilapidated constitutions, as well as great bodily weakness, warned us that it was high time to think of retirement, and of a preparation for another and a still more momentous change. Accordingly in the beginning of 1835 I applied for my discharge, and the necessary papers being made out, I began, in the month of February, in company with invalids from many other corps, my march towards Calcutta. It is not worth while to describe at length the particulars of that journey. It was not a pleasant one, for it was performed chiefly by water; and of invalids whom no officer looks after, even native boatmen take less care than they might do. Nevertheless, after suffering various inconveniences, we reached the capital of British India, just in time to learn that the last ship of the season had sailed. The consequence was that up to the month of January in 1836 we lingered amid the heat and squalor of Calcutta. Then, however, berths being found for us on board the teak-built ship the Hungerford, such of us as had survived the miseries of the last ten months embarked for England.

We had upon the whole a pleasant passage. Some trifling accidents occurred, such as the death of a man whom a shark devoured while bathing, and the loss of another who fell overboard; and we had our own share of enjoyments, especially when at anchor off the Cape, whence supplies of fresh provisions, wines, and vegetables were brought to us. But why continue these details? On the 25th of May we disembarked at Gravesend; from that place we marched to Chatham, and there, after an interval of three weeks I at length obtained my discharge. I cannot say that the remuneration allotted to me was too great; for my pension, after so many years service, amounts only to tenpence a day, and I am by far too much worn out to add to it greatly by personal exertion.

ALSO FROM LEONAUR
AVAILABLE IN SOFTCOVER OR HARDCOVER WITH DUST JACKET

EW2 EYEWITNESS TO WAR SERIES
CAPTAIN OF THE 95th (Rifles) *by Jonathan Leach*

An officer of Wellington's Sharpshooters during the Peninsular, South of France and Waterloo Campaigns of the Napoleonic Wars.

SOFTCOVER : **ISBN 1-84677-001-7**
HARDCOVER : **ISBN 1-84677-016-5**

WFI THE WARFARE FICTION SERIES
NAPOLEONIC WAR STORIES
by Sir Arthur Quiller-Couch

Tales of soldiers, spies, battles & Sieges from the Peninsular & Waterloo campaigns

SOFTCOVER : **ISBN 1-84677-003-3**
HARDCOVER : **ISBN 1-84677-014-9**

EWI EYEWITNESS TO WAR SERIES
RIFLEMAN COSTELLO *by Edward Costello*

The adventures of a soldier of the 95th (Rifles) in the Peninsular & Waterloo Campaigns of the Napoleonic wars.

SOFTCOVER : **ISBN 1-84677-000-9**
HARDCOVER : **ISBN 1-84677-018-1**

MCI THE MILITARY COMMANDERS SERIES
JOURNALS OF ROBERT ROGERS OF THE RANGERS *by Robert Rogers*

The exploits of Rogers & the Rangers in his own words during 1755-1761 in the French & Indian War.

SOFTCOVER : **ISBN 1-84677-002-5**
HARDCOVER : **ISBN 1-84677-010-6**

Lightning Source UK Ltd.
Milton Keynes UK
UKOW04n2216060915

258158UK00002B/34/P